Virtue and the Promise of Conservatism

Virtue and the Promise of Conservatism

The Legacy of Burke and Tocqueville

Bruce Frohnen

 University Press of Kansas

Published by the University Press of Kansas (Lawrence, Kansas 66049), which was organized by the Kansas Board of Regents and is operated and funded by Emporia State University, Fort Hays State University, Kansas State University, Pittsburg State University, the University of Kansas, and Wichita State University

Library of Congress Cataloging-in-Publication Data

Frohnen, Bruce.
    Virtue and the promise of conservatism : the legacy of Burke and Tocqueville / Bruce Frohnen.
        p.   cm.
    Includes bibliographical references and index.
    ISBN 0-7006-0558-4 (hardcover)
    1. Burke, Edmund, 1729–1797—Contributions in political science. 2. Tocqueville, Alexis de, 1805–1859—Contributions in political science. 3. Conservatism—History. I. Title.
JC176.B83F76   1992
320.5'2—dc20   92-13803

British Library Cataloguing in Publication Data is available.

Printed in the United States of America
10 9 8 7 6 5 4 3 2 1

The paper used in this publication meets the minimum requirements of the American National Standard for Permanence of Paper for Printed Library Materials Z39.48-1984.

For those who have taught me
especially my parents

Contents

Acknowledgments

This book began as a doctoral thesis, written for the Government Department at Cornell University under the chairmanship of Isaac F. Kramnick. I would like to express my appreciation to Theodore J. Lowi of Cornell, whose professionalism and courtesy rendered our philosophical differences relevant only as spurs to my intellectual growth. I owe a special debt of gratitude to Werner J. Dannhauser, also of Cornell, without whose intellectual guidance, professional advice, and many personal kindnesses this book would never have come to be. I also must acknowledge the contributions of Jeremy A. Rabkin and Henry Shue, both of Cornell, in reading and commenting on portions of the dissertation.

My work was aided greatly by the kind assistance of the Lynde and Harry Bradley Foundation, which provided me with research grants for two successive summers while I was in graduate school. Fellow graduate students Leslie Feldman, Victor Morales, and Rachel Reiss gave me much needed advice and encouragement.

A number of men and women helped in the not inconsiderable task of transforming my student thesis into this book. Thomas S. Gryboski and Charles J. Reid, Jr., of Emory University read portions of the manuscript and rendered sound advice when it was sorely needed. Peter J. Steinberger of Reed College and Sister Elizabeth Kolmer of Saint Louis University showed me what is demanded by current academic standards of excellence. Robert and Gretchen Sutherland of Cornell College gave me invaluable advice, support, and sustenance. Theodore L. Putterman of California State University, Sacramento, first got me interested in political philosophy, and in Burke in particular. As is fitting, his influence on this work has been at times obscure and often ironic, but always pronounced.

I also would like to thank my editor, Michael Briggs, and everyone at the University Press of Kansas for their efforts, advice, and expressions of confidence in my work. In addition, I was blessed with two editorial readers who showed an uncommon concern for advancing the quality of the work rather than their own projects or opinions. Gordon J. Schochet of Rutgers University gave valuable advice and even-handed criticism at a crucial stage in the development of the manuscript, and Peter Augustine Lawler of Berry College went beyond the call of duty in his efforts to make my arguments coherent and readable. Of course, any confusions and mistakes remaining are my own.

Finally, I must thank Rob Waters of the University of Mississippi. He has left his mark throughout this work, in part through his tireless editorial efforts but most important by showing me the true meaning, and the true virtue, of friendship.

Introduction

Of course, conservatism always has the worst of the argument, is always apologizing, pleading a necessity, pleading that to change would be to deteriorate; it must saddle itself with the mountainous load of the violence and vice of society, must deny the possibility of good, deny ideas, and suspect and stone the prophet.
—Ralph Waldo Emerson, "The Conservative"

Emerson, spiritual leader of the American transcendentalists, owed his position in large measure to his ability to sum up the attitudes of his fellow intellectuals. It is unfortunate that, as in so much else, his summation of intellectual opinion concerning conservatism has proved accurate. The notion that conservatives seek only to point out the fallacies of more "progressive" thinkers and to make do with our current "unjust" arrangements has come to dominate discussions of conservatism, even among conservatives themselves. Thus recent works on the topic generally are based on the assumption that although conservatism may have a history (certain men have called themselves conservatives or have been so labeled by others), it has no fundamental essence transcending advocacy of prudent policy positions and a general hostility toward rapid change.[1]

Emerson did have one good thing to say about conservatism: It gave birth to that splendid, rational creature called the "innovator."[2] High praise indeed. Yet the notion that we are fully human only when we judge the world and change it to fit our own notions of abstract justice has done much to undermine the traditions and the beliefs necessary for any good life.

1

Whatever Emerson and other innovators might argue, conservatism does not constitute a defense of violence and vice. It constitutes an admonition that violence and vice are produced by the prideful reliance on individual reason and will for which progressive thinkers stand. Indeed, man has followed "prophets" and innovators with increasing frequency in the modern age, and the results have been anything but splendid.

Only now are we witnessing the unraveling of the rationalistic innovations set forth by the philosophical prophet Jean Jacques Rousseau in the eighteenth century and first instituted, with murderous efficiency, by the French revolutionary despot Robespierre. The French Revolution, like its Marxian progeny in Russia and elsewhere, was essentially an attempt to substitute man's will for God's. French revolutionary Jacobinism promised to free man from bondage and want, but because it was concerned with its own perfection rather than with the needs and nature of man, it brought systematic mass murder followed by a living death of lies, oppression, and a nightmarish monotony owing much to the pointlessness and futility of the project itself. Millions of lives have been wasted, particularly over the last two centuries, on the adolescent fantasy of a world in which childish self-indulgence would magically combine with spontaneous "caring"—aided, of course, by a miraculously beneficent nature that would feed, clothe, and shelter her wards as they followed their whims of the moment.

The conservative need not apologize for throwing stones at the false prophet who would sacrifice us to the god of his own delusions. The conservative does not defend what some would-be innovator in his pride calls man's "true," supposedly rational nature. Instead the conservative defends the abiding character of man and his true, if necessarily limited, capacity to do right by his fellow man.

It is clear to anyone not blinded by love of his own utopian illusions that the great rationalistic experiment of socialism was a horrifying flop. All the terror and indoctrination that state socialism could muster did nothing to bring to life the "new socialist man." All the horrors of the last decades have not erased man's inherent need to find God, to take care of his family, and to belong to a community of neighbors before he can belong to the community of man.

We are now seeing in the nations of Eastern Europe the reemergence of man's permanent character. The dangers of ethnic rivalry and nationalist extremism remain great in Eastern Europe and central Asia—socialist ideology and coercion only fed ethnic resentments. But the true hope of Western Civilization may now lie in the East, where so many men unabashedly profess their love of God, their hopes for freedom, and their desire to rebuild their own communities. In the West meanwhile, we remain locked in a meaningless debate between those who bemoan the lack of "distributive justice" in the free market and those who defend human liberty on the grounds that it is profitable.

Our materialistic debate has been as debilitating as it has been meaningless. It has kept us—conservatives and nonconservatives alike—from asking what we must do to lead a good life. It has done much to transform virtue, in the minds of most Americans, from the proper standard of conduct and the essence of any good life to the "quaint" maintenance of premarital virginity. And conservatism's unphilosophical reputation owes much to our abuse of the word virtue. Virtue is, in fact, the very basis of conservative political philosophy. The conservative, far from defending whatever happens to be old, recognizes that societies are good only if and to the extent that they promote right conduct. He believes, moreover, that essentially all societies possess certain arrangements that have endured over time, and therefore need not be "rationally" imposed, that make it possible for men to behave as they should.

To act rightly, to do as God wills in one's own life, is to act virtuously. But one cannot judge by the light of one's independent reason what it is to act rightly. One needs the guidance of revelation (most prominently the Ten Commandments and the golden rule), the guidance of principles that are self-evident to all men (rather than merely "obvious" to one prideful individual), and the guidance of traditional institutions, beliefs, and practices. Because societies are in large measure products of circumstances, including historical events, geography, and numerous other factors, each possesses different appropriate rules of right conduct. Having stood the test of time and changing circumstances, these societies and their standards of virtue should not be dismissed merely because they do not fit some preconceived notion of what is rational.

The conservative may defend highly divergent institutions and practices, but he does so because they are integral parts of the same conservative good life—the life in which man fulfills his nature through affectionate service to those he knows and loves. The conservative approaches his life and society with the attitude of a friend, more concerned with fostering and treasuring what is good than with eliminating what he finds unpleasant. It is the pursuit of a good life and the virtue that is its lifeblood that gives to conservative political philosophy its purpose and its essential connection with the eternal standards of natural law. The practice of conservative virtue—that accepting virtue dedicated to the service of the good that already exists—is severely weakened in a society that judges utility in material terms and considers virtue itself a charming museum piece, a fraudulent cover for class or gender domination or an echo from an unrecoverable past.

It is the dilemma of the contemporary conservative that he must defend and find virtue within a society whose members have discarded virtue itself in their pursuit of material comfort. Our society's latent virtue is often difficult to detect because it is obscured and weakened by a rampant egalitarianism that confuses equality of material conditions with freedom and justice, that sees the proper goal of politics and life itself as the pursuit, not of happiness in a good life, but of material well-being in a *comfortable* life. Whatever their behavior, all men now claim their right to monetary support from the government, along with the security for self-esteem provided by assurances that all actions will be deemed equally moral. Thus the contemporary conservative must find a basis on which to defend a society tragically divorced in its very spirit from the pursuit of the good life, for in any good life happiness means having the character to do what is right and not merely the material means to do what one wishes.

Unfortunately, today even conservatives all too often eschew defense of the good in order to defend the practical. Yet it is not practical to leave virtue undefended or to acquiesce in the use of materialistic criteria in debates over the goodness of our way of life. Man cannot live without ends. Thus, if virtue is not shown to be man's proper end, material comfort will take its place. Because he knows that radical innovation is destructive, the conservative's only alternative to despair is to call upon his fellows to reform their own characters and actions—and thence their own society. There is much that remains good in our society, and only by fostering our latent decency may we recover the life of virtue.

If the good life is not explained and defended, the comfortable life will come to be seen as the only good life available. Thus it is not surprising that the equality and "fairness" that so many men from all parts of the political spectrum deem necessary for a good society today are matters of the bureaucratic distribution of material goods. What is "comparable worth" if not an attempt—either through legislation or judicial decree—to direct bureaucrats to determine how much money a given task is "worth?" What are arguments over social welfare programs if not arguments concerning the level of income to which all Americans are "entitled"? And what is "affirmative action," so often defended as reparation for past injustice and lack of opportunity, if not an outright dismissal of standards of excellence in the name of a "fair" (that is, race- and sex-based) distribution of jobs and wages? That the good life is in some sense the just life is irrefutable, but the equation of the just life with the life in which material goods are distributed equally is an illusion inimical to the soul whose very existence it denies.

Natural law, that body of standards for human conduct best summed up in the command to love one's neighbor as oneself, dictates that men care for the spirit of their communities and the souls of their fellow men. Unrestrained exercise of the human will, even if limited by contract, degrades the soul as it warps the mind and corrupts the body by sanctifying the pursuit of a life of sensual pleasures. Even those who seek to defend their community, to love their neighbors as themselves, degrade themselves and those they seek to serve when service is rendered only in material terms, toward merely material ends.

One need not be a conservative to recognize the failings of the modern world, but such a recognition lends support to the conservative opposition to egalitarian materialism and its utopian projects. Perhaps the two most famous academic critics of modernity to write in America were Leo Strauss—the defender of classical philosophy—and the religious thinker Eric Voegelin. Neither was a conservative in any conventional sense and each differed from the other in many ways, but Strauss and Voegelin both argued that, tragically, we have replaced the good with the comfortable as the goal of life. Both men observed that the birth and progress of modernity have been characterized by two interdependent developments: the emergence of a view of politics as the pursuit of secular salvation (the achievement of a materially defined paradise on earth) and the concomitant loss of transcendent standards and goals.

For Voegelin the "eschatology of the realm," first given clear and comprehensive expression by Joachim of Flora,[3] brought about an "immanentization of the Christian eschaton"—a transference of the pursuit of salvation from the next, spiritual, world to the present, material, world.[4] Joachim in effect rejected Christian recognition of the transhistorical, supernatural and fundamentally mysterious character of God and human salvation. He and his successors replaced faith in God with faith in man's ability to build heaven on earth. The new earthly faith depended upon the fallacious notion that history itself has a purpose: the achievement of human perfection.[5] Salvation was to be sought in this world, through the pursuit of temporal achievements aimed at making material the transcendent world of God.[6]

According to Voegelin, Thomas Hobbes sought to defuse the revolutionary nature of Joachim's version of gnosticism, a nature made apparent to Hobbes by the English Civil War, by remaking the earthly paradise in material terms. Hobbes disposed of both philosophy and Christianity in the interest of peace. "But how can one dispose of them without abolishing the experiences of transcendence which belong to the nature of man? Hobbes was quite able to solve this problem, too; he improved on the man of God's creation by creating a man without such experiences."[7] Remaking man in the image of the machine, Hobbes sought to destroy the desire for transcendence by denying its very existence. The Joachimite and Hobbesian profanizations of salvation brought about the rise of Western Civilization and its ultimate embodiment in totalitarianism—the empire (and the church) of material progress. In this empire those men who are useful are canonized, and those who pursue God are condemned. Voegelin found the rise of Western Civilization impressive, but "the death of the spirit is the price of progress."[8]

Strauss shared Voegelin's conviction that it was Hobbes who most successfully promoted pursuit of an earthly paradise. According to Strauss, Hobbes's primary accomplishment was the equation of the pleasurable with the good and the verifiable with the true.[9] The fundamental goal of all human beings, according to Hobbes, is self-preservation. Thus self-preservation is an empirical natural law on which all other acts rest. Lacking any transcendent standards of knowledge and conduct (lacking natural law in the traditional sense), individuals are the only possible judges of what is conducive to their own preservation. "Everything may legitimately be regarded as required for self-preservation: everything is by nature just."[10] Peace is the only universal necessity and is to be maintained by the equation of justice with the keeping of contracts—with adherence to expressions of individual will.

Following Hobbes, the individual's will became self-justifying, as did the political pursuit of material well-being, for the virtues that had served to check the appetites sprang neither from contract nor from individual will and so were themselves no longer justified.[11] The pursuit of higher goals, and the self-restraint necessary for such pursuits, were discarded in the pursuit of peace and pleasures of the moment. Hobbesian political hedonism, necessarily linked with political atheism, substituted "the right kind of human government" for the state of grace as man's means of salvation from his fallen state—a state now defined as the dangerous and incommodious state of nature.[12] The search for an ordered life and for wisdom itself became lost in the pursuit of material goods and the exercise of a generalized "benevolence." The ruler's duty was no longer to make men good but to provide for "commodious living."[13]

For both Strauss and Voegelin, the profanization of politics, the descent from the pursuit of wisdom to the pursuit of an earthly paradise, was furthered greatly by the fact/value distinction imported from the natural into the social sciences. Reliance on this distinction served to eliminate the search for truth in the name of a search for the useful or the "scientifically verifiable." Reaching its logical conclusion in Max Weber's social thought, this distinction in effect denigrated the essential ordering truths by which man must live, labeling them "demons" with no objective content. One's "values," for Weber, were merely self-chosen principles of action to be accepted as first principles but not to be accorded any intrinsic merit or standards of merit.[14] Because standards of virtue were methodologically unverifiable, the scientific method proclaimed them unsound and even unimportant. Utility and material progress, on the other hand, could be measured scientifically. Thus science reinforced the equation of the useful or the pleasurable with the good.

Man's pride led him to attempt to understand the universe in its entirety, to make himself divine.[15] His self-divination, along with his childish pursuit of pleasures of the moment, caused man to lose, or rather to reject, natural law. Discarding transcendent standards of right and wrong, forsaking knowledge of the good of man and of the questions of life (the answers to which generally lie beyond our ability to grasp), man fell into a self-flattering view of his own intellectual resources and an almost equally degrading view of his *right* to limitless satisfactions.

The fundamental change in the goals of human society noted by Voegelin and Strauss was not the result of any human strength. Voegelin argued that the "immanentization of the eschaton" was an act of human weakness: "The more people are drawn or pressured into the Christian orbit, the greater will be the number among them who do not have the spiritual stamina for the heroic adventure of the soul that is Christianity." Christian faith, in particular the acceptance of facts that are not scientifically derived, is an act of heroism of which most men are not capable.[16] Strauss argued that the supposed realism of Hobbes was based on the abandonment of the search for true wisdom. Incapable of achieving (or accepting) the wisdom of Socrates—to know that we know nothing and thus to know the nature of, though not the solutions to, the fundamental mysteries of life—men accepted the Hobbesian doctrine that what we cannot know is not knowledge. What we cannot sense is not real, in this view, and since only our senses can tell us what is good, only that which gives us pleasure can be deemed good.[17]

For both Voegelin and Strauss, the materialistic project of Hobbes and his followers has impoverished our lives. The true ends of life, which Strauss defined in philosophical and Voegelin in theological terms, have been thrust aside in the pursuit of material goods. Combating attempts to bring heaven to earth with pictures of a material, earthly paradise, Hobbes and his followers obscured and constructed dangerous arguments against the life of the spirit—the pursuit of the eternal rather than of the merely material.

Voegelin and Strauss set forth powerful visions of the contemporary materialist dilemma, only the broadest outlines of which I have given here, with which conservatives today must treat in order to find and defend the life of accepting virtue. However, while I will make occasional references to Strauss in particular in discussing the nature of conservatism, I will not deal at any length with the attempts of either thinker to address our predicament. Both Voegelin and Strauss give elegant and necessarily complex readings of the "progress of history"; I cannot hope to do justice to these theories here. Moreover, neither Voegelin nor Strauss accepted conventional conservatism. Strauss rejected conservatism because he thought it was based on the notion that men seek by nature the ancestral but not the good.[18] Voegelin, though observing that conservatives during the French Revolution were trying to salvage the Christian tradition, argued that even they were attempting the fatal project of bringing heaven to earth.[19] Voegelin in fact rejected Western Civilization itself—the civilization the (Western) conservative accepts as the source of virtue and the guardian of any good life. Because neither Strauss nor Voegelin was in any conventional sense conservative, extensive discussion of their work would detract from the central goals of this book: to describe the elements of the conservative good life and to examine attempts to find and defend this life of accepting virtue in contemporary Western society.[20]

I shall instead present a particular interpretation of the thought of the eighteenth-century British statesman and writer Edmund Burke—the acknowledged founder of modern conservatism—and of Alexis de Tocqueville, the nineteenth-century French statesman and theorist of democracy. In both cases, I will argue, we are given sustained, philosophical arguments for the conservative good life. Burke and Tocqueville defended their own societies and others on the grounds that existing institutions and practices, varied as they were, allowed for a life in which service to the community—service in one's given capacity, out of affection for those with whom one has lived one's life—was promoted. Burke and Tocqueville defended the conservative good life, the life of accepting virtue, wherever they found it. My goal is to show that the conservative good life has been expounded in coherent form and can (and should) be so expounded again. Burke's and Tocqueville's arguments for accepting virtue, like virtue itself, have been submerged in the sea of egalitarian materialism spawned most prodigiously by Hobbes. Yet by renewing our commitment to the life of the spirit, we may regain our understanding of God's will and our need to follow it if we are to live a good life. Many men claim that conservatism, because it prescribes no single blueprint for the best society, is unphilosophical and thus incoherent. My aim is to show that this charge rests on an exaggeration of the powers of human reason and on an excessively narrow vision of the nature and purpose of philosophy. Conservative political philosophy rests on recognition of man's God-given limits. It unabashedly asserts man's need for God, as well as for tradition and the natural attachments arising from the fundamental institutions of family, church, and neighborhood. It recognizes that any good life depends at least as much upon goodness of heart as upon brilliance of mind.

In reconstructing the arguments of Burke and Tocqueville concerning the nature of man, the proper scope and limits of reason, and the requirements for a virtuous life, I seek to show that the fundamental elements of conservative political philosophy remain coherent and meaningful when applied to radically different circumstances. Until relatively recently, philosophers themselves acknowledged that, in pursuing the good life, the need for goodness exceeds the need for brilliance. Aristotle recognized that all societies depend upon mutual affection, the friendship that grows from habitual intercourse, for their very existence. Burke and Tocqueville added to this the recognition that we must acknowledge the sovereignty of God if we are to accept our duty to serve our fellow men as friends rather than use them as the tools of our own ambitions. Conservatives today seek, often only half-wittingly, to resuscitate our understanding of and our aspiration for virtue. I aim to show that this resuscitation is necessary, and that it is possible even in the corrupt times in which we live.

In attempting to reconstruct the conservative vision of the good life, I court controversy even in my choice of philosophical guides. Although Burke's conservatism is almost unquestioned, Tocqueville is claimed by adherents to a number of political positions as one of their own. But it is indicative of the philosophical affinity between Burke and Tocqueville that interpretations, and misinterpretations, of their work overlap in important ways. Both men often are seen as apologists for existing material interests and the "Liberal" status quo;[21] both are also often seen as utilitarian politicians concerned only with pragmatically determining the best way to maintain stability and prosperity in the given circumstances.[22] Differences in interpretation of Burke and Tocqueville lie primarily in moral and religious readings of their work. Those who view Burke as a natural law theorist often praise him for his espousal of prudence. Burke is seen as arguing for the pragmatic application of practical remedies to particular problems in accordance with existing circumstances—and within the confines of preexisting norms. On this reading, Burkean natural law rules out both tyranny and uniformity of government, since different circumstances give rise to different traditions, institutions, and rights.[23] Although some scholars also see Tocqueville in this light,[24] others attempt to connect him with classical republicanism. For these latter interpreters, Tocqueville's lament over the loss of Frenchmen's desire for glory shows his desire to resuscitate a classical (political and military) virtue, tying citizens to the state through the use of honors.[25]

I will argue that both Burke and Tocqueville sought to promote the same, conservative good life within the confines of their given circumstances. The problems and institutions faced by Tocqueville in postrevolutionary France were different from those faced by Burke in late eighteenth-century Britain, and both thinkers encountered circumstances far different from those we confront today. Thus it should not be surprising that conservatives, committed to promoting right action, should defend different specific institutions and remedies. But then a thinker is a conservative because he seeks to preserve the traditional institutions, practices, and beliefs promoting a good life in a given society—not because he promotes any particular utopian blueprint.

Perhaps ironically, conservatism's hostility toward abstractions, its supposed lack of a substantive prescription for man and society, is the source of its universality. Burke's view that institutions should be made to fit the circumstances and natures of the people involved allowed him to defend, without inconsistency, the American Revolution as well as traditional Irish society and the Indian caste system as well as the mixed constitution of Great Britain.[26] Tocqueville argued that an affectionate and virtuous community requires that, wherever possible, we accept and attempt peacefully to improve the institutions given us by Providence. This view led him to make peace and to work with the Bourbon restoration, Louis-Phillippe's "bourgeois" monarchy, and the republic overthrown by the dictator Louis Napoleon. Louis Napoleon, however, was an innovating tyrant responsible for the destruction of French liberty, a tyrant with whom Tocqueville refused to deal.[27]

Burke's adherence to the natural law, as well as Tocqueville's, and Tocqueville's espousal of honor and glory, as well as Burke's, are both part of a coherent and consistent prescription for the conservative good life. For Burke and Tocqueville, only in societies whose citizens serve the existing order because they love it and believe it to be good can the conservative good life exist and human nature be fulfilled. Contemporary conservatives who deny the existence of or the need for accepting virtue in effect deny their own philosophical roots and the possibility of achieving their own inherent goal.

Contemporary thought is not completely bereft of any vision of a conservative good life. George F. Will writes of the need for conservative virtue: "By virtue I mean nothing arcane or obscure. I mean good citizenship, whose principal components are moderation, social sympathy and willingness to sacrifice private desires for public ends."[28] Apparently much more common, however, is a contemporary conservative lament for a virtue that has, according to Irving Kristol, lost "all her loveliness."[29] In many cases, conservative skepticism has become a kind of fatalism that does not accept society because it is good, but rather acquiesces in what is seen as an inevitably tragic fate.

If the conservative is to carry out his task as the defender of the good that exists, he must remain committed to the notion that what exists is good. His vision is not utopian; he does not posit a perfect community and regime that must be instituted immediately in the name of abstract "justice." But a reasonable comprehension of virtue includes the understanding that one need not be a utopian to value, and to defend, a particular way of life which is proper for man—pleasing to God and so inherently good. It is no paradox that the conservative good life depends upon rejection of the contemporary attempt to build an earthly paradise, for such enthusiasms discard the good of customary arrangements in pursuit of a perverse and unattainable human perfection.

In examining recent conservative thought I shall focus on the writings of three prominent figures: British philosopher Michael Oakeshott (often referred to as a "libertarian" or "liberal-conservative"), neoconservative journalist Irving Kristol, and traditionalist scholar Russell Kirk. Each of these writers is generally acknowledged to be a conservative, yet each holds seemingly divergent views on the nature of man and society, and on the proper role and nature of politics. My goal in examining their work is to show that very different thinkers within the conservative movement do in fact share a common attachment to a recognizably conservative vision of human nature and the good life. Each of these thinkers acknowledges our dilemma, and each seeks to address it in a recognizably conservative manner, emphasizing the role of traditional institutions, beliefs, and practices in any good life. Not all these thinkers succeed in constructing a powerful defense of existing society and a conservative approach to rebuilding the good life, nor do all of them reject materialist arguments in favor of appeals to accepting virtue. I contend that all contemporary conservatives *should* do both, and that the latter is necessary for the former.

Because my goal is to show prominent and varied responses to the practical reality of our dilemma, I have not made my choices of contemporary conservative thinkers on the basis of their generally accepted philosophical standing; instead I have chosen figures who thoughtfully represent major sectors of the contemporary conservative movement. In this way I seek to show the essential thread unifying the various forms of conservative thought: attachment to a conservative good life.

Oakeshott, Kristol, and Kirk approach our dilemma and its solution on very different terms, but each man sees a very real problem in our loss of virtue. Each also sees the need for a spiritual rebirth in contemporary society. Briefly, Oakeshott seeks to persuade us to virtuous self-restraint, using what he sees as the myth of the Tower of Babel to show the disastrous nature of attempts to "steal" heaven. By defending capitalism's performance, Kristol seeks to prevent our materialistic predicament from growing even worse by degenerating into collectivism. Kirk seeks to resuscitate traditional beliefs and educational concerns in order to reestablish our links with the fundamental "permanent things." Each of these responses to our dilemma has weaknesses as well as merits. Oakeshott and Kristol both seem to lack a full vision of the conservative good life, and Kirk's educational prescription appears to lack a concrete basis in conservative habituation. Yet each thinker speaks from within the tradition and for the goals first fully explicated by Burke and first fully applied to democratic society by Tocqueville.

In discussing Oakeshott, Kristol, and Kirk I shall turn also, in less detail, to the writings of Catholic thinker Michael Novak, who provides an all-too-rare defense of existing institutions and practices in terms of the spiritually based good life that they make possible. "The spirit of democratic capitalism" for Novak is embodied in the beliefs and practices of our everyday life. America's free society, according to Novak, fosters right action because it allows communities to form on the basis of mutual interest and affection rather than out of necessity and coercion.

Despite the promise of freedom, conservative acceptance is difficult today because as a society we have chosen egalitarian materialism instead of virtue. Yet Burke, the enemy of parliamentary and imperial corruption, and Tocqueville, the opponent of the dictator Louis Napoleon, found it possible to oppose elements of existing practice while supporting the existing society—its essential institutions, beliefs, and practices. The task of contemporary conservatives would seem, then, to be that of regaining the ability to defend what exists without losing their commitment to virtue. We must find the bases for the life of accepting virtue in our society and make prudent reforms where necessary to promote its fulfillment. The conservative's unchanging task is to maintain the eternal order in the face of changing circumstances.

Conservatism is, as many have noted, more of an attitude or a disposition than an ideological defense of a particular political blueprint. Yet unfortunately, the conservative attitude—that of the friend—is no longer given.[30] True friendship now must be defended, and even promoted, on the grounds that it is proper and necessary if man is to live the way of life proper to him. Only through self-examination and commitment to the service of what is good in our society may conservatism regain the motive force necessary to bring about the rebirth of the spirit in the temporal world.

Uncomfortable as many conservatives might be at the prospect of "preaching" in the name of virtue, men must be *called* to right action. That illusory "universal benevolence" that, as Burke said, "makes a man a lover of mankind but a hater of his kindred" is destructive. But it is as necessary to revive belief in the inherent goodness of kindred feelings as it is to free from materialistic reformers the natural institutions of family, church, and neighborhood that are the source of kindred feelings. Only men of sound character, men who value others as themselves and pursue their mutual good in a reasonable manner, can be free and virtuous. Only a society that places friendship before abstract and often bizarre notions of fairness can be said to allow for a good life.

1 • Natural Law and Virtue

Understanding is the reward of faith. Do not therefore try to understand in order that you may believe; but believe in order that you may understand.
—St. Augustine, *On the Gospel of St. John*

HEARTS AND MINDS

It would seem odd that there should be a political philosophy that does not assert the primacy of reason. Indeed, conservatism's insistence that human reason is quite limited in its capacity and its proper status renders it philosophically empty to many interpreters. But philosophy—the love of wisdom—has been given rather too narrow a meaning in our materialistic age. If it is true that one must believe in order to understand, that God's truth is revealed to the heart and not merely to the mind, then to ignore this truth in favor of the exercise of independent reason is to reject wisdom in favor of folly.

Augustine's statement of the relationship between faith and understanding has fallen into disuse, in large part because the good of man to which he pointed—salvation—is no longer seen as the proper one, particularly in the transcendent form he envisioned. Even many of those men who decry the corruption of our age disagree fundamentally with the notion that the soul is different from and superior to the intellect. To many men, valuing the soul over the intellect means valuing an immaterial and unknowable (and possibly nonexistent) next life and denigrating the human needs and potentials of this life. These men see dedication to transcendent norms as little more than an abandonment

15

of man's intellectual capacities and an acquiescence in terrestrial pain and injustice.

But the intellect—"reason" as that term has come to be understood—is in fact merely a limited human faculty. Reason is the means by which man discovers the appropriate solution (or lack thereof) to a given problem. Only when the problem, or more precisely the question as formulated by the inquirer, is stated in purely rationalistic terms does reason in the narrow sense of formulaic logic become of paramount importance. Thus when Descartes asserted that mathematics was the only "true" science, he was correct only in a very limited sense. Mathematics provides clear, verifiable answers only because it is inherently redundant—it is a man-made system providing the inquirer with questions, as well as with answers, that are stated solely in its own terms. Such a system is ideal for the man who seeks to feed his own pride, but it does not necessarily provide the important answers to life's questions.

The relationship between mathematics and the "real" world around us appears clear because we have been taught from our youth that "if you start with three apples and give one to your friend, you are left with two." This focus shows the limits as well as the utility of mathematical science because the question must be posed in terms of material objects that can be added or subtracted from one another, or else there will be no answer. Any attempt to subtract apples from oranges will be dismissed as incoherent.

Despite its limitations, in particular its inability to deal with differences in kind among the objects of study, mathematics has been applied to varying "objects" far more complicated than mere fruit. All the social sciences share mathematics' "rational" commitment to reducing life to a limited number of categories wherein all objects and experiences are interchangeable. Bentham's measurement of the utility of public policies according to a "calculus" of pleasure and pain was the paradigmatic attempt to reduce human behavior itself to mathematics. But, because it is based solely on human reason, a "rational" science cannot address the most important questions of life.

Although "rational" science aims to discover what is true, the truly wise man seeks to discover what is good. And the distinction between true and good is far from irrelevant. Nor does this distinction necessarily favor the use of reason over adherence to the dictates of the soul. One is being reasonable when one recognizes that all men die. One is wise only to the extent that one has discovered how one ought to meet one's death. The good, though based on a recognition of what is "true" in given circumstances, goes beyond the mere recitation of facts—or the drawing of often false analogies (for example, from man's natural desire for physical pleasures to the identification of physical pleasure as the proper goal of life)—to an examination of what is morally correct in the given circumstances. Such an examination cannot properly be based on the mere weighing of one's particular wants of the moment to discover which want should be given the most weight. To find the morally proper response to given circumstances one must recognize that some wants are by nature more important than others, that human appetites and the human will must often be denied so that God's will may be done. To act wisely is to act on the recognition that man should seek a higher good than satiation of his appetites. One should seek the happiness that is known only in a life that is properly—though not necessarily pleasantly—lived.

Men increasingly have come to reject their duty to accept God's will because they have come to identify the good, not with the holy, but with the pleasant. The corrupting notion that that which does not feel good is not good has led to the charge that those men who defend acceptance of that which is (and that may be materially or physically unpleasant) are "insensitive" to human suffering. Thus those men who see the material arrangements of this world as paramount in importance fault conservatives for their lack of outrage over "existential injustices," such as inequalities of income.

Much has been made over the centuries of the admonition rendered by Thomas Aquinas that "all human power is from God . . . *therefore he that resisteth the power,* in matters that are within its scope, *resisteth the ordinance of God;* so that he becomes guilty according to his conscience."[1] This admonition, divorced from the context of Thomistic philosophy, has been misinterpreted widely as a "conservative" rejection of the exercise of reason in favor of acquiescence in whatever happens to exist.

It is true that, for the conservative, the will of God is superior to the whims (however "rationally" arrived at) of man. The conservative shares with Aquinas, and with Augustine, a recognition of the unbreakable bond between God and man—between the transcendent and the merely material—as well as a recognition that this bond must be kept in proper order if man is not to be corrupted. Thus what God has given, including temporal forms of human power, must be accepted because such is

God's will. Because God Himself is good, that which He wills also must be accepted as good.

But the conservative attachment to existing institutions, beliefs, and practices has been criticized, not just by materialists concerned only with the distribution of material comforts, but also by those men with extra-temporal concerns. Philosophers may criticize the conservative for dei-fying history and circumstance and thereby foreclosing the pursuit of true human ends. Even as thoughtful a critic as Leo Strauss argued that con-servatism lacks positive content beyond attachment to the familiar and so has come to share in the corruptions of modernity. Thus "what goes now by the name of conservativism has in the last analysis a common root with present-day liberalism and even with Communism."[2]

For Strauss, classical political philosophy is distinct from conservatism since "it is guided by the awareness that all man [sic] seek by nature, not the ancestral or traditional, but the good." Although conservatives offer only what is or has been seen as the good, classical political philosophy offers a "substantive principle. It asserts that the society natural to man is the city, that is, a closed society that can well be taken in in one view or that corresponds to man's natural (macroscopic, not microscopic or telescopic) power of perception."[3]

Seemingly in accord with the conservative attachment to the famil-iar and the particular, Strauss's classical political philosophy also posits a conservative-sounding need for limited horizons of human perception and experience. "Less literally and more importantly, it asserts that every political society that ever has been or ever will be rests on a particular fundamental opinion which cannot be replaced by knowledge and hence is of necessity a particular or particularist society. This state of things imposes duties on the philosopher's public speech or writing which would not be duties if a rational society were actual or emerging; it thus gives rise to a specific art of writing."[4]

Strauss's theory that philosophers engage in "esoteric writing," with meanings understandable only to the initiated, stems from the role he ascribed to the philosopher within the imperfectly rational city. Since most men are not philosophers, they require "a particular fundamental opinion" upon which to base their institutions and their very lives. The philosopher knows that this opinion does not correspond to the truth, but he also knows that truth is unobtainable in this world and that to reveal the falsity of society's bases is to destroy the city and to make im-possible the life that is natural to man. For Strauss, there are no fundamental, unchanging principles upon which all societies must be based—save that the society's given principles must be held to the exclusion of all others. Morality itself is malleable and will vary radically according to the "particular fundamental opinion" upon which a particular city is based.

Strauss may seem conservative to some scholars because he emphasizes man's sociability and need for accepted fundamental beliefs. But Strauss himself resisted this identification because conservatism rejects the special status of the philosopher. Strauss's view of the philosopher's ability and role—to stand outside and analyze, if not fundamentally to change, the existing society—rests upon a confidence in and an attachment to independent reason that is not conservative. Strauss's philosopher must hide his rational project from the masses because they are incapable of grasping its truth and worth.

For the conservative, the Straussian philosopher's project itself is fundamentally misguided because it is based on a mistaken belief that traditions are exclusive and arbitrary and that man's reason can and should fully transcend his social nature and context.[5] Human nature, with all its limits and circumstance-driven variety, is more stable for the conservative than for Strauss because fundamental, unchanging principles do exist upon which all societies must be based. But these principles may be found only through the social interaction and faith that the Straussian philosopher rejects (for himself, although not for the masses) in favor of the pursuit of rational truth.

The conservative need not, indeed cannot, be antirational. Aquinas himself, the most exhaustive and eloquent theorist of natural law (the very basis of conservative political philosophy), argued from rational proofs for the existence of God.[6] But reason, for the conservative, is by nature limited and must be exercised within a social and, more importantly, an *emotional* context. There is no true external, Archimedean point possible from which society may be judged. And the search for such a vantage point is the product, not of virtue, but of the vice of overweening philosophical pride. For the conservative, reason must be guided by an emotion or passion fundamentally different from that of pride—namely affection. Love of God and of His creations is the necessary prerequisite for the proper use of reason. God is beyond reason; neither He nor His works may be understood fully by mere mortals. But God gave reason to man—to be used in order to discover and follow His will.

The Thomistic recognition of three forms of law—divine, natural, and manmade—leaves ample room for, indeed in each case depends upon, the use of human reason. If one is to understand these laws, which to-gether rule all of life, one must acknowledge human limits and the need, in the very exercise of reason, to look outside the self (to the divine au-thority of Scripture, to the natural world explained by both revelation and reason, and to scientific truths necessarily based upon "naturally known, indemonstrable principles"[7]) in order to find, as well as mere mortals can, the natural order. Divine and natural law certainly pro-vide standards "outside" the given structures and horizons of a society, but they also command that we apply these standards with humility and a gentle care for what God, nature, our ancestors, and our neighbors have wrought.

The philosopher, whether Plato in ancient Greece or Nietzsche in the last century, who presumes to judge societies, let alone to create or de-stroy them, on the basis of his own reason is in fact mad. He assumes the place of God and so explodes the limits within which any sane man must live. Thus Nietzsche, who announced the demise of God, ended his days in an asylum, claiming to be Christ. And even the philosopher whose madness goes unrecognized pursues a mad life divorced from the intercourse of humanity. He rejects man's natural sociability in order to pursue an independent reason that does not exist.

Aquinas argued that human reason is a limited and practical faculty, much more limited and fallible than (divine) knowledge.[8] The major function of reason is to control the passions so that one may discern prop-erly that which lies outside the self—the God-given nature of things—and thus determine what is fitting, given the current circumstances.[9] The nature and function of Thomistic proper reason is shown by Aquinas's term *synderesis*, generally rendered as "conscience."[10] Natural law is based on certain principles that are self-evident to sane men—most fundamentally that man should do good and avoid evil. Aquinas iden-tified the good with the natural. That which is natural to man—to which he will incline if not corrupted—is good.[11] The most basic good of man is sociability. Man naturally seeks the society of his kind, and it is to make possible and to enhance this natural good that human law arises.

Since law by nature is useful to man, it must (1) foster religion, (2) be "helpful to discipline," and (3) "further the commonweal." Each of these characteristics, fulfilling divine, natural, and practical human requirements, respectively, inheres in any true law. But specific forms of law must vary since "the general principles of the natural law cannot be applied to all men in the same way on account of the great variety of human affairs."[12] To serve man, the laws must fit his particular circumstances as well as his inherent nature.

The circumstances of a society—the history and preexisting institutions and practices that characterize it—determine in large measure what laws will be natural to it. But human laws must fulfill their natural functions as set forth in higher law if they are to be judged worthy of obedience. Far from justifying any government that happens to exist as the will of God, Aquinas, explicitly following Augustine, argued that "the force of a law depends on the extent of its justice . . . every human law has just so much of the nature of law, as it is derived from the law of nature. But if in any point it deflects from the law of nature, it is no longer a law but a perversion of law."[13]

The supposed passivity of Thomistic doctrine stems from Aquinas's insistence that laws should not be changed at the mere whim of individuals. But for Aquinas the duty of obedience itself is based upon the dictates of natural law. One resists God only when one resists human power acting *within its proper scope*. One is not bound to obey wicked laws, "provided he avoid giving scandal or inflicting a more grievous hurt."[14] Wicked laws are to be obeyed only when, and to the extent, necessary to avoid harming others or society itself.

Possessed of both soul and body—partaking of the angelic and the beastly—man is capable of both good and evil. It is society that, by prohibiting the vicious indulgence of base appetites, allows man's natural inclination toward virtue to develop (within the natural sphere of the family) and to be put into practice.[15] And virtue—the habit of choosing correctly[16]—is the proper goal of man. Virtuous, moral action, although not sufficient for salvation (which requires the grace of God), is pleasing to God and necessary if salvation is to be possible. Thus virtue serves both to make this life more perfect (in the sense of achieving an inherent rather than a willfully determined nature) and to make the highest goal of man—to be close to God—possible.[17]

Aquinas argued that "Grace does not abolish Nature but perfects it."[18] Man's peculiar nature places him in a position between angels and beasts—both of whose natures are inherent and unchanging. Man's nature is malleable; he requires society if he is to avoid corruption and achieve his nature. And it is this conception of man's particular social nature, and its requirements, that lies at the heart of conservative political philosophy. The conservative argues that each of us must act within a *particular* society—but a society whose particular laws and customs are derived from a universal natural law.

The conservative reading of natural law owes much to Aquinas. But the conservative goes beyond Aquinas in his insistence that reason's basis lies in faith and revelation.[19] As Augustine argued that one must believe in order to understand, so the conservative bases his view of man and society on an understanding that conscience is not merely rational but, more fundamentally, moral. Put bluntly, Moses gave the Jews God's Ten Commandments—not ten rationally self-evident principles. It is man's God-given nature or proper, natural end to lead the moral life best summed up in the golden rule—the commandment to love your neighbor as yourself.

Natural law was not, of course, the invention of Aquinas. The Thomistic vision of man's nature and place in the order of the universe is perhaps the most comprehensive and powerful, but it was formulated within a tradition as old and as important as human thought itself. In his path-breaking study *Edmund Burke and the Natural Law*, Peter Stanlis has traced the influence of natural law doctrine from ancient to modern times. From Aristotle to Cicero to Justinian to Bracton to Aquinas and on up to Jefferson, certain fundamental beliefs were shared by all men of thought and good will.[20] For these thinkers, natural law was an emanation of the will of God, providing self-evident principles that man must follow and that transcend particular human laws. Although the content of natural law doctrine varied over time in emphasis and to some extent in particular elements, the literature and the tradition of natural law established as fundamental principles the unity of human nature and the need for (varying forms of) human society if man is to control his vices and achieve his nature.

Stanlis quotes Strauss in arguing that Hobbes corrupted man's vision of natural law, transforming it in men's minds from a statement of eternal standards to "a series of 'rights,' of subjective claims, emanating from the human will."[21] Thus the language of natural law came to be used within various materialist ideologies as mere cover for individual appetites. Yet the tradition of natural law continued, particularly within canon law, and served as the very basis for the common law of England.[22]

It is to the traditional, uncorrupted doctrine of natural law that the conservative turns in facing the corruptions of his day.[23] The Thomistic conception of the natural hierarchy of the universe has had a powerful and lasting influence upon conservative philosophy. Burke in particular emphasized man's subordinate position in the order of creation and, from this, the limits of human reason. According to Burke, man has neither the right nor the means to question the bases of his own society, let alone to cure all the world's ills.[24] Each man has a specific place in the natural, hierarchical Great Chain of Being, be he peasant, squire, or monarch. And each man must accept his place, itself often bestowed at birth in aristocratic societies, as a manifestation of the will of God.[25] We each have our own station in life, a station that determines the nature and extent of our capacity and of our right to act.

Because human reason is by nature limited, Tocqueville argued that "for society to exist and, even more, for society to prosper, it is essential that all the minds of the citizens should always be rallied and held together by some leading ideas; and that could never happen unless each of them sometimes came to draw his opinions from the same source and was ready to accept some beliefs ready made."[26] Man must accept his own limitations and the rightness of his society's fundamental beliefs, or civilization will become impossible.

For the conservative, as for Aquinas, society is *the* force that civilizes man by taming his passions.[27] Human laws may vary, but human society is natural and thus necessary. As Tocqueville put it, "Man creates kingdoms and republics, but townships seem to spring directly from the hand of God."[28] Hierarchy also is a naturally occurring phenomenon, necessary for society. While Tocqueville commented throughout his *Democracy in America* on the spontaneous production of class distinctions,[29] Burke concerned himself most with defending their necessity. "To destroy hierarchy would have all the decent drapery of life rudely torn off . . . all which is necessary to cover the defects of our naked, shivering nature."[30] It was Burke's view of the weakness of a human nature bereft of social institutions that informed his insistence upon prescription, or "the natural and dutiful reverence to any institution that has existed through the ages and persists to the present day."[31]

But societies and given beliefs are not wholly self-justifying. The conservative seeks to preserve existing institutions *because* they allow for and foster the practice of virtue. Institutions and indeed entire social systems (such as Communist states) that do not allow for the practice of conservative virtue are morally wrong and best abolished because they fit the nature of no man. Natural law dictates that history and circumstance take leading roles in forming the institutions that in turn perfect—or bring to proper fulfillment—human nature. "Since man in every state is by nature a political animal, the real natural rights of man are a matter of practical political reason, and are to be found only within the objectives and conventions of civil society."[32] But if human nature is to be fulfilled, society must allow for the stable, familiar, and affectionate life that teaches men to love and to serve their neighbors and thence their communities.

Conservative political philosophy seems vague and even nonexistent to many men because it is based, not on a particular blueprint of the perfect political order, but on an attachment to a way of life. And a way of life need not be dependent upon a particular political regime. Conservatism is no more the defense of one particular regime than it is the defense of whatever regime happens to exist. Conservatism entails the defense of all regimes (but *only* those regimes) respectful enough of customary institutions, beliefs, and practices to allow for a conservative good life. Natural law requires that we accept society's pivotal role in the formation of proper character. By the same token, natural law provides criteria by which to judge the ability of particular societies to promote the proper goal of man: the life of accepting virtue.

FORMS OF VIRTUE

Only now are we beginning to reconstruct the concept of virtue torn asunder by centuries of materialistic preoccupation. Moreover, this reconstruction is taking place in a time when Western Civilization itself is being pronounced dead and helped into an untimely grave by intellectuals and others claiming the right to transform our way of life. It seems apparent, then, that any coherent discussion of the conservative good life requires some initial examination of the forms of virtue propounded by thinkers working within our tradition.[33]

The rebirth, such as it is, of the notion of virtue as a political idea in recent years owes much to scholars of classical republicanism. In interpreting political philosophers as diverse as Machiavelli and Harrington, republican scholars such as J. G. A. Pocock have emphasized the role of "civic virtue"—the provision of public service in pursuit of honors—in the republican political community. Theorists of republicanism share with conservatives a reliance on what is fundamentally a natural law con-

ception of man's social nature and his fulfillment of that nature in social life. Not surprisingly, then, there is a conflation, notably by some of
Tocqueville's interpreters, of conservative with republican virtue. But
conservative virtue is distinct from republican virtue in that it emphasizes social rather than political or military action. To make this distinction
clear, it first is necessary to examine the classical, Aristotelian conception of virtue on which Aquinas himself relied, and on which both republicanism and conservatism rely so heavily.

Aristotle

Aristotle argued that all men aim at the good of life, which is happiness.[34] And the happy or good life is lived by practicing "active" virtue.
"The Good of man is the active exercise of his soul's faculties in conformity with excellence or virtue, or if there be several human excel-
lences or virtues, in conformity with the best and most perfect among
them."[35]

The nature of virtue, for Aristotle, is also the problem of virtue;
virtue's nature makes its practice difficult. Virtue is a mean, "because it
aims at hitting the middle point in feeling and in actions. This is why
it is a hard task to be good, for it is hard to find the middle point in anything: for instance, not everybody can find the centre of a circle, but only
someone who knows geometry. So also anybody can become angry—that
is easy, and so it is to give and spend money; but to be angry with or give
money to the right person, and to the right amount, and at the right time,
and for the right purpose, and in the right way—this is not within everybody's power and is not easy; so that to do these things properly is rare,
praiseworthy, and noble."[36] Virtue is in part the product of consideration and circumstance. If one's anger is to be virtuous, one must be angry
with the right man and for the right reason rather than at everyone and
all the time because it is abstractly or metaphysically correct to be angry.

Because virtue requires that we conform our actions properly to our
given circumstances, it requires prudence. "Prudence is a truth-attain-
ing rational quality, concerned with action in relation to the things that
are good for human beings."[37] Prudence is not concerned with general
principles only; it is also able to "take account of particular facts, since
it is concerned with action, and action deals with particular things."[38]
Thus, "Prudence as well as Moral Virtue determines the complete per-

formance of man's proper function: Virtue ensures the rightness of the end we aim at, Prudence ensures the rightness of the means we adopt to gain that end."[39]

Aristotle identifies moral virtue with justice. Justice is the practice of virtue toward others; the just man acts as the law bids, takes the proper share of good and bad things, and gives the proper share of good and bad things to those around him.[40] But the phrase "those around him" does not denote everyone. The practice of justice requires prudence so that we may know how to treat others properly, that is, in light of their particular characteristics. "For there is no such thing as injustice in the absolute sense towards what is one's own; and a chattel, or a child till it reaches a certain age and becomes independent, is, as it were, a part of oneself, and no one chooses to harm himself; hence there can be no injustice towards them, and therefore nothing just or unjust in the political sense. For these, as we saw, are embodied in law, and exist between persons whose relations are naturally regulated by law, that is, persons who share equally in ruling and being ruled."[41] The nature of those men with whom one is dealing—their status as free or slave, or their age and thus their ability to be treated as fully competent men—determines not only what justice is in relation to them, but whether justice in the true sense may exist in one's dealings with them.[42]

Prudence is the necessary tool for the attainment of virtue; it is the practical wisdom necessary if one is to judge rightly how to respond to particular circumstances. Prudence, and not the theoretically superior philosophical wisdom, provides the guidance necessary for virtue. Thus habituation rather than metaphysical knowledge is the surest road to virtue. "Virtue being, as we have seen of two kinds, intellectual and moral, intellectual virtue is for the most part both produced and increased by instruction, and therefore requires experience and time; whereas moral or ethical virtue is the product of habit. . . . And therefore it is clear that none of the moral virtues is engendered in us by nature, for no natural property can be altered by habit. . . . The virtues therefore are engendered in us neither by nature nor yet in violation of nature; nature gives us the capacity to receive them, and this capacity is brought to maturity by habit."[43]

What is more, "acts done in conformity with the virtues are not done justly or temperately if they themselves are of a certain sort, but only if the agent also is in a certain state of mind when he does them: first he must act with knowledge; secondly he must deliberately choose the act, and choose it for its own sake; and thirdly the act must spring from a fixed and permanent disposition of character."[44] A single good deed done, as it were, by accident, is not virtuous. One's disposition determines the character of one's actions. One acts virtuously because one is disposed to do so. And one acquires a virtuous character or disposition through habituation. Indeed, the virtues themselves *are* dispositions.[45] "Only an utterly senseless person can fail to know that our characters are the result of our conduct."[46] A man becomes careless by acting in a careless manner, by allowing himself to fall into bad habits such as drinking to excess. A man may become virtuous by living, that is acting, in the proper manner until he does so automatically, or from habit. As for natural law thinkers who followed him, for Aristotle society's natural role is to provide the discipline necessary for virtue.

One practices virtue only in one's relations with those whom one rules and is ruled by in turn. Thus, according to Aristotle, "the Supreme Good was the end of political science, but the principal care of this science is to produce a certain character in the citizens, namely to make them virtuous, and capable of performing noble actions."[47] Political science determines the proper institutions for society, the proper relations between men, and the proper way to habituate men to the proper dispositions—the dispositions that *are* moral virtue.

Man cannot be made virtuous solely through intellectual instruction. "Theory and teaching are not, I fear, equally efficacious in all cases: the soil must have been previously tilled if it is to foster the seed, the mind of the pupil must have been prepared by the cultivation of habits, so as to like and dislike aright. For he that lives at the dictates of passion will not hear nor understand the reasoning of one who tries to dissuade him; but if so, how can you change his mind by argument?"[48] And it is here that political science must enter, and that the statesman's performance becomes all-important.

It is difficult to obtain a right education in virtue from youth up without being brought up under right laws; for to live temperately and hardily is not pleasant to most men, especially when young; hence the nurture and exercises of the young should be regulated by law, since temperance and hardiness will not be painful when they have become habitual. But doubtless it is not enough for people to receive the right nurture and discipline in youth; they must also practice the lessons they have learnt, and confirm them by habit, when they are grown up. Accordingly we shall need laws to regulate the discipline of adults as well, and in fact the whole life of the people generally; for the many are more amenable to compulsion and punishment than to reason and to moral ideals.[49]

It is perhaps his view of the needs and limitations of the many that led to Aristotle's statement that, where the law is concerned, "what it does not expressly sanction it forbids."[50]

The statesman's task is difficult because citizens have varied characters and so require varied treatment if they are to be made virtuous. This is why the statesman must have both scientific wisdom (dealing with universals) and practical wisdom or prudence. He must have knowledge of both the universal (especially the nature of man) and the specific (the nature of particular circumstances) if he is to legislate properly.[51] "Prudence is indeed the same quality of mind as Political Science, though their essence is different. Of Prudence as regards the state, one kind, as supreme and directive, is called Legislative Science; the other, as dealing with particular occurrences, has the name, Political Science, that really belongs to both kinds."[52]

Political science is prudence as applied to relations between men. Because it provides the means with which to mold virtuous citizens, political science is also that science which aims most directly toward the good. This means that, for Aristotle, statesmen are most able to practice moral virtue and to attain the highest moral virtue because they practice it on behalf of the entire community. The state is all-important and essentially all-encompassing in Aristotle's view because its dictates are to control the lives of its citizens.

But it is important to note that, for Aristotle, it is not moral virtue but speculative wisdom which is the heart of the best life attainable by man. He argued that

> contemplation is at once the highest form of activity (since the intellect is the highest thing in us, and the objects with which the intellect deals are the highest things that can be known), and also it is the most continuous, for we can reflect more continuously than we can carry on any form of action. And again we suppose that happiness must contain an element of pleasure; now activity in accordance with wisdom is admittedly the most pleasant of the activities in accordance with virtue: at all events it is held that philosophy or the pursuit of wisdom contains pleasures of marvellous purity and permanence, and it is reasonable to suppose that

the enjoyment of knowledge is a still pleasanter occupation than the pursuit of it.[53]

Indeed, the life of contemplation transcends the merely human because it partakes of something in man that is actually divine—the intellect.[54] The life of contemplation is also one of leisure, self-sufficiency, relative freedom from fatigue, "and all the other attributes of blessedness: it follows that it is the activity of the intellect that constitutes complete human happiness."[55]

> The life of moral virtue, on the other hand, is happy only in a secondary degree. For the moral activities are purely human: Justice, I mean, Courage and the other virtues we display in our intercourse with our fellows, when we observe what is due to each in contracts and services and in our various actions, and in our emotions also; and all of these things seem to be purely human affairs. And some moral actions are thought to be the outcome of the physical constitution, and moral virtue is thought to have a close affinity in many respects with the passions. Moreover, Prudence is intimately connected with Moral Virtue, and this with Prudence, inasmuch as the first principles which Prudence employs are determined by the Moral Virtues, and the right standard for the Moral Virtues is determined by Prudence.[56]

The moral virtues (and prudence) are inferior and secondary to the life of contemplation. They partake only of what is purely human—including even the passions—and so do not constitute the fully human, self-sufficient life. This means that man naturally seeks the life of contemplation. The Aristotelian good life is the life of contemplative wisdom or what we now exclusively call "philosophy."

The life of self-sufficiency and contemplation is best, for Aristotle, and therefore is to be aimed at, not only by individuals, but by statesmen on behalf of their communities. In the *Politics*, Aristotle argued that contemplation is the highest good for the state as well as for the individual since it is "clear that the same way of life which is best for the individual must also be best for the state as a whole and for all its members."[57] The good statesman will arrange the institutions of the city to maximize the leisure available to the citizens so that they may pursue the life of contemplation.[58]

Accepting many of his arguments concerning the nature of man and of moral virtue, the conservative rejects Aristotle's assertion that philosophical contemplation is the true good of life. The philosopher all too often is a dangerous madman who may corrupt or destroy society with his faith-sapping speculations. The conservative does not necessarily reject the Thomistic revision of the Aristotelian good, however. The greatest good for Aquinas was beatitude (or "blessedness"). To achieve the transcendent happiness of beatitude—to be close to God—one must leave behind merely temporal concerns. The monastic life is not the social life, at least in the way in which most men conceive of it. But few men are called to monasticism—to "die" to this world and live as much as possible in the next. What is more, the man who seeks beatitude is far different from the one who seeks to transform this world in supposed imitation (or "immanentization") of the next. The true saint is much less a danger to society than is the "true" (Aristotelian or perhaps Platonic) philosopher. The saint in fact shows by his example that virtue is possible. Recognizing that few men are saints, the conservative attempts to foster virtue among those of us who must dwell in this world by defending our fundamental institutions, beliefs, and practices. The conservative does not seek to maintain the given merely for its own sake, but rather to make possible a life of virtue—a life that is proper for man because it is pleasing to God.

Republicanism

In republican theory, the concerns of this world are not merely the most obvious objects of immediate attention, they are the only proper objects of attention. The republican legislator is the greatest practitioner, not of moral, philosophic or Godly virtue, but of civic virtue. And civic virtue appears to be the only virtue available. Virtue for the republican is inherently political and overtly active. Virtuous action does not include active thought, but only political acts in direct service to the state. This is why Machiavelli could value his city more than his soul: For the republican, the state provides the only real moral and thus (in its own terms) spiritual life.

But the republican does not reject Aristotelian philosophy. Pocock asserts that "there are several ways of reading Aristotle's *Politics*, and this greatly complicates the task of assessing its place in Western tradition."[59] The *Politics* may be seen as a treatise on natural law or grace. "But it may also be read as the originator of a body of thought about the citizen and his relation to the republic, and about the republic (or polis) as a community of values," and this is how its importance to republicanism is uncovered. For the republican, Aristotle taught that all human activity "aimed at some theoretically identifiable good," a good necessarily pursued by men "in association with one another." The republic was the highest association because it made possible the pursuit of other, lesser ends. Thus participation in the political association of the republic was a higher good than the pursuit of more particular goods.[60] Association was itself a good of high order. The highest mode of life was that of "the citizen who ruled as head of his . . . household, and ruled and was ruled as one of a community of equal heads making decisions which were binding on all. He took part in the determination of the general good, enjoying in his own person the values made attainable by society while contributing by his political activity to the attainment of values by others."[61]

The goal of the republic was that of "allocating priorities"—determining what particular goods should be enjoyed or pursued at what times and to what extent, given the conflicts between different particular goods and between the particular and the universal good. But, in its efforts to provide for both the particular and the common good, the republic was to treat groups of men, not just as members of particular groups categorized according to their particular qualities, but also as the few and the many. The separating criterion was the ability to rule. Those men considered to have the quality of rulers were counted among the few, those found wanting in this area were counted among the many. In this way ruling became a quality and a goal separated from other, more particular goals.[62] Decision making was not reserved solely for those men counted among the few, however. Given the interdependent nature of community life, the evil most to be avoided was the domination of the whole by one—any—particular group. Each group had to exercise power and have power exercised upon it; otherwise, particular values would come to dominate and displace the common good.[63]

Aristotle argued that the problem of power distribution could best be solved through the institution of the polity, a regime that prescribed the inclusion of all groups in the decision-making process. The polity's balanced government was aimed at preventing the subversion of the general by the particular. But the polity, a highly varied society with an unlimited number of possible groups and corresponding political roles, generally has been simplified into the single idea of a government that balances the roles of the few and the many. The theoretical and political problems of such an oversimplification—as well as those of a system such as Aristotle's in which there are so many possible groups that the regime's institutionalization may be impossible—were the focus of the republican attempt to reconcile the activities of men who are "moral only in their relations with each other."[64]

In the republic, conflicts between the particular and the common good were to be settled by the condition of each man ruling and being ruled in turn "or—more rigorously—[being ruled by] the moral and political laws that governed all of them."[65] Since all its citizens were in some sense rulers, the polity was intimately concerned with their virtue and legislated to provide for it. "Humanist political thought excelled at this sort of analysis, and subordinated the consideration of power to it; liberty, virtue, and corruption, rather than the location of authority, were its prime concerns."[66] And it was liberty, in the republican sense, that provided for virtue and guarded against corruption. Only "free" citizens, that is citizens with their own arms (Machiavelli's citizen militia, later expanded by Harrington to mean citizen freeholders owing their arms to no one save the state), were in a position to learn and to practice virtue.

The danger to republican liberty, and to virtue, was not excessive social control. Indeed, according to Forrest McDonald,

> The vital—that is life-giving—principle of republics was *public virtue.* . . . Public virtue entailed firmness, courage, endurance, industry, frugal living, strength, and above all, unremitting devotion to the weal of the public's corporate self, the community of virtuous men. It was at once individualistic and communal: individualistic in that no member of the public could be dependent upon any other and still be reckoned a member of the public; communal in that every man gave himself totally to the good of the public as a whole. . . . Every matter that might in any way contribute to strengthening or weakening the virtue of the public was a thing of concern to the public—a *res publica*— and was subject to regulation by the public. Republican liberty was totalitarian: one was free to do that, and only that, which was in the interest of the public, the liberty of the individual being subsumed in the freedom or independence of his political community.[67]

Thus the republic controlled the daily lives of its citizens, providing for the circumstances under which civic virtue, defined as service to the state, could be practiced. Sumptuary laws and stiff penalties for bribery and sedition were only the most obvious of means to the end of civic virtue.

In order to survive and prosper, the republic would have to construct a system of honors allowing its more able and thus more ambitious citizens to achieve the rewards they desired through service to the state.[68] The republic, whether Aristotle's, Machiavelli's, or Harrington's, aimed at maintaining a balance among groups such that the common interest would be served. This balancing act had to include attention to the tension between private and public virtues—with public virtues given precedence and encouragement in the form of specific institutions (such as militia, public honors, and freehold land).

There is another important aspect of the republican perception of man's role in history and society, however—the relationship between *virtù* and *fortuna*: "By the exercise of a partly nonmoral *virtù*, the innovator imposes form upon *fortuna*: that is to say, upon the sequence of happenings in time disordered by his own act."[69] The founder, or legislator, achieves the highest level of virtue since he is the one who forms the polis out of the disorder that surrounds him, balancing the virtues of the citizens he creates.[70] Civic virtue is subordinate because it is derived from the creative virtue of the founder.

Because of its emphasis upon the founder, republican virtue is dangerous, even deadly, in the eyes of the conservative. Republicanism promotes the molding of virtuous citizens through the act of political foundation. It calls only political acts truly virtuous and therefore allows only one final, ultimate goal for the ambitious: the setting up of political institutions. This means that society will be unstable—made up of conflicting, ambitious, would-be founders, whose powers must be carefully balanced in a republic in which there is only one good. And "founding" is a dangerous good, the pursuit of which may destroy society itself.

The role of political action, the requirement for active civic virtue, is not nearly so great in the conservative as in the republican concept of virtue. Indeed, conservatism's rejection of the primacy of the Aristotelian and republican goods (speculative wisdom and strictly political action) may be seen as the basis for arguments that conservatism is without a conception of the good or virtuous life. Most men today recognize only philosophy and politics as possible alternatives to material comfort as the good of man. The conservative, rejecting material comfort as a degrading goal, is skeptical of the abstract goodness of its commonly noted alternatives. Both abstract reason and political action are dangerous. Indeed, they may undermine the essential moral institutions of society—tradition (particularly religion), prejudice and manners.

Conservative, Accepting Virtue

Conservative virtue does not presume to be "creative." The purpose of the conservative statesman is not (as it is for his republican counterpart) to found a republic, to mold the citizens according to a particular conception of civic virtue. The purpose of the conservative statesman also is not (as it is for his Aristotelian counterpart) to mold institutions and citizens to produce moral virtue and to allow for intellectual virtue. The statesman simply is not the central figure in conservative thought. Indeed, it would appear that there is no central figure. Instead there are central institutions, beliefs and practices which have existed from time immemorial, which are historical and natural to the society in question. The statesman is to tend to arrangements, to protect society as it faces changing circumstances, so that social institutions may do their socializing work.

The founder/legislator is the man whose actions the conservative seeks to prevent or to counteract. While republican thought expends much time and praise on the founder, the man who shapes fortune into a social whole, conservatism is more concerned with maintaining the good of existing arrangements in the face of attempts to reform radically or to refound a given society. For the conservative, the idea that one man—or one group of men—has the wisdom necessary to create a new society and new citizens rather than to take what circumstance and history have given reflects, not virtue, but hubris. It is a manifestation of that overweening pride that urges man to replace his own will for the will of God.

According to Harvey Mansfield, "for Aristotle, the possibility of a legislator is crucial for the possibilities of man: it is the link between the best life of man—the life of reason—and the usual, necessary life of man—the life of politics." For the conservative, "This link does not exist"[71]—because it need not exist. Prudence and tradition give the statesman the guidance he needs, without the dangers of hubristic pure reason. Conservative natural law makes the Aristotelian distinction between moral and intellectual virtue politically unnecessary because nature's laws are sufficiently obvious for all to see. Moreover, the conservative would, whenever possible, eschew political action itself in favor of supportive social action within already existing communities.

The creative republic in fact demands a particular form of government—the mixed regime or polity—and the particular form of (martial) virtue appropriate to that form of government. For Tocqueville (himself a supporter of French colonialism), martial virtue is intimately connected with a feudal aristocratic society. It is based upon the dominance of one class over all others. As a guiding principle it is antithetical to any free and democratic society. "The feudal aristocracy was born of war and for war; it won its power by force of arms and maintained it thereby. So nothing was more important to it than military courage. It was therefore natural to glorify courage above all other virtues. Every manifestation thereof, even at the expense of common sense and humanity, was therefore approved and often even ordained by the manners of the time. The fantastic notions of individuals could affect only the details of such a system."[72] Whatever our abstract imaginings might tell us, for Tocqueville martial virtue was a brutal reality, supporting an often brutal system.

Burke also opposed any monolithic notion of human virtue and the good society. He praised ancient legislators for forming governments that disposed "their citizens into such classes, and [placed] them in such situations in the state, as their peculiar habits might qualify them to fill, and to allot to them such appropriated privileges as might secure to them what their specific occasions required, and which might furnish to each description such force as might protect it in the conflict caused by the diversity of interests that must exist, and must contend, in all complex society."[73] Dispensing with the wisdom of the ages, the French revolutionaries paved the way for tyranny by leveling men—by abolishing classes. The rash, rationalistic actions of the Jacobins destroyed the traditional balance of forces (or classes), which once reflected divergent interests and offered resistance to would-be tyrants.[74]

Burke did not praise the *creation* of different men through deliberate action on the part of legislators. Class distinctions are necessary because men's differing circumstances promote differing habits and in turn different types (or "classes") of men. Wise, ancient legislators recognized that they "were obliged to study the effects of those habits which are communicated by the circumstances of civil life. They were sensible that the operation of this second nature on the first produced a new combination,—and thence arose many diversities amongst men, according to their birth, their education, their professions, the periods of their lives, their residence in towns or in the country, their several ways of acquiring and of fixing property, and according to the quality of the property itself, all which rendered them, as it were, so many different species of animals."[75]

Human differentiation is not planned; it occurs in the course of human events. The role of the legislator is to construct (or more correctly to oversee the growth of) a state that reflects naturally acquired human differences rather than to create such differences. Natural law commands rulers to fit human laws to differing human circumstances rather than to create differing human natures, for example, by founding militias for the express purpose of fostering martial virtue among citizen freeholders. Monarchy, polity, or moderate democracy—in short, the institutional form of the regime—matters only in that it should fit (be natural to) the people involved. Institutions and peoples must grow together so that man may perfect his nature—that is, attain his proper virtue. "He who gave our nature to be perfected by our virtue willed also the necessary means of its perfection: He willed, therefore, the state."[76]

Conservatism gains from Aristotle the understanding that the political community is the product of natural attachments. For Aristotle, of course, attachment to one's family naturally grows into attachment to the household, the village, and finally to the highest and most important association: the polis.[77] Likewise for the conservative, local attachments—such as those in the townships on which Tocqueville argued American democracy was based—form out of the habitual interactions of daily life. And from local attachments and habits grow the particular characters of particular men. This is why prudence dictates, for Aristotle and the conservative, that circumstances be met with local differentiation so that particular men may achieve their natures.

Conservative virtue appears more worldly than that of Aquinas and more quiet and humble than that of either republicanism or Aristotle because it is concerned principally with fostering right conduct in the given circumstances of this world. For the conservative, virtuous acts necessarily will take place within the confines of existing institutions and practices. Provided they allow for the operation of the institutions (principally religion, family, and local associations) habituating man to virtue, societies are good. Thus the virtuous man must love and serve his society along with his fellow man.

Conservative virtue is more social than political. It is concerned with promoting a way of life rather than a formal structure. The man of accepting virtue accepts that which life (or Providence) has given to him. His station in life, his family, and community—his beliefs and primary practices—are given to him in the literal sense; they are presented to him at birth. Virtue, in this context, consists of accepting the gift of a given way of life and doing one's best to be worthy of it. The virtuous man, for the conservative, lives up to his duties and fulfills his nature in large part through the often difficult task of seeing to it that his community is preserved as it was given to him.

A given way of life, for the conservative, is not mere material to be reworked and improved. A way of life is a precious gift that must be valued for its own sake lest the divine giver be displeased, lest the receiver take on the despicable character of an ingrate. To be worthy of a great gift is more difficult than to be worthy of one which is humble. Thus, for Burke, the responsibilities of an aristocrat are greater than those of a peasant. To accept a humble gift is more difficult than to accept one that is grand. Thus, for Burke, the most important duty of a hairdresser is to refrain from untoward political action. But all men have the duty to accept and to use the gift of their lives both wisely and reverently.

One's social and economic position is not the sole gift of life, however. One also is given the gift of free will and the corresponding duty to do one's best with one's capacities and opportunities. Economic and social advancement are just goals if pursued properly, through the provision of service to one's fellow man. And service might take many forms. Progress can rightly be had through commerce and manufacturing as well as through service in politics, the sciences, the military, or the clergy. Virtue is not limited to a particular group but to those men who live up to the dictates of the profession in which circumstance, ability, and choice have placed them.

Both Burke and Tocqueville led political lives. Burke served in Parliament for most of his adult life, and Tocqueville even attained the position of foreign minister for a brief time. Yet both men sought to conserve the goodness of their societies rather than to refound them through political action. They sought political lives, but they also recognized the honor properly attaching to other callings. That the conservative thinker should be drawn to political life is not surprising, for it is in politics that the circumstances threatening one's given society will be most apparent in our political age. Nonetheless, Burke and Tocqueville both defended the varied splendor of virtues and callings that makes up the conservative good life.

The conservative good life is not static; one may advance one's position within this life in many ways. But a society can survive the rigors of a just liberty only if its members are attached to and seek to act in the interests of what is familiar and so loved. Indeed, if man is to survive the rigors of liberty, he must recognize that freedom must be exercised well, lest man himself be degraded. A free life, if it is to be a good life, requires that man recognize and act upon his duty to love and serve those with whom Providence has linked his existence. In a life of accepting virtue, the enlightened self-interest often deemed the basis of Tocqueville's thought has only a marginal connection with egalitarian materialism. Tocqueville recognized that self-regard is the unchanging basis of human nature. But he also recognized that human attachments naturally expand from this self-regard—from the self to the family, to neighbors, and thence to the nation and mankind. It is in practical interaction with those one knows, those whose respect and love one covets, that one learns how to act properly.

Conservative virtue is accepting virtue. It is possible only when there is that attitude of friendship that allows one to accept, "warts and all" he, and that, which is familiar and so loved. In particular, prejudice, now strongly identified with racism, is a fundamental part of any society rightly constituted. Prejudice is nothing more (and nothing less) than belief based on history and social convention rather than on independent rational judgment. Virtue begins with acceptance of preexisting arrangements, and if the beliefs on which society's arrangements depend are called into question, the arrangements themselves soon will be imperiled. To dismiss unquestioned beliefs along with the injustices of racial bigotry is, then, to dismiss the basis of any social consensus—and thus of any society.

Accepting virtue here will be discussed in terms of five virtues meant to indicate (rather than schematically exhaust) what is, after all, an organic conception of the elements of a good life. Particular goods may be weighed somewhat differently in light of given circumstances (this is, after all, the proper goal of right reason or prudence). And particular labels may or may not be used by particular conservatives to denote given modes of right action. But virtues that may usefully be termed "accept-ingness," "public service," "independence," "prudence," and "local af-fection" represent the fundamental elements of the conservative good life.

The conservative virtues are much less specific than those of repub-licanism or of Aristotle. To say that one should be accepting might be seen as demanding piety, patriotism, or loyalty. But the distinction be-tween these terms has more to do with the object of acceptance than with the act itself. The pious accept religion and the need for faith. The patriotic accept the supremacy and goodness of the nation. The loyal support their friends and neighbors. All accept and defend that which is *given* or that which already exists. This is the tenor of conservative virtue—the objects of virtuous action are *accustomed* goods.

Action is virtuous because it supports the preexisting moral order rather than attempts to create a new and supposedly better order. Only when the other virtues are made impossible will the conservative admit that it is necessary to give up the virtue of acceptingness, for acceptingness represents the heart of the conservative good life. And to accept is not merely to acquiesce because acceptance requires that one believe—with one's heart as well as one's mind—that the existing arrangements of so-ciety are good and not merely inevitable. Beginning from a belief in the goodness of our given way of life, we may come to understand how it provides for a life that is proper for man, in accordance with his limited nature and the will of God.

Like acceptingness, public service also may take many forms, ac-cording to the given circumstances. But public service must be based on the desire to serve one's community in a capacity fitting for one's own character and in keeping with the real needs of one's society—not the requirements of any utopian vision of the good of man. The crucial fac-tor is the individual's willingness to go outside himself, to serve not just his own interest but the public interest. We all are called upon to act for the good of our fellow man, according to the best of our abilities—within existing rules and arrangements.

One must read correctly the given circumstances, and the available responses to these circumstances, in order to act virtuously. Thus rea-son plays a crucial role in the conservative good life. But the ability to discern what natural law dictates—what is fitting in the given circum-stances—is generally termed "prudence" in order to distinguish it from the more prideful "pure" reason. One's passions must be calmed if one is to discern the dictates of natural law. But passion is necessary for, not inimical to, prudence. One can see the requirements of natural law only when one is motivated by affection—by the proper desire to serve one's community. Since natural law is moral, prudence is an explicitly moral virtue—entailing the (truly rational) determination of the requirements for moral action in the given circumstances.

The man who wishes to be free from the demands of his community cannot act virtuously, for he seeks to divorce himself from the attachments that are the basis, and the very embodiment, of virtue. Nonetheless, the virtuous man cannot be the mere creature of his circumstances. He must judge for himself, independently, what is best for the community he would serve. Uncorrupted by monetary or other rewards accruing to those men who serve the interests of patrons instead of the public, the virtuous man judges for himself how best to serve his community, without attempting to transcend his proper place in that community.

Accepting the goodness of one's society, one must discern for oneself the dictates of natural law (not merely of one's own circumstances). But natural law will almost never dictate radical change—such prescriptions denote individual hubris or overweening pride and not independent reason. Independence, like all the virtues, must begin with acceptance. Given the limits of human nature, acceptance, and from it public affection, must begin close to home. It is within the local community that one learns the habits of affection—that one learns to value the affections of others and even to love one's neighbor as oneself. Through constant interaction one is forced to accommodate the needs and desires of others—even in pursuit of one's own ends. Local attachment—whether to a social group or to one's physical neighbors—provides the only reasonable means by which one may learn affection for one's fellow man.

Local attachment is good because it leads men to transcend selfish, material desires and to act on behalf of, as well as in concert with, those around them. Local affection produces public service, but it also produces men who are better than they would otherwise be because they act in the public interest out of public affection. The leveling systems of supposedly egalitarian intellectuals destroy the very basis of society and particularly of liberty by tearing men apart from one another. The man who advocates such a system is thus in love, not with his fellow man, but with his rationalistic creation.

Human action is necessarily more the product of habit than of "abstract," disembodied reason. But habit and emotion must be controlled and guided by the standards of right conduct set forth in natural law if man is to lead a good life. When man rejects natural law, virtue still retains all her loveliness, but man is blinded by his base appetites and by the illusory creations of his pride. "Rational" man cannot see virtue for what she truly is—man's link with God. To the extent that we abandon our pursuit of virtue, we abandon the necessary link between ethics and politics, and between the transcendent and the material—between God and man—which is the basis of any truly good life.

2 • Philosophy, Man, and Society: Burkean Political Philosophy

We shall say the imitative poet produces a bad regime in the soul of each private man by making phantoms that are very far removed from the truth and by gratifying the soul's foolish part, which doesn't distinguish big from little, but believes the same things are at one time big and at another little.
—Plato, *The Republic*

Strepsiades: What are they doing over there who are so stooped over?
Student: They are delving into Erebus under Tartarus.
Strepsiades: Why then is the anus looking at the heaven?
Student: It itself by itself is being taught astronomy.
—Aristophanes, *The Clouds*

"There is an old quarrel between poetry and philosophy."[1] So Socrates asserted soon after banishing poets from his model city. Poets, according to Socrates, corrupt men's souls by teaching them that the apparent or, more precisely, the conventional, is true. They half-wittingly enslave men to their passions and to the partial and false perceptions embodied in traditional institutions, beliefs, and practices. Poets have returned the philosopher's compliments in kind. Socrates, founder of the Western philosophical tradition, was portrayed in his own time as little more than an arrogant dimwit by the comic poet Aristophanes. For Aristophanes, Socrates's foolish search for an absolute, rational truth independent of human circumstance is dangerous, not because it may succeed and so transform the city, but because it teaches a prideful disregard for the traditions and even for the gods that make life in the city possible. For the poet, Socrates's search for a truth independent of the circumstances making up our social natures is not just dangerous, but also silly. By constantly searching for some independent, abstract truth the philosopher ends up with his head in the ground and his anus sticking up in the air, pathetically attempting to learn "by itself."

The philosopher believes that our concern with circumstances—with the things we believe are at one time big and at another little—corrupts our nature by distracting us from the unchanging truths revealed by philosophical reason. But if he disregards the varying circumstances of life, Aristophanes tells us, man is incapable of truly rational action. The "rational" philosopher is capable only of corruption, impiety, and foolishness. His rejection of circumstance entails rejection of our family, our God, and our community—those things that make us truly human.

Traditions of thought and action—our codes of conduct or manners and our accepted beliefs or prejudices—essentially are responses, developed and refined over time, to the circumstances of our communities. Circumstances—from the weather to the current state of our family or nation—and our often habituated responses to these circumstances make up a large part of our lives. Thus they also make up a large part of our natures. For Burke, who was confronted with a *movement* of impious "philosophy," namely French revolutionary Jacobinism, habituated responses to circumstances *are* human nature. "Art is man's nature" because mere rational thought is incapable of maintaining society.[2] Rational thought, disconnected from habit and circumstance, would destroy convention and thereby man himself.

Burke preferred the poet to the philosopher because the poet must apply himself to "the moral constitution of the heart" in his audience.[3] The heart, when not subverted by rationalistic philosophies, is less critical of society and accepted moral standards than is philosophical reason. Where philosophical reason may see only age, infirmity, and imperfection, the heart may see an old, familiar, and dear friend.

Philosophical (or speculative) reason is more dangerous than the passions themselves, for "there is a boundary to men's passions, when they act from feeling; none when they are under the influence of imagination. Remove a grievance, and, when men act from feeling, you go a great way towards quieting a commotion. But the good or bad conduct of a government, the protection men have enjoyed or the oppression they have suffered under it, are of no sort of moment, when a faction, proceeding upon speculative grounds, is thoroughly heated against its form. When a man is from system furious against monarchy or episcopacy, the good conduct of the monarch or the bishop has no other effect than further to irritate the adversary."[4]

Speculative reason is more dangerous than passion because it respects no limits save its own internal logic. Immoderate by nature, this reason may blind men to the good in their society and so destroy it and themselves. Only if one loves one's society (and love is, after all, a passion) may one see that its goodness transcends merely "rationalistic" criteria.

ABSTRACTION AND IDEALIZATION

Burke gave early warning of the dangers of Jacobinism. Before the French Terror had begun, Burke observed that French society, like all societies, was fragile. This fragile society was destroyed by the rational principles of the Jacobins. Their schemes to impose their notions of "liberty, equality, and fraternity" on their nation, without reference to its preexisting circumstances, left no room for traditional forms and practices, no room even for humanity or simple pity. The fruit of Jacobin rationalism was mass murder. And, Burke observed, the poison was spreading. English radicals now justified their own monarchy on the grounds that it was, in fact, "elective." They thereby called into question the traditional foundations of the British Constitution, undermining the very bases of British society. But why is it so dangerous to legitimize a monarchy by recasting it in terms dictated by abstract democratic principles? What differentiates the use of bad, abstract philosophical criteria from the reason whose use Burke said "is not to revolt against authority?"[5] The answer seems to lie in the kind of questions that may be asked while still serving true reason. For Burke, reason "is a friend who makes an useful suggestion to the court, without questioning its jurisdiction. Whilst he acknowledges its competence, he promotes its efficiency."[6]

One uses reason properly when one seeks to improve the already existing structure of society, without calling its fundamental bases into question. The proper use of reason is based upon the acceptance of society as it stands. Proper reason takes into account, not its own coherence, but its probable effects on that which it is supposed to serve—the existing, virtuous way of life and the fundamental institutions, beliefs, and practices making that good life possible.

Whether they were used in the service of increased liberty or of increased governmental power, Burke abhorred metaphysical arguments of abstract, idealized right. For Burke, "Circumstances are what render every civil and political scheme beneficial or noxious to mankind."[7] Thus, in discussing the French revolutionaries, Burke asked, "Is it because liberty in the abstract may be classed amongst the blessings of mankind, that I am seriously to felicitate a madman who has escaped from the protecting restraint and wholesome darkness of his cell on his restoration to the enjoyment of light and liberty?"[8]

Liberty, for Burke, is not bad as an ideal. But when liberty is judged in practice, the nature of those who are to enjoy it and the uses to which it is to be put must be taken into account; and this account must take human nature as it is, not as one might wish it to be.

> The effect of liberty to individuals is, that they may do what they please: we ought to see what it will please them to do, before we risk congratulations, which may be soon turned into complaints. Prudence would dictate this in the case of separate, insulated, private men. But liberty, when men act in bodies, is *power*. Considerate people, before they declare themselves, will observe the use which is made of *power*,—and particularly of so trying a thing as *new* power in *new* persons, of whose principles, tempers, and dispositions they have little or no experience, and in situations where those who appear the most stirring in the scene may possibly not be the real movers.[9]

The quality of its practitioners determines the quality (good *or bad*) of the liberty at their disposal. The only reasonable course, then, is to entrust men with only that liberty that their natures and circumstances fit them to exercise properly. "Men have no right to what is not reasonable, and to what is not for their benefit."[10]

Loathing philosophers, Burke had to refute them with necessarily philosophical argument. According to John MacCunn, Burke's hatred was aimed not so much at philosophy as at abstraction.[11] But a key distinction must be made between the kind of abstraction that cannot be avoided if philosophical, or even practical political, discussion is to take place and the kind of rationality that conservatives such as Burke find abhorrent.

Onora O'Neill points out that "abstraction, taken literally, is a matter of selective omission, of leaving out some predicates from descriptions and theories." Even in differentiating dog from cat we are engaging in abstraction. The categories "dog" and "cat" are themselves abstract—

they are not fully determinate. When we want to refer to the category "dog" we say "dog," not "small brown dog with white paws" let alone "quadruped, standing so high, weighing so much" and so on. Such rigid criteria for differentiation would make categorization, and thus discourse, impossible.

To communicate without abstraction is impossible. What is more, to minimize abstraction beyond a certain point is undesirable. "The less abstract our reasoning the greater the likelihood that it hinges upon premises that others will dispute, and that its conclusions will seem irrelevant to those others."[12] Is a Great Dane a dog? According to some overly specific criteria, it may be too big to be a dog, yet we *know* that a Great Dane is a dog.

A reasonable man, Burke did not attack abstraction per se; to do so would have rendered his own arguments incomprehensible. Burke's attacks upon "metaphysical" arguments and "abstract" rights were actually attacks upon idealization. According to O'Neill, "an idealised account or theory not merely *omits* certain predicates that are true of the matter to be considered, but *adds* predicates that are false of the matter to be considered."[13] Such an account not only abstracts human nature from its particular circumstances, but posits hypothetical human actors with abilities, motives, and capacities not necessarily reflecting *any* reality. At the root of Burkean political philosophy lies the conviction that any attempt to study men without reference to their particular historical and cultural positions is idealized; it is to argue that universal truths may be found that do not rely upon and act themselves out through circumstance; it is to deny, not only that man is fallible, but that he is a creature of circumstance and convention.

Jacobin theories of the abstract rights of men ignore the role of circumstance in forming human nature and thus the variety of human characters and capacities.

> Men are qualified for civil liberty in exact proportion to their disposition to put moral chains upon their own appetites,—in proportion as their love to justice is above their rapacity,—in proportion as their soundness and sobriety of understanding is above their vanity and presumption,—in proportion as they are more disposed to listen to the counsels of the wise and good, in preference to the flattery of knaves. Society cannot exist, unless a controlling power upon will and appetite be placed somewhere; and the less of it there is within, the more there must be without. It is ordained

in the eternal constitution of things, that men of intemperate minds cannot be free. Their passions forge their fetters.[14]

The amount of liberty which a people should have is the amount which they may use without becoming licentious. The amount of liberty must fit the character of those who are to enjoy it. For Burke, circumstances determine what is a good and what is a bad policy. However, it is what makes for a circumstance which distinguishes Burke's view of man and society from the metaphysical philosophers he despised.

Just as idealized theories may be used to undermine existing authority, they also may be used to extend it to the point of tyranny. And the result may well be rebellion. Urging British moderation toward the American colonies, Burke argued against all uses of idealized theory. "I am not here going into the distinction of rights, nor attempting to mark their boundaries. I do not enter into these metaphysical distinctions; I hate the very sound of them. . . . But if, intemperately, unwisely, fatally, you sophisticate and poison the very source of government, by urging subtle deductions, and consequences odious to those you govern, from the unlimited and illimitable nature of supreme sovereignty, you will teach them by these means to call that sovereignty itself in question."[15]

Actions based upon idealized principles are extreme by their very nature. Based on "metaphysical distinctions" rather than reality, these principles lead their adherents to ignore circumstance and may lead to ruin by calling the existing order into question. Abstract doctrines contemn tradition, and because they contemn reality itself, their practical failures lead only to redoubled destructive efforts. The French revolutionaries had their doctrine of the rights of men. This doctrine made them supremely dangerous since against these rights "there can be no prescription; against these no argument is binding: these admit no temperament and no compromise: anything withheld from their full demand is so much of fraud and injustice."[16]

Particularly when cast in metaphysical terms, the act of questioning may itself cause destruction because "it may be truly said, that 'once to doubt is once to be decided.'"[17] To doubt the goodness of a particular institution or belief is to fail to support it and thus to let it fall. Doubt is, in a very real sense, opposition. "They who do not love religion hate it."[18] Thus the system set up by the French revolutionaries was not merely irreligious; it was a system of atheism. "Whilst everything prepares the body to debauch and the mind to crime, a regular *church of avowed atheism*, established by law, with a direct and sanguinary persecution of Christianity, is formed to prevent all amendment and remorse. Conscience is formally deposed from its dominion over the mind. What fills the measure of horror is, that schools of atheism are set up at the public charge in every part of the country."[19]

For Burke, "Man is by his constitution a religious animal."[20] By rejecting religion the French revolutionaries rejected a fundamental part of human nature. By establishing a state which was not religious, they set themselves up as the creators of a new human nature. Since there is no fundamental, uncorrupted nature of man that can exist completely divorced from institutions and circumstance (since art is man's nature), to reject one, in this case religious, institution is to advocate its replacement by another. By rejecting their established church, the French revolutionaries necessarily set up an official "church" of atheism. They established an institution that taught bad morals but that taught a certain set of morals, nonetheless.

The prudent thinker recognizes that human nature is malleable. His reason is a tool in the search for ways to benefit the community, in accordance with preexisting circumstances and conventions. After all, these gifts of history and Providence are the basis, not only of society, but of man himself.

CIRCUMSTANCE, CONVENTION, AND FITTINGNESS

For Burke, the abstract rights of men are all-encompassing—and therefore useless. Everyone cannot enjoy everything in peace. What is more,

> The moment you abate anything from the full rights of men each to govern himself, and suffer any artificial, positive limitation upon those rights, from that moment the whole organization of government becomes a consideration of convenience. This it is which makes the constitution of a state, and the due distribution of its powers, a matter of the most delicate and complicated skill. It requires a deep knowledge of human nature and human necessities, and of the things which facilitate or obstruct the various ends which are to be pursued by the mechanism of civil institutions. . . . What is the use of discussing a man's abstract right to food or medicine? The question is upon the method of procuring and admin-

istering them. In that deliberation I shall always advise to call in the aid of the farmer and the physician, rather than the professor of metaphysics.[21]

Society is the product of convention, and "if civil society be the offspring of convention, that convention must be its law."[22] The guiding force for society is and ought to be a combination of accepted opinion (existing conventions and prejudices) and a practical wisdom that uses preexisting tools to face new and continuing circumstances.

Because conservatism emphasizes the use of what already exists, scholars such as Mansfield have termed it uncreative. Unlike the republican, the conservative must make do with society as it is and with the tools it provides. The conservative may not create a particular society and particular kinds of citizens in order to fit his needs or desires. Republican, "creative" virtue is impossible and undesirable because so much already exists. Man may not and should not be reduced to a block of clay to be molded and remolded. Man already has a nature, the character of which is the result of preexisting institutions and experiences.

Burke viewed the role of the statesman, and even of the original legislator in those rare cases where he may exist, as that of seeing to it that social institutions fit the preexisting dispositions of the people to be governed. But these dispositions are themselves the results of preexisting institutions and arrangements, such as social status at birth, education, occupation, and religion—in short, circumstances over which the individual has, and should have, little or no control.[23] "Man is by nature reasonable; and he is never perfectly in his natural state, but when he is placed where reason may be best cultivated and most predominates."[24] True reason and the natural state that perfects it act, not through the creation of new institutions, but through habituation to old ones. Thus for Burke,

> A true natural aristocracy is not a separate interest in the state, or separable from it. It is an essential integrant part of any large body rightly constituted. It is formed out of a class of legitimate presumptions, which, taken as generalities, must be admitted for actual truths. To be bred in a place of estimation; . . . to be habituated to the censorial inspection of the public eye; to look early to public opinion; to stand upon such elevated ground as to be enabled to take a large view of the wide-spread and infinitely diversified combinations of men and affairs in a large society; to have leisure to read, to reflect, to converse; to be enabled to draw the court and

attention of the wise and learned, wherever they are to be found; to be habituated in armies to command and to obey; to be taught to despise danger in the pursuit of honor and duty; . . . to be led to a guarded and regulated conduct, from a sense that you are considered as an instructor of your fellow-citizens in their highest concerns, and that you act as a reconciler between God and man; to be employed as an administrator of law and justice, . . . to be a professor of high science, . . . to be amongst rich traders, . . . these are the circumstances of men that form what I should call a *natural* aristocracy, without which there is no nation.[25]

Nature dictates a hierarchical structure for society. But nature produces this necessary Chain of Being by operating "in the common modification of society." That is, nature produces the particulars of man's nature through convention. Natural law dictates that there be hierarchy, but the nature and makeup of particular classes is produced by a number of forces. Hierarchy is an "array of truth and Nature, as well as of habit and prejudice."[26]

Living in a particular way forms habits that in turn form a character appropriate to a given way of life. The aristocrat is brought up to respect himself and to pursue honor with the knowledge that he is by nature a public figure. He has the leisure and the means to cultivate his mind and character so that he may become that which his station dictates. And the same rules of character formation apply to the other, less august stations in life that complete the Great Chain of social Being.

Society is not a reflection of pure or, more properly for the conservative, mere reason. Reason is only one tool to be used in confronting circumstance. The rational faculties must be guided by prudence and affection so that man may aid his society to fit the nature of its people and the dictates of natural law in the face of changing circumstances.

The character of a people is determined, not by some metaphysical human nature, but by particular experiences. History produces a particular set of institutions and prejudices within a given society, and these institutions and prejudices determine, in large measure, the nature of the people of that society. They also largely determine the appropriate responses within that society to changed circumstances. In dealing with current problems, men must look to experience and seek to preserve society's inheritance from history.

HISTORY AND THE LIMITS OF REFORM

Burke argued that man is in large part that which society, over the course of history, has made him. This is not to say that man is somehow part of a "spirit" of history that has little to do with him and that has goals of its own, which man unknowingly carries out; the Burkean view of history is not so abstract. For Burke, divine will is worked out through circumstance and the ways in which men and societies choose to respond to it. History is a proving ground, testing institutions through circumstance and so producing the wisdom of the ages. Thus Burke praised

> the uniform policy of our Constitution to claim and assert our liberties as an *entailed inheritance* derived to us from our forefathers, and to be transmitted to our posterity,—as an estate specially belonging to the people of this kingdom, without any reference whatever to any other more general or prior right. By this means our Constitution preserves an unity in so great a diversity of its parts. We have an inheritable crown, an inheritable peerage, and a House of Commons and a people inheriting privileges, franchises, and liberties from a long line of ancestors.
>
> This policy appears to me to be the result of profound reflection,—or rather the happy effect of following Nature, which is wisdom without reflection, and above it.[27]

On the other hand, those, like the French revolutionaries, "whose principle it is to despise the ancient, permanent sense of mankind, and to set up a scheme of society on new principles, must naturally expect that such of us who think better of the judgment of the human race than of theirs would consider both them and their devices as men and schemes upon their trial."[28]

Burke argued that man's reason is limited, subject to his passions and the inevitable mistakes of idealization. Thus, rather than trusting independent wisdom, we should trust the wisdom of the ages: those institutions, practices, and beliefs that have grown up over time through interaction between nature ("wisdom without reflection"), the limited reason or prudence that reads the dictates of natural law, and circumstance. When faced with a crisis, those men who are in a position of authority should look to their ancestors for guidance, and should use the tools that history has placed in their hands, rather than their own weak reason.

Even kings may be accused of foolish hubris for failing to follow the wisdom of the ages. Addressing a member of the French National Assembly, Burke criticized the reforms made by the French king during the events leading up to the revolution, asserting that

> I am constantly of opinion that your States, in three orders, on the footing on which they stood in 1614, were capable of being brought into a proper and harmonious combination with royal authority. This constitution by Estates was the natural and only just representation of France. It grew out of the habitual conditions, relations, and reciprocal claims of men. It grew out of the circumstances of the country, and out of the state of property. The wretched scheme of your present masters is not to fit the Constitution to the people, but wholly to destroy conditions, to dissolve relations, to change the state of the nation, and to subvert property, in order to fit their country to their theory of a Constitution.[29]

The French king had at his disposal the means of proper reform. This reform would have been based upon the historical arrangements of French society. The circumstances of French history had produced a particular hierarchy of French classes and a representational system predicated upon this hierarchy. By basing his new actions upon old institutions and old relations among Frenchmen, the king would have been acting according to French history and thus the French nature. By grounding his actions upon a false, metaphysical view of human nature the king contributed to the downfall of his nation—and of himself.

History provides the proper guide to action, even, and perhaps especially, in the face of severe crises. But it is important to note that for Burke history is not a collection of known facts and institutions that should be studied scientifically to find answers to all of society's problems. History's validity should not be questioned, and neither should the extent to which existing institutions and practices are in accordance with ancient practice. Such questioning would constitute reliance upon independent reason rather than on the collective wisdom of the ages.

Taking his political opponents in Britain to task for asserting the right of Englishmen to form their own government, Burke argued that their mistakes were the result of an improper view of history. Contrary to his opponents, who viewed the English Revolution of 1688 as the source of a number of rights belonging to the people, for Burke "the Revolution was made to preserve our *ancient* indisputable laws and liberties, and that *ancient* constitution of government which is our only security for law and liberty. If you are desirous of knowing the spirit of our Constitution, and the policy which predominated in that great period which has secured it to this hour, pray look for both in our histories, in our records, in our acts of Parliament and journals of Parliament, and not in the sermons of [radical dissenters], and the after-dinner toasts of the Revolution Society."[30]

Claims to the right of fabricating new governments are based on opinions directly contrary to those of the English people at large. It was Burke's feeling, and in his view the feeling of the English people, that the revolution was a *preserving* one, forced upon the nation by the actions of a bad king and aimed solely at protecting ancient rights. Indeed, for Burke the preserving impulse was the primary force behind all actions of the English people in relation to their governors.

> Our oldest reformation is that of Magna Charta. You will see that Sir Edward Coke, that great oracle of our law, and indeed all the great men who follow him, to Blackstone, are industrious to prove the pedigree of our liberties. They endeavor to prove that the ancient charter, the Magna Charta of King John, was connected with another positive charter from Henry the First, and that both the one and the other were nothing more than a reaffirmance of the still more ancient standing law of the kingdom. In the matter of fact, for the greater part, these authors appear to be in the right; perhaps not always; but if the lawyers mistake in some particulars, it proves my position still the more strongly; because it demonstrates the powerful prepossession towards antiquity with which the minds of all our lawyers and legislators, and of all the people whom they wish to influence, have been always filled, and the stationary policy of this kingdom in considering their most sacred rights and franchises as an *inheritance*.[31]

Burke emphasized, not the fact of historical continuity, but the impulse toward it in both historical action and in the interpretation of historical action. Burke praised the habituated desire of Englishmen to establish and to justify their rights. These rights were to be justified, not through appeals to abstract theories, but through appeals to the actual practice and history that, in their view, produced the specific rights of Englishmen.

The backward-looking, legal frame of mind cultivated by the English established the concrete bases of English society. A profession and a people that seek in their historical practices both the justifications for and the origins of their rights will not discard their inheritance in favor of abstract notions of absolute, ideal rights. As Pocock asserts, "What [Burke] is saying, then, is not a piece of antiquarian's lore, but an account of contemporary practice. This is how we conduct our politics, he is saying; how we have always conducted them. He is not calling upon his contemporaries to return to a seventeenth-century habit of mind, but assuming that it is still alive and meaningful among them."[32]

The purpose of reform, for Burke, must always be the preservation of ancient and established liberties. This does not mean, however, that reform itself is ruled out.

> A state without the means of some change is without the means of its conservation. Without such means it might even risk the loss of that part of the Constitution which it wished the most religiously to preserve. The two principles of conservation and correction operated strongly at the two critical periods of the Restoration and Revolution, when England found itself without a king. At both those periods the nation had lost the bond of union in their ancient edifice: they did not, however, dissolve the whole fabric. On the contrary, in both cases they regenerated the deficient part of the old Constitution through the parts which were not impaired. . . . At no time, perhaps, did the sovereign legislature manifest a more tender regard to that fundamental principle of British constitutional policy than at the time of the Revolution, when it deviated from the direct line of hereditary succession. The crown was carried somewhat out of the line in which it had before moved; but the new line was derived from the same stock. It was still a line of hereditary descent; still an hereditary descent in the same blood, though an hereditary descent qualified with Protestantism. When the legislature altered the direction, but kept the principle, they showed that they held it inviolable.[33]

Those men who are entrusted with governmental power in times of great national need have the duty to rejuvenate the old when facing new circumstances. They must resist the hubristic impulse to create a new government or, even worse, to create a new human nature or national character. Human reason is limited, and man is fallible; but history, collective wisdom, and the forms of the existing constitution provide the necessary guidance for prudent action. If followed, these guides will lead to the preservation of the existing, good society.

PREJUDICE

Burke emphasized the wisdom of man over the wisdom of men. He argued that men must enter into corporate societies and be treated as corporate beings if they are to live properly. "He who gave our nature to be perfected by our virtue willed also the necessary means of its perfection: He willed, therefor, the state."[34] Burke did not argue only that the state as an abstract entity is the necessary means to virtue. He insisted upon the maintenance of the *parts* of the British Constitution—including its *categories* of individuals. The Great Chain of Being dictates for every member of society a specific place, but this place is itself corporate, not individual. As one has the place of a man rather than of an angel or a beast, one also has the place of a peasant, a businessman, or a member of the landed gentry. Habits of both opinion and action are formed in the particular circumstances of each station in life, and the resulting characters are themselves integral parts of a society's constitution.

For Burke our views of the world are the results of our experiences, and these necessarily depend in great measure upon the place in society into which we are born. The nobleman is habituated into his proper role by his corporate experiences: Seeing nothing mean, he has no mean feelings. Feeling that society looks up to and depends upon him, the nobleman comes to recognize his importance and his responsibility. All that is required is that the nobleman be educated properly and protected from metaphysical teachings that disregard the importance of place and circumstance. These, then, are the bases of that great guiding force of proper human action Burke called prejudice.

According to Burke the French revolutionaries enslaved the people in the name of the rights of men, or, more properly, in the name of revolutionary "reason." British humility produced better results.

> We are afraid to put men to live and trade each on his own private stock of reason; because we suspect that the stock in each man is small, and that the individuals would do better to avail themselves of the general band and capital of nations and of ages. Many of our men of speculation, instead of exploding general prejudices, employ their sagacity to discover the latent wisdom which prevails in them. If they find what they seek, (and they seldom fail,) they think it more wise to continue the prejudice, with the reason involved, than to cast away the coat of prejudice, and to leave nothing but the naked reason; because prejudice, with its reason,

has a motive to give action to that reason, and an affection which will give it permanence.[35]

Commonly painted as a great scourge today, prejudice or unexamined belief, according to Burke, embodies a wisdom superior to that of individual reason. If prudent thinkers find no reason behind the prejudice, they will doubt themselves rather than the wisdom of nations and of ages. Prejudice is a rich source of right thinking and a necessary basis for right action. "Prejudice is of ready application in the emergency; it previously engages the mind in a steady course of wisdom and virtue, and does not leave the man hesitating in the moment of decision, skeptical, puzzled, and unresolved. Prejudice renders a man's virtue his habit, and not a series of unconnected acts. Through just prejudice, his duty becomes a part of his nature."[36] Prejudice, then, is the proper guide to action because it is more reliable than individual reason. Based upon collective experience, it has an intimate connection, strengthened over time, with the object of its concern—be it society, class, or a more universal category. It is the proper educator of mankind because, as the product of the ages, it is ever ready for use in current circumstances.

But the idealized programs of would-be founders, by opposing all accepted beliefs, do not endanger a mere useful tool; they endanger man himself. "The moral sentiments, so nearly connected with early prejudice as to be almost one and the same thing, will assuredly not live long under a discipline which has for its basis the destruction of all prejudices, and the making the mind proof against all dread of consequences flowing from the pretended truths that are taught by their philosophy."[37]

Prejudices are the guardians of the moral sentiments. Bereft of accepted beliefs, men no longer can choose to act properly and are reduced to less than truly rational beings. If one sets up a system, such as that of the French revolutionaries, that is not based upon the people's natural prejudices, "everything depends upon the army in such a government as yours; for you have industriously destroyed all the opinions and prejudices, and, as far as in you lay, all the instincts which support government. Therefor the moment any difference arises between your National Assembly and any part of the nation, you must have recourse to force."[38] It is prejudice that allows men to deal with one another in a peaceful, mutually beneficial manner, that binds a society together, and that guards the moral sentiments and the public affections necessary if men are to live with one another on any basis other than fear and violence.

As prejudices must be protected as the guardians of morality and human society itself, so must the bases of prejudices also be protected. And the bases of these prejudices are to be found in the local arrangements that naturally induce affection in the individual. Local affection, "to love the little platoon we belong to in society,"[39] is a virtue in and of itself, but it is also good because it is necessary for the unquestioned ("prejudiced") attachments which hold together any stable society. For this reason, respect on the part of those in power for family, locality, class attachments, the idea of nation—and even the idea of a European commonwealth based upon common history and Christianity[40]—is necessary if society is to be maintained.

Aristotle constructed his polis as a hierarchy of attachments from the family to the household to the village and then to the polis itself. Burke also constructs the necessary attachments and affections of men from the more local to the more universal. Society itself depends upon the continued good health of the family. Thus, for Burke, liberal French revolutionary divorce laws were designed to produce "the total corruption of all morals, the total disconnection of social life."[41] Burke's own life and career were guided by his desire to achieve his concept of the proper, ultimate goal (and reward) of a life of virtuous public service: the founding of a great family of power, influence, and inheritable prestige. A great family, of course, is an institution built upon and held together by natural attachments.[42]

Human sociability, in all its forms, rests upon the affections, attachments, and prejudices that arise naturally from shared, local experience.

> Men are not tied to one another by papers and seals. They are led to associate by resemblances, by conformities, by sympathies. It is with nations as with individuals. Nothing is so strong a tie of amity between nation and nation as correspondence in laws, customs, manners, and habits of life. They have more than the force of treaties in themselves. They are obligations written in the heart. They approximate men to men without their knowledge, and sometimes against their intentions. The secret, unseen, but irrefragable bond of habitual intercourse holds them together, even when their perverse and litigious nature sets them to equivocate, scuffle, and fight about the terms of their written obligations.[43]

The old proverb "like to like," which Socrates ignored, was restated by Burke in describing the very nature of human affections. We like what is familiar, and familiarity grows from common experience, and this is as it should be.

In arguing against the repression of Catholicism in Ireland, Burke pointed out with regret that there existed in England and Ireland

> a number of persons whose minds are so formed that they find the communion of religion to be a close and an endearing tie, and their country to be no bond at all,—to whom common altars are a better relation than common habitations and a common civil interest,—whose hearts are touched with the distresses of foreigners, and are abundantly awake to all the tenderness of human feeling on such an occasion, even at the moment that they are inflicting the very same distresses, or worse, upon their fellow-citizens, without the least sting of compassion or remorse. To commiserate the distresses of all men suffering innocently, perhaps meritoriously, is generous, and very agreeable to the better part of our nature,—a disposition that ought by all means to be cherished. But to transfer humanity from its natural basis, our legitimate and home-bred connections,—to lose all feeling for those who have grown up by our sides, in our eyes, the benefit of whose cares and labors we have partaken from our birth, and meretriciously to hunt abroad after foreign affections, is such a disarrangement of the whole system of our duties, that I do not know whether benevolence so displaced is not almost the same thing as destroyed, or what effect bigotry could have produced that is more fatal to society.[44]

Attachments—even religious attachments—that do not have their basis in habituated affection, in the daily interactions of men with a common background, are perverse if not kept in their proper place. And this place is less exalted than that of local attachments. Religious attachments, if bereft of closer ties, are too metaphysical, too divorced from daily life, to bind men to one another properly. Dogmatic religious attachments may destroy the natural, habituated attachments of common experience that are the bases of society and of moral life. Man is by nature a religious animal, but he is not necessarily an Anglican animal. The particulars of dogma and ritual must not be allowed to overshadow and destroy the local circumstances and attachments that bind together a society.

Prejudice is good because men, their reason, and their affections are limited. We are not capable of making attachments or of developing the proper affections on purely rational grounds. Instead, men's natural attachments grow from their locality, their occupation, and their station in life. Habituation is the rule in affection as well as in behavior, and since God's will has dictated the hierarchy of society as well as the nature of man, both must be accepted.

GOVERNMENT, RELIGION, AND MANNERS

Society, history, and the human race possess great wisdom; men, for Burke, by and large do not. Burke also argued that government's capacity for wise action is easily overestimated. Society and government, according to Burke, are not the same thing—in many ways they are quite different. Government is the weaker entity, best confined to the tending of existing arrangements. The ability of a government to see to the needs of its people is quite limited; indeed, "A frost too long continued or too suddenly broken up with rain and tempest, the blight of the spring or the smut of the harvest will do more to cause the distress of the belly than all the contrivances of all statesmen can do to relieve it."[45]

The moderation that Burke demanded of the statesman he also demanded of the government itself. Severely limited in their ability to help those they govern, statesmen must see to it that government does not harm them. This is why Burke praised balanced government and justified his own career on the grounds that he had opposed "all the various partisans of destruction, let them begin where or when or how they will."[46] All attempts to destroy the proper power and role of one or another of the branches of England's balanced monarchy eventually would end by destroying the British Constitution and British society. The British Constitution was based upon balance and properly limited liberty—both for individuals and for branches of government. Because governors are no more omniscient or perfectly moral than are those whom they govern, those who govern are no more to be trusted with unlimited power or liberty than the governed. Power must counteract or, more properly, limit power lest one branch grow beyond its proper bounds and cause the entire structure to topple.

As the proper power of each branch is limited, so is the power of government itself. "The coercive authority of the state is limited to what is necessary for its existence." Rather than pursuing some metaphysical ideal of human perfection, the good government "does bear, and must, with the vices and the follies of men, until they actually strike at the root of order. This it does in things actually moral. In all matters of speculative improvement the case is stronger, even where the matter is properly of human cognizance. But to consider an averseness to improvement, the not arriving at perfection, as a crime, is against all tolerably correct jurisprudence; for, if the resistance to improvement should be great and any way general, they would in effect give up the necessary and substantial part in favor of the perfection and the finishing."[47] Should man's government attempt to give him an ideal nature, his nature would be corrupted. The role of government is not to create a virtuous people; it does not possess the means to produce human perfection and will succeed only in destroying society if it makes the attempt.

Burke seems to advocate a government that does very little and that acts according to rather utilitarian rules. He insisted that "there are two, and only two, foundations of law; and they are both of them conditions without which nothing can give it any force: I mean equity and utility."[48] According to Burke, equity means that all men shall be treated equally according to the law, and utility means that all laws shall be in the general interest. Any idea of human interconnection, let alone virtue, seems to have no place within Burke's materialistic/utilitarian governmental structure. This makes all the more seemingly strange Burke's statement that, in the production of the great English people of "high mind and a constancy unconquerable" and in the establishment of English preeminence under the reign of King William, "government gave the impulse."[49]

Burke himself answered the question of whether improvement may be "brought into society? Undoubtedly; but not by compulsion,—but by encouragement,—but by countenance, favor, privileges, which are powerful, and are lawful instruments."[50] Government is, then, somehow concerned with social improvement and has some duty beyond the mere tending of arrangements. It seems clear, however, that the role of government in this area is purely secondary, that government is not the true teacher of virtue but the guardian of the true teachers: tradition, manners, and prejudice.

Limited in its ability to act in the public interest without endangering it, government acts best when it merely tends to arrangements. These arrangements, then, do most of society's work in perfecting man in the only way reasonable: by showing him the possibility of virtue and by habituating him to virtue's modes. This does not mean, however, that the government plays no role in the moral life of the nation. The institutions that inculcate virtue require governmental protection from atheists, experimenters, and those men who do not recognize the need for the maintenance, and supremacy, of existing traditions, manners, and prejudices.

Burke opposed atheism, not just because he believed that it is incorrect and wrong, but also because it corrupts all morals. For Burke, man's natural religiosity is of supreme importance. Religious beliefs or prejudices help shape human behavior, and religious institutions embody the traditions of a people while teaching a particular set of practices (manners) and beliefs. This is why religions, like governments, must be viewed as historical institutions, closely connected with the national life. Like governments, particular religions require historical justification and unquestioning acceptance, but they need at least one other support if they are to play their proper role in society: official recognition. As Burke related,

> some years ago, I strenuously opposed the clergy who petitioned, to the number of about three hundred, to be freed from subscription to the Thirty-Nine Articles [of the Episcopal Church], without proposing to substitute any other in their place. There never has been a religion of the state (the few years of the Parliament only excepted) but that of *the Episcopal Church of England*: the Episcopal Church of England, before the Reformation, connected with the see of Rome; since then, disconnected, and protesting against some of her doctrines, and against the whole of her authority, as binding in our national church: nor did the fundamental laws of this kingdom (in Ireland it has been the same) ever know, at any period, any other church *as an object of establishment,*—or, in that light, any other Protestant religion. Nay, our Protestant *toleration* itself, at the Revolution, and until within a few years, required a signature of thirty-six, and a part of the thirty-seventh, out of the Thirty-Nine Articles. So little idea had they at the Revolution of *establishing* Protestantism indefinitely, that they did not indefinitely *tolerate* it under that name.[51]

Episcopalianism, like the mixed and limited monarchy, has been the established rule in Britain from time immemorial. Like the government, it must remain unquestioned. Episcopalianism is natural to England because it is an integral part of it, having gone through time and trial with it, guiding the nation through its troubles with its moral teachings.

Religion does not provide only a shared set of beliefs. Shared forms of worship and prescriptive religious conduct also form men's actions.

For Burke, behavior is guided from the surface inward. That is, habituation acts upon the outward forms of behavior and thence inward affections and opinions. Affections and opinions in turn affect concrete behavior—and thence society. Proper thought and proper action are related intimately, and religion aids both.

Good government supports religion because religion is a primary support of proper government—and because both are integral elements of any good society. Religion supports good government by habituating the people, through manners, to act and to believe in such a way as to make government stable. More important, religion promotes modes of thought and action that are intrinsically *good* in the society's given circumstances. In listing the French revolutionaries' crimes, Burke argued that

> when to these establishments of Regicide, of Jacobinism, and of Atheism, you add the *correspondent system of manners*, no doubt can be left on the mind of a thinking man concerning their determined hostility to the human race. Manners are of more importance than laws. Upon them, in a great measure, the laws depend. The law touches us but here and there, and now and then. Manners are what vex or soothe, corrupt or purify, exalt or debase, barbarize or refine us, by a constant, steady, uniform, insensible operation, like that of the air we breathe in. They give their whole form and color to our lives. According to their quality, they aid morals, they supply them, or they totally destroy them.[52]

Manners are more important than laws because they have a greater effect on men's actions. Men always act in relation to the given set of manners. Thus they are habituated in accordance with a given set of rules and forms. Their behavior is directed by a given set of precepts that correspond to, but are not the same as, political and religious establishments. The "rationalistic" radicalism and atheism of the French revolutionaries produced a corrupt system of manners. The Jacobins destroyed the old system of proper manners and replaced it with an immoral one that habituated men into the wrong modes of activity.

The doctrines of Jacobinism and atheism are barbaric; they reject all notions of prescription and deference to established hierarchy. Supplemented by the uncouth egalitarianism of their corresponding system of manners, Jacobin and atheist doctrines produced a society in which the sanctity of rights, and even of life itself, was unrecognized by the unchastened mob. This was to be expected, because a mob, undirected by a confining system of manners that support and are supported by an unquestioning belief in the goodness of existing hierarchical relations, is capable only of destruction.

The importance of convention in promoting proper behavior extends even to the realm of taste. For Burke, "Taste and elegance, though they are reckoned only among the smaller and secondary morals, yet are of no mean importance in the regulation of life. A moral taste is not of force to turn vice into virtue; but it recommends virtue with something like the blandishments of pleasure, and it infinitely abates the evils of vice."[53] Men require encouragements to right action. Standards of taste produce social and thence internal pressure to act according to their dictates, which properly correspond to society's religious, moral, and political norms. Elegance, by showing men the rewards of right action in secondary matters, inculcates proper habits and so helps men to act rightly in matters of greater importance.

Government, for Burke, should support the more capable guardians of human nature: tradition, manners, prejudice, and the greatest embodiment of all three—religion. Social institutions act upon man in his daily activities. They reward and punish the individual according to how well he acts in relation to the dictates of his particular religion, locality, and station in life. Social institutions teach men to accept unquestioningly the prescriptive role of preexisting modes of conduct. That is, they habituate men to proper conduct. And habituation is the only reasonable method by which to produce right action because "prescriptions" not based in historical practice are not truly prescriptive.

Prescriptions based upon idealized models fail to take into account the fundamental natures of philosophy, man, and society. They fail to recognize that the natural function of philosophy is to discern the role of appropriate conventions in habituating men to right action. They do not recognize that man is by nature a creature of habit and circumstance. They ignore the fact that society is naturally fragile and that its natural role is to provide prescriptive, conventional criteria by which to judge the virtue of men's actions. Social institutions and conventions require unquestioning acceptance if they are to survive and function properly. Purely metaphysical prescriptions may destroy the social fabric and cannot possibly produce virtue.

NATURAL LAW

Since convention rules most of our lives, our conventions must be proper or they will corrupt rather than perfect human nature. Burke's emphasis upon the need for fitting conventions brings into focus the basis of the Burkean reading of natural law in a particular view of divine will. Although philosophy must limit itself to recognizing man as a creature of particular circumstances—including history and convention—history is not philosophically self-justifying. The course of history may produce abomination as well as virtue, and there is a kernel of human nature that is not the mere product of convention.

Man is religious by nature. He is limited by nature—that is, he is incapable of ultimate perfection. He has only limited rationality and so must be guided by prejudice. He is best treated as the member of a corporate body, for this is where his nature may achieve its fulfillment. Divine will intends that man be in society—where his true perfection, or virtue, may be attained. The Great Chain of Being is an instrument of divine will, providing the possibility of human virtue by allowing men to come together and so rely on a greater stock of human reason than that afforded by any individual. Society also is the realm in which virtue may be practiced, for right action is action that accepts the natural hierarchy arising from the circumstances of society and that acts according to its basic dictates so as to further its interests (the common good) in accordance with divine will.

Both "creative" and "rationalistic" reason are dangerous since they lead to hubris and perhaps to the destruction of society itself. But there is a safe and proper reason: the reason (in truth the wisdom) of conservatism, based upon the unchanging wisdom of natural law. Conservative wisdom dictates the prudent tending of existing arrangements so that men will not be corrupted. It also dictates prudent defense of the moral institutions of society against idealized theories and against the circumstances that history inevitably produces. Most of all, conservative wisdom dictates faith in the goodness of God's will and in what He has given. Any proper defense of society must grow from a desire to serve that which is old, familiar, and accepted as the will of God. And virtue is acting in ways that promote and provide the means for this defense.

3 • Accepting Virtue in Burke

The awful Author of our being is the Author of our place in the order of existence,—and . . . having disposed and marshalled us by a divine tactic, not according to our will, but according to His, He has in and by that disposition virtually subjected us to act the part which belongs to the place assigned us. We have obligations to mankind at large, which are not in consequence of any special voluntary pact. They arise from the relation of man to man, and the relation of man to God, which relations are not matters of choice. On the contrary, the force of all the pacts which we enter into with any particular person or number of persons amongst mankind depends upon those prior obligations. In some cases the subordinate relations are voluntary, in others they are necessary,—but the duties are all compulsive.
—Edmund Burke, *Appeal from the New to the Old Whigs*

Perhaps the most famous passage from Burke's writings, the discussion of hierarchy quoted above is more fundamentally a discussion of the nature of divine will and man's proper response to it. We must accept our place in the Great Chain of Being lest we defy the will of God. The virtuous man works humbly and to the best of his ability, within the existing arrangements of society and without questioning the legitimacy of these arrangements, to fulfill the obligations of his station in life.

Men must accept the existing structure of society as a given, not only because such acceptance is necessary for social stability but also because unquestioning adherence to traditional forms and practices is itself a virtue. Acting selflessly in the interests of a community whose nature took shape without one's consent is the ultimate act of conservative self-transcendence; acting in this way is acting virtuously. One gives one's all in

65

the service of a community that one loves without having taken part in its creation.

Men have some control over their lives—some "subordinate relations" are voluntary. But only when men recognize the moral necessity of obedience to God's will as communicated through natural law and historical circumstance may they attain their true nature. Only when men acknowledge the primacy of the will of God over the will of man may they lead a good life. Since God has willed that man seek society, to reject one's society lightly is to be impious. Since God has willed that man's reason be limited, to question the goodness of the given society before it is clear that the society makes human virtue—and therefore the will of God—impossible is to commit hubris.

One must look at one's community, not through the eyes of some cold, calculating scientist who reduces everything to its illusory numerical equivalents, nor through the eyes of some abstract philosopher, seeking to test or to fulfill his own notions of the true and the good, but through the affectionate eyes of a friend. Like a friend, the good man views the faults of his society as the accustomed foibles of a trusted and loved companion, to be gently corrected where necessary and prudent or else to be forgiven—unless some fundamental degeneration of character renders the friendship itself impossible. Only societies worthy of affection ought to be defended, but only the attitude of the friend can make virtue possible.

ACCEPTINGNESS, HUMILITY, AND STANDARDS OF VIRTUE

> Unsuspecting confidence is the true centre of gravity amongst mankind, about which all the parts are at rest. It is this *unsuspecting confidence* that removes all difficulties, and reconciles all the contradictions which occur in the complexity of all ancient puzzled political establishments. Happy are the rulers which have the secret of preserving it![1]

Society is fragile, and if its foundations are dug into the entire edifice may come crashing down. For Burke, the liberties of Englishmen depend upon the unquestioning acceptance of the legitimacy of the hereditary monarchy. "When such an unwarrantable maxim is once established, that no throne is lawful but the elective, no one act of the princes who preceded this era of fictitious election can be valid."[2] The Petition of Right, habeas corpus, and the very rule of law would be swept away should the legitimacy of their royal originators be denied. But for Burke acceptance is morally good (and excessive questioning morally bad) not merely in light of the probable results of each but because of the *nature* of each. To accept is to act rightly in and of itself. To question beyond the point of helping to strengthen what already exists is to act wrongly in and of itself. To accept is to show proper humility and respect for God's will; to question and seek to replace is to show overweening pride. "True humility, the basis of the Christian system, is the low, but deep and firm foundation of all real virtue. But this, as very painful in the practice, and little imposing in the appearance, [the Jacobins] have totally discarded. Their object is to merge all natural and all social sentiment in inordinate vanity. In a small degree, and conversant in little things, vanity is of little moment. When full-grown, it is the worst of vices, and the occasional mimic of them all. It makes the whole man false. It leaves nothing sincere or trustworthy about him. His best qualities are poisoned and perverted by it, and operate exactly as the worst."[3] The goodness, or virtue, of the Christian system rests in its humility. A humble, accepting attitude is necessary if virtue is to be possible, let alone achieved. The man who accepts does what is natural (and therefore good) for him by believing in the goodness of accustomed (and therefore natural) conventions.

Even bad men are to be judged in part according to their acceptance of the existing order. Burke himself defended "great bad men" such as the regicide Oliver Cromwell who, while wielding illegitimate, tyrannical power, still did not seek to destroy the existing form of society.

These disturbers were not so much like men usurping power as asserting their natural place in society. Their rising was to illuminate and beautify the world. Their conquest over their competitors was by outshining them. The hand that, like a destroying angel, smote the country communicated to it the force and energy under which it suffered. I do not say (God forbid), I do not say that the virtues of such men were to be taken as a balance to their crimes; but they were some corrective to their effects. . . . It is a thing to be wondered at, to see how very soon France, when she had a moment to respire, recovered and emerged from the longest and most dreadful civil war that ever was known in any nation. Why? Because among all their massacres they had not slain the *mind* in their country. A conscious dignity, a noble pride, a generous sense of glory and emulation was not extinguished. On the contrary, it was kindled and inflamed. The organs also of the state, however shattered, existed. All the prizes of honor and virtue, all the rewards, all the distinctions remained.[4]

The crimes of a Cromwell or of a Richelieu arose from their insistence that they be accorded their proper place in society, whatever the cost. Pride itself may be noble, if kept within proper bounds. The violent and demanding pride of Cromwell and Richelieu was bad and damaging. Yet the pride (the excessive civic virtue) of these great bad men was less bad and less damaging than that of the would-be founder because it was taken to less of an extreme. Cromwell, evil regicide that he was, nonetheless stopped short of destroying Britain because he retained both the common law and the great judges who maintained and interpreted this embodiment of English tradition.[5] The crimes of Cromwell and Richelieu lay in their subversion of substantial parts of the social order. Their crimes were mitigated by their retention of the *minds* of their nations— the fundamental institutions, practices, and beliefs that give a people its character.

To found a society upon unnatural, untraditional bases is impossible, and he who attempts to do so will succeed only in destroying the society that already exists. Society is not merely a collection of political mechanisms; its character is more fundamentally composed of the spirit of its members. "Nothing is more certain than that our manners, our civilization, and all the good things which are connected with manners and with civilization have, in this European world of ours, depended for ages upon two principles and were, indeed, the result of both combined: I mean the spirit of a gentleman and the spirit of religion."[6]

Chivalry and piety, the spirit of a gentleman and the spirit of religion, were the most important elements of European society. Society could survive diminishment in its other aspects—including the commercial and trading interests some accuse Burke of defending single-mindedly[7]—so long as its spirits remained healthy. But, if the natural relations that make for trade, commerce, and thus prosperity were lost in the attempt to live without chivalry and piety, Europe would be a ruin: "What sort of a thing must be a nation of gross, stupid, ferocious, and at the same time poor and sordid barbarians, destitute of religion, honor, or manly pride, possessing nothing at present, and hoping for nothing hereafter?"[8]

Burke urged his countrymen to overthrow the Jacobins because he believed that the French revolutionary system was an abomination, against the nature of man and corrupting to all whom it touched. The Jacobins' atheism, their destruction of prejudice in favor of idealized philosophy, and their reliance upon force as the sole tool of governance made virtue impossible because they necessarily made men something less than human. The beginning of being human lies, for Burke, in the ability to accept the given order on a basis other than force—on a basis of religious piety and gentlemanly chivalry. "Manly" or "noble" pride is in fact humble because it rests on acceptance of society as it exists.

According to Burke, the modern effects of ancient chivalry made Europe superior to the ancient states of Asia—possibly even to the greatest states of the ancient world. The demands of honor and chivalry made societies out of despotisms. The chivalric code fostered sentiments that made the relationships between men good rather than merely necessary. Burke lamented the loss of chivalry in the metaphysical revolution of French "sophisters, economists, and calculators." "It was this [chivalry], which, without confounding ranks, had produced a noble equality, and handed it down through all the gradations of social life. It was this opinion which mitigated kings into companions, and raised private men to be fellows with kings. Without force or opposition, it subdued the fierceness of pride and power; it obliged sovereigns to submit to the soft collar of social esteem, compelled stern authority to submit to elegance, and gave a domination, vanquisher of laws, to be subdued by manners."[9] Chivalric opinion caused men to *submit* to the requirements of their station in life, as well as those of society in general. Chivalry set up a code of manners and morals that encouraged right action through the provision of honors.

The chivalric code was concerned in part with the requirements of each station in life. Its standards varied according to the particular needs of given classes of men. But it should be noted that Burke called for *all* members of society to submit to the dictates of the existing order. It is a positive good that sovereigns are compelled to submit to "the soft collar of social esteem." Submission is good, not merely because it is necessary for the maintenance of society, but because it is in the nature of a good sovereign to obey the dictates of social estimation, when it is within reason. The good ruler accepts as good the familiar dictates of tradition and the prejudices of public opinion. This is why Burke lamented the loss in France of "that generous loyalty to rank and sex, that proud submission, that dignified obedience, that subordination of the heart, which

kept alive, even in servitude itself, the spirit of an exalted freedom!"[10]
This *exalted* freedom was the essence of virtue.

Closer to home, Burke attacked the Duke of Bedford in his "Letter to
a Noble Lord" because the duke had betrayed his class. Bedford not only
failed to live up to the requirements of his station in life, he also committed treason against the standards of his station and thus against his
society itself. Supporting the egalitarian doctrines of the French Revolution, Bedford sought to undermine the very structures and opinions
whose (unearned) benefits of wealth, power, and prestige he abused so
liberally.

Of course, Burke castigated the Jacobins themselves for their subversion of accepted standards—for their ill-treatment of the French clergy
and their claims that such treatment was justified because these clergy-
men lacked virtue. "When we talk of the heroic, of course we talk of
rare virtue. I believe the instances of eminent depravity may be as rare
amongst [the French clergy] as those of transcendent goodness. Examples of avarice and of licentiousness may be picked out, I do not question it, by those who delight in the investigation which leads to such
discoveries. A man as old as I am will not be astonished that several, in
every description, do not lead that perfect life of self-denial, with regard
to wealth or to pleasure, which is wished for by all, by some expected,
but by none exacted with more rigor than by those who are the most at-
tentive to their own interests or the most indulgent to their own passions."[11] The virtue of a clergyman consists in living up to the expectation
that he will live a life of self-denial. But those who observe the clergyman do not act virtuously when they demand too much self-denial. We
should accept that the clergy do their best in most cases and not demand
perfection. Indeed, the acceptance of imperfection is the basis of both
social stability and virtue. To demand perfection is to set oneself up as
the sole judge of others, and this is hardly humble.

The French revolutionaries destroyed their nation in pursuit of a corrupt, utopian vision. The good subject, for Burke, "should approach to
the faults of the State as to the wounds of a father, with pious awe and
trembling solicitude. By this wise prejudice we are taught to look with
horror on those children of their country who are prompt rashly to hack
that aged parent in pieces and put him into the kettle of magicians, in
hopes that by their poisonous weeds and wild incantations they may re-
generate the paternal constitution and renovate their father's life."[12] Again,
in opposing efforts to reform radically his own House of Commons,

Burke accused his opponents of being would-be parricides, in contradistinction to which "I look with filial reverence on the constitution of my country, and never will cut it in pieces, and put it into the kettle of any magician, in order to boil it, with the puddle of their compounds, into youth and vigor. On the contrary, I will drive away such pretenders; I will nurse its venerable age, and with lenient arts extend a parent's breath."[13]

Virtuous action requires that we accept society's authority because any action that is not based on this acceptance is not properly aimed. By refusing to accept the dictates and standards of his society, the bad man, like the rebellious child, throws aside the proper relationship between himself and authority and the *only* basis upon which one may pursue virtue. As he would have us deem a child virtuous who is deferential to the authority and wishes of his father, so Burke would have us deem virtuous the subject who is deferential to the authority and wishes of his society: its code of conduct and the institutions, practices and beliefs from which this code grows.

We must find our happiness and our virtue in acceptance of our circumstances. Only by accepting with humility the will of God and the judgment of the ages, which have placed us in a particular society and in a particular station within that society, may we pursue virtue. We must do our best to live up to the demands, duties and standards placed upon us by our society and by our station. By doing so we achieve the particular virtues of our station. By accepting the preexisting authority of society (and God) we achieve the virtue of acceptingness, and make possible the achievement of other virtues as well.

THE MANY MEANS OF PUBLIC SERVICE

A society that serves the true interests of its people deserves their support, but it is in the nature of a good society to promote (properly directed) public service. Indeed, the interests of society dictate that public service and rewards go together whenever possible. In his "Letter to a Noble Lord," Burke defended the pension he had received for his parliamentary service against the attacks of the Duke of Bedford. Unlike the duke, whose position and influence were given to him because of and essentially at his birth, "at every step of my progress in life, (for in every step was I traversed and opposed), and at every turnpike I met, I was obliged to show my passport, and again and again to prove my sole title to the honour of being useful to my country, by a proof that I was not wholly unacquainted with its laws, and the whole system of its interests both abroad and at home. Otherwise no rank, no toleration even, for me. I had no arts but manly arts. On them I have stood, and please God, in spite of the Duke of Bedford and the Earl of Lauderdale, to the last gasp will I stand."[14]

Burke did not attack the right of aristocrats—presumed virtuous—to judge the merits of those seeking honors. Instead Burke defended his own pension as the rightful reward for his writings and his parliamentary activities in defense of the British Constitution. By questioning Burke's passport to honorable station, the duke risked calling into question his own prerogatives and, more important, the means by which Britain encouraged public service.

Aristocrats as well as commoners must act in the public interest—they must make themselves worthy of their honors and their station. Burke frequently chastised his superiors in the Rockingham parliamentary opposition, including his mentor Lord Rockingham himself, for their failure to live up to their responsibility to provide effective public service. Shortly before the war with the American colonies began in earnest, Burke wrote to Rockingham, "This is no time for taking publick business in its course and order, and only as a part in the Scheme of Life, which comes and goes at its proper periods and is mixed in with other occupations and amusements. It calls for the whole of the best of us. . . . Indeed my Dear Lord you are called upon in a very peculiar manner. America is yours. You have saved it once; and you may very possibly save it again."[15] We are called upon to act for the good of the nation, according to the best of our abilities, and within existing arrangements. Great status brings great responsibility, as well as great capacity, to serve the public interest.

Burke was a man of politics, and politics traditionally is seen as the realm of civic, republican virtue. But public service may take many forms. As Burke earned his passport to high station through his political service to the commonweal, so other men might earn distinction through nonpolitical means—religious, military, or in some other activity. Although the specifics of one's duties vary according to station and circumstance, the duty to fulfill one's role remains. Discussing the proper role of a good citizen confronted with the party divisions inseparable from free government, Burke observed:

It appears to me, that this question, like most of the others which regard our duties in life, is to be determined by our station in it. Private men may be wholly neutral, and entirely innocent: but they who are legally invested with public trust, or stand on the high ground of rank and dignity, which is trust implied, can hardly in any case remain indifferent, without the certainty of sinking into insignificance; and thereby in effect deserting that post in which, with the fullest authority, and for the wisest purposes, the laws and institutions of their country have fixed them. However, if it be the office of those who are thus circumstanced, to take a decided part, it is no less their duty that it should be a sober one. *It ought to be circumscribed by the same laws of decorum, and balanced by the same temper, which bound and regulate all the virtues.* In a word, we ought to act in party with all the moderation which does not absolutely enervate that vigor, and quench that fervency of spirit, without which the best wishes for the public good must evaporate in empty speculation.[16]

One's duties, and possibilities for the practice of virtue, differ according to one's position in society. But man's proper goal remains public service. As Burke's career attests, a virtuous man need not die in the social position into which he was born. Burke emphasized the need for hereditary aristocrats whose presumed virtue gives them a position from which to judge the virtue of others. He also argued that "a true natural aristocracy is not a separate interest in the state, or separable from it. It is an essential integrant part of any large body rightly constituted."[17]

A natural aristocracy arises, not from the mind of some founder, nor even directly from the hand of nature, but from habituation. Indeed, it is in accustoming oneself to one's position in the Great Chain of Being that one gains the ability to perform public service. Some public service may be done by those in many positions in life. The natural aristocracy, capable of achieving great public service, seems to include a varied group of professions. Certain occupations habituate one to a high place in the natural, hierarchical order of society. The circumstances that accustom men to their esteemed positions include "to be employed as an administrator of law and justice, and to be thereby amongst the first benefactors to mankind; to be a professor of high science, or of liberal and ingenuous art; to be amongst rich traders, who from their success are presumed to give sharp and vigorous understandings, and to possess the virtues of diligence, order, constancy, and regularity, and to have cultivated an habitual regard to communitative justice,"[18] as well as membership in the armed forces, the clergy, or the hereditary aristocracy. These are positions of honor within the structure of society. Habits are developed in the interaction between the individual and his particular circumstances; if he acts in a manner appropriate to his circumstances, the individual will gain the means as well as the duty to provide public service.

The most visible form of public service is that provided by public spirited statesmen, but even those in search of private gain may serve the public good. Thus "it is never . . . wise to quarrel with the interested views of men, whilst they are combined with the public interest and promote it: it is our business to tie the knot, if possible, closer."[19] Burke was in fact quite willing to recognize the beneficial possibilities of self-interest—rightly understood. "The love of lucre, though sometimes carried to a ridiculous, sometimes to a vicious excess, is the grand cause of prosperity to all states." In pursuing wealth, monied men serve the state, in a manner that is natural, reasonable, and powerful, if used properly to promote the national interest.[20] This is not to say that all callings are equally honorable. In his *Reflections on the Revolution in France*, Burke used biblical quotations concerning the need for leisure if one is to be wise and worthy and capable of ruling, in order to justify his statement that "the occupation of a hair-dresser, or of a working tallow-chandler, cannot be a matter of honor to any person,—to say nothing of a number of other more servile employments. Such descriptions of men ought not to suffer oppression from the state; but the state suffers oppression, if such as they, either individually or collectively, are permitted to rule. In this you think you are combating prejudice, but you are at war with Nature."[21]

For Burke certain "low" occupations require obedience and do not allow for the contemplation and high-minded interaction of aristocratic responsibility and leisure. The hairdresser's occupation does not provide him with the habits necessary for public office. Clearly, one may argue with the idea that a lack of leisure disqualifies certain men from exercising political rights. One might point out that ruling, too, requires certain habits best developed in the *doing* rather than in the contemplation of political life. But Burke's position is in keeping with his view that nature is fulfilled through a habituation that is itself largely dependent upon circumstance; nature precludes certain classes of men from providing public service in politics. Thus the Jacobins made a great mistake in attempting to turn men of low birth into public servants and legislators: "No name, no power, no function, no artificial institution whatsoever, can make the men, of whom any system of authority is composed, any other than God, and Nature, and education, and their habits of life have made them. Capacities beyond these the people have not to give. Virtue and wisdom may be the objects of their choice; but their choice confers neither the one nor the other on those upon whom they lay their ordaining hands. They have not the engagement of Nature, they have not the promise of Revelation for any such powers."[22] Indeed, where public assemblies are concerned, "nothing can secure a steady and moderate conduct in such assemblies, but that the body of them should be respectably composed, in point of condition in life, of permanent property, of education, and of such habits as enlarge and liberalize the understanding."[23] Aristocrats have a duty to serve the public in a public capacity. Members of low orders can only do their jobs. Men of ability (like Burke) can fulfill many occupations honorably and so further the public good. "The place of every man determines his duty."[24]

For some men their duty is that of obeying, for others it is that of pursuing their profession according to the dictates and within the confines of existing prejudice and convention. Some men may provide direct public service through governmental participation; others may perform it more indirectly. But wherever virtue and wisdom are found, their possessors "have, in whatever state, condition, profession, or trade, the passport of Heaven to human place and honour. Woe to the country which would madly and impiously reject the service of the talents and virtues, civil, military, or religious, that are given to grace and to serve it; and would condemn to obscurity everything formed to diffuse lustre and glory around a state!"[25] The state's glory and its lifeblood, virtue must be called for in all aspects of life—military, religious, economic, and political—if a society is to be worthy of conservation.

Man's proper goal, for Burke, is to live up to the dictates of his place in the Great Chain of Being. A hairdresser can achieve very little in the way of honor because his condition itself is not, in Burke's view, honorable. But even the hairdresser may achieve a kind of virtuous life. The hairdresser's virtue will be less august than that of the aristocrat who lives up to the imposing dictates of his presumptive status, but nonetheless it will be real virtue. The hairdresser may accept his position in life, and this is virtuous; he may show the proper deference to his superiors, and this also is virtuous.

For Burke it is possible that even certain "menial" workers may have the means and nature necessary to render more visible public service. They may be men of inventive or of economic genius—members of the natural aristocracy who will give economic benefit to society and so earn an honorable station. Members of "low" orders also may be capable of rendering public service in the military in time of need. There is room for advancement in Burke's view of society, but it must be gained through deeds done in the public interest. And the public interest cannot be determined through the use of speculative reason or the will of majorities of the moment; it can be discovered only with the guidance of prudence.

PRUDENCE AS VIRTUE'S GUIDE

Prudence is often seen as little more than timorous caution. To act swiftly and decisively, before all the elements of a given situation have been considered and all possible courses of action weighed would not be "prudent." Such a prudence, however useful in preventing short-term disaster, hardly seems virtuous. But Burkean prudence does not merely follow events; it guides action. Prudence is the virtue necessary for the proper reading of natural law, for the determination of what is needed to maintain the existing, virtuous society. It is the proper guiding principle for the statesman whose responsibility it is to tend public establishments and for all members of society in their daily lives.

Clearly, prudence is concerned with finding the proper course in given circumstances. In chastising the British government for its harsh treatment of its American colonies, Burke observed,

> ideas of liberty might be desired more reconcilable with an arbitrary and boundless authority. Perhaps we might wish the colonists to be persuaded that their liberty is more secure when held in trust for them by us (as their guardians during a perpetual minority) than with any part of it in their own hands. But the question is not, whether their spirit deserves praise or blame,—what, in the name of God, shall we do with it? You have before you the object, such as it is,—with all its glories, with all its imperfections on its head. You see the magnitude, the importance, the temper, the habits, the disorders. By all these considerations we are strongly urged to determine something concerning it.[26]

To deal properly with given circumstances is to be a prudent and there-fore a virtuous actor. To do otherwise is to act against the interests of the nation and so betray one's trust.

A society's circumstances include—in large part consist of—the gen-eral opinions of the people to be governed. "In effect, to follow, not to force, the public inclination,—to give a direction, a form, a technical dress, and a specific sanction, to the general sense of the community, is the true end of legislature."[27] A statesman who acts against the public inclination fails the test of prudence. By acting against the prejudices of the people, he calls into question the very authority of the legislature and perhaps of society itself.

A certain state of mind is necessary for the practice of virtue. The fevered mind, or society, distracted by utopian visions or base appetites, cannot read the dictates of natural law—cannot act prudently. Throughout his life and work Burke sought to foster and promote a society that is calm in its very roots. Calmness is particularly necessary in those men who render public service in government because they are the most capable of harming society by acting upon idealized errors, but they are not the only ones called upon to be prudent. After all, public service "ought to be circumscribed by the same laws of decorum, and balanced by the same temper which bound and regulate all the virtues."[28]

The temper Burke saw binding and regulating all the virtues was one of moderation. Moderation, which entails decorum, attention to the forms of discourse and civility, and especially the calm cast of mind necessary for proper decisions, is a great good. A moderate temper is particularly important in the dealings of those men who seek to do public service in positions of public life, but it is to "bound and regulate all the virtues."

Moderation is a good. The calm ability to look at the world without one's passions being violently engaged, the temperate control of one's desires that makes civilization possible, the restraint that is the basis of society is dictated by prudence as a necessary element of the life of virtue. Moderation is not prudence, however; prudence may at times dic-tate that moderation be cast aside. Prudence—that wisdom which rec-ognizes what circumstances dictate for the preservation of the existing order—may, in some instances, demand that the good society, the soci-ety of moderation and accepting virtue, be defended through decidedly immoderate means.

Revolutionary France, for Burke, exemplified all that was wicked.

More important, France corrupted all who viewed it and was actively expanding its boundaries. The French cancer had to be destroyed, through whatever means necessary, if European civilization was to survive.

> Dreadful is the example of ruined innocence and virtue, and the completest triumph of the completest villainy that ever vexed and disgraced mankind! The example is ruinous in every point of view, religious, moral, civil, political. It establishes that dreadful maxim of Machiavel, that in great affairs men are not to be wicked by halves. This maxim is not made for a middle sort of beings, who, because they cannot be angels, ought to thwart their ambition, and not endeavor to become infernal spirits. It is too well exemplified in the present time, where the faults and errors of humanity, checked by the imperfect, timorous virtues, have been overpowered by those who have stopped at no crime. It is a dreadful part of the example, that infernal malevolence has had pious apologists, who read their lectures on frailties in favor of crimes,—who abandon the weak, and court the friendship of the wicked. To root out these maxims, and the examples that support them, is a wise object of years of war. This is that war. This is that moral war.[29]

The extremism of Machiavelli was given life by the Jacobins. It was thus the duty of the British to put the Frenchmen's extremist regime to death so that man's moderation, his search for the nonwicked, might be restored. The most immoderate of means, a "Battle of Giants,"[30] was necessary so that Europe and the virtues for which it stood and which it made possible might survive.

Prudence, like public service, is most visible in the public sphere; it is also most needed in the dealings of statesmen. The natural guardians of the virtues—tradition, prejudice, and manners—must be protected from the speculative notions that will destroy them. Since society generally promotes to the rank of statesman those men who wish it well and have some actual or presumptive virtue, moderate means generally are sufficient for society's protection. If the danger comes from outside or is not realized until late in the game, however, prudence may dictate that moderation be set aside until the crisis has passed. Immoderation may be necessary to protect and maintain the natural moderation of society.

> They who go with the principles of the ancient Whigs, which are those contained in Mr. Burke's book [the *Reflections*], never can go too far.

They may, indeed, stop short of some hazardous and ambiguous excellence, which they will be taught to postpone to any reasonable degree of good they may actually possess. The opinions maintained in that book never can lead to an extreme, because their foundation is laid in an opposition to extremes. The foundation of government is there laid, not in imaginary rights of men, (which at best is a confusion of judicial with civil principles,) but in political convenience, and in human nature,—either as that nature is universal, or as it is modified by local habits and social aptitudes. The foundation of government (those who have read that book will recollect) is laid in a provision for our wants and in a conformity to our duties: it is to purvey for the one, it is to enforce the other. These doctrines do of themselves gravitate to a middle point, or to some point near a middle. They suppose, indeed, a certain portion of liberty to be essential to all good government; but they infer that this liberty is to be blended into the government, to harmonize with its forms and its rules, and to be made subordinate to its end. Those who are not with that book are with its opposite; for there is no medium besides the medium itself.[31]

Burke's self-avowed purpose in the *Reflections* was to protect the moderate, virtuous life of the British, those men who live according to the dictates of nature (and are *therefore* moderate[32]), against the immoderate, unnatural system of the Jacobins and of their allies in Britain. Prudence dictates the defense of the British Constitution against the Jacobin onslaught, and the virtuous statesman—the statesman who uses his practical wisdom to preserve existing institutions from changing circumstances—will not be afraid to act immoderately in defense of "the middle path."[33]

Prudence determines the value of particular virtues in particular circumstances. The balancing that must be done, not only between institutions but between virtues, is neither simple nor metaphysical in nature. Prudence allows one to discern what natural law dictates in given circumstances. Although natural law is not beyond the ability of the normal man to comprehend, it must be read carefully, through the use of a practical reason grounded in affectionate attachment to society as it exists. Acceptingness, if taken to its extreme, is slavish. Moderation dictates its limitation as well as the limitation of all virtues. But the particular circumstances in which acceptingness must take precedence over independence or vice versa, though perhaps clear in their broad outlines, may change, just as the need to be moderate or immoderate may change in extreme circumstances. Prudence is not the basis of the life of virtue, as acceptingness is, but it is its guide.

INDEPENDENCE AND THE PRINCIPLE OF PARTY ATTACHMENT

Politics was the center of Burke's life, and Burke considered Parliament to be the center of political life in Britain. Although politics is certainly not the central, let alone the only, avenue for the pursuit of virtue, it is in politics that independence becomes most important and most conspicuous in Burke's writings. Independence is the ability (both economic and intellectual) and the willingness to make decisions on the basis of a principled view of the public interest. The public interest is never served by utopian reform, and almost never by immoderation. Thus independence by itself leads to the crimes of the French Revolution. But its lack leads to servitude. Independence is a virtue when it is principled and when it is used in the provision of public service.

In the name of principled independence, Burke sought to promote principled party government. He argued repeatedly for the maintenance of connections between men that are based upon shared views of what is best for the nation. Indeed, early in his career, Burke defended existing British political arrangements on the grounds that numerous and strong examples could still be found "of an unshaken adherence to principle, and attachment to connection, against every allurement of interest," among members of Parliament.[34]

Burke argued that there is an economic requirement for the independence of members of Parliament. He opposed triennial elections because he "should be fearful of committing, every three years, the independent gentlemen of the country into a contest with the treasury."[35] The royal party, controlling the king's treasury, could outspend and eventually defeat all but its wealthiest principled opponents. Elections, "too frequently repeated [would be] utterly ruinous, first to independence of fortune, and then to independence of spirit."[36] Attempting to limit the crown's ability to exert corrupt influence on Parliament, Burke proposed reforms intended to minimize payments from the treasury for which there was no accounting.[37] He also spoke out against the actions of the "court cabal" that was seeking to institute its policies, over Parliament's objections, through the use of corruption, intrigue, and the improper use of the royal name and prerogative.[38]

Of course, the crown was not the only source of corrupt and unprincipled action by members of Parliament. Burke was heavily involved in attempts to prosecute officers of the East India Company and in efforts to reform that company on the grounds that the illegal procurement of funds in India had corrupted Parliament. British adventurers, having made their fortunes in India, would bring their funds and influence home to Britain and use them to purchase protection from members of Parliament, thus escaping justice and corrupting their protectors.[39]

Clearly, separation of powers and independence from corruption were both politically useful in Burke's view. But the man who acts independently is not a mere cog in governmental machinery. He is a maker of important party and individual choices. Party government embodies the Burkean ideal of political independence. This may seem contradictory at first, since party members must act in concert if they are to be effective. But party government is necessary for the party *attachment* with which Burke was most concerned.

The good statesman is independent of the mob "out of doors," even if they are friends because the puppet of the mob violates the dictates of both prudence and independence.[40] The good statesman is independent from monarchical influences derived from the king's ability to bribe, reward, deny rewards, or use royal money, lands, and honors against him. His attachment is to a particular party on the basis of a common view of the public interest. Indeed, Burke defined party as "a body of men united, for promoting by their joint endeavours, the national interest, upon some particular principle in which they are all agreed."[41]

Because differences between parties are inevitable, so are attempts by one party to gain advantage over another. Yet "if no system for relieving the subjects of this kingdom from oppression, and snatching its affairs from ruin, can be adopted, until it is demonstrated that no party can derive an advantage from it, no good can ever be done in this country." Party rewards properly belong to the party that has as its own interest the protection of those directly affected by the legislation. The proper party to receive rewards for reforming India is the party that "has its reputation, nay, its very being, pledged to the protection and preservation of that part of the empire."[42] Rewards rightly accrue to men who take principled positions, and the only proper basis of party connection is itself principle. Thus, if a statesman "does not concur in these general principles upon which the party is founded, and which necessarily draws on a concurrence to their application, he ought from the beginning to have chosen some other, more conformable to his opinions."[43]

In his *Observations on a Late Publication on the Present State of the Nation*, Burke defended his notion of principled party government against the attacks of an opponent attached, in Burke's view for reasons of interest, to the ruling, nonparty, administration. Examples of honor and virtue were still to be found in Britain, and they were "not furnished by the great alone; nor by those, whose activity in public affairs may render it suspected that they make such a character one of the rounds in the ladder of ambition; but by men more quiet, and more in the shade, on whom an unmixed sense of honor alone could operate."[44] According to Burke, the men whom his opponent attacked

> are many of them of the first families, and weightiest properties, in the kingdom; but infinitely more distinguished for their untainted honor, public and private, and their zealous, but sober attachment to the constitution of their country, than they can be by any birth, or any station. If they are the friends of any one great man rather than another, it is not that they make his aggrandizement the end of their union; or because they know him to be the most active in caballing for his connections the largest and speediest emoluments. It is because they know him, by personal experience, to have wise and enlarged ideas of the public good, and an invincible constancy in adhering to it; because they are convinced, by the whole tenor of his actions, that he will never negotiate away their honor or his own: and that, in or out of power, change of situation will make no alteration in his conduct. This will give to such a person in such a body, an authority and respect that no minister ever enjoyed among his venal dependents, in the highest plenitude of his power; such as servility never can give, such as ambition never can receive or relish.
>
> This body will often be reproached by their adversaries, for want of ability in their political transactions; they will be ridiculed for missing many favorable conjunctures, and not profiting of several brilliant opportunities of fortune; but they must be contented to endure that reproach; for they cannot acquire the reputation of *that kind* of ability without losing all the other reputation they possess.[45]

Honor is the requirement and the reward of the statesman. And to act upon a desire to serve the public interest is infinitely more important than birth or political effectiveness. Deference, that conservative value that many most fault Burke for emphasizing, is due, not to those men who merely hold high position, but to those who hold it with honor. The virtuous statesman is more concerned with doing what is right, according to his considered view of the public interest, than with doing what is rewarding or expedient.

One is not to act solely on the basis of one's own wisdom. This would be unforgivably prideful, imprudent, and damaging to the nation. But if one is to be worthy of the name "independent gentleman" one must act according to one's view of the national interest—to make one's choice of party on the basis of independent judgment. The party chosen must be beyond reproach of corruption, and the choice itself must be based on shared principles. Thus the severing of party ties may be necessary (as it was for Burke during the French Revolution) when disagreement over principles becomes too great. It is through the choice of party on the basis of principle that one acts as a virtuous, independent statesman. And it is in this way that the statesman may live up to his duty to perform public service, the performance of which is itself a virtue.

Independence is a very limited virtue for Burke. He was acutely aware of the dangers of unimpeded intellect and action. The independence of Parliament for which he argued was needed so that power might be limited rather than extended. Not trusting the king's men to act in the national interest, Burke argued that Parliament's traditional role as protector of the people demanded independence from the royal favorites.

One's independence is not to be separate from one's station in life. The properly independent man acts according to conscience, upon his own prudential view of natural law and the national interest, but within the confines of existing norms and institutions. Independent action proper for one man may be folly or rank servitude for another. Nor is independence purely a matter of situation. One is not independent merely because one is not financially dependent upon another. Financial independence may be necessary, but it is certainly not enough. Statesmen are not dependent upon their friends "out of doors." Yet to follow blindly the wishes of these friends, though perhaps consistent with a certain view of the statesman's responsibility, is not in keeping with Burke's insistence upon the statesman's duty to use his *own* judgment in matters of state as elsewhere.[46]

Proper independence of thought is rare; perhaps this is why it is a virtue. Moreover, too much independence leads to license and the tyranny of the passions.[47] Most men do not think reasonably, instead following their passions or the popular opinion of the day. But it is the public-spirited man of independent thought who may do his nation great service, through wise public positions on political issues, or in whatever sphere his ability to provide public service may be manifested.

LOCAL AFFECTION: VIRTUE AT ITS SOURCE

> To be attached to the subdivision, to love the little platoon we belong to in society, is the first principle (the germ, as it were) of public affections. It is the first link in the series by which we proceed towards a love to our country and to mankind.[48]

Burke attacked British laws intended to repress Irish Catholicism because they rewarded one group in Irish society and punished another solely for their religious beliefs. The Popery Laws, as they were called, were unnatural and unjust because affections growing from local attachments are more natural and therefore more fundamental than those based on the particulars of religious dogma. Natural affections grow from familiarity, from the living of one's daily life in concert with one's neighbors— those with whom one shares locality, circumstance, and belief (including religious belief).

Local attachments must be nurtured because they make possible the conservative good life of affectionate public service. The conservative life of public affection is different from the life of civic participation sought by republican theorists because it does not necessarily mean self-conscious service to the state as a political entity. As we have seen, public service may take many forms, not the least of which is religious service. What is essential, for the conservative, is the desire to serve the friends, neighbors, and society one knows and loves.

Prejudice also may be seen in terms of the virtue of local affection because it is, in a sense, its embodiment. When men live together in harmony, they develop a set of norms and opinions by which they live their lives. These norms and opinions, these prejudices, are good in the

Burkean view because they are the natural outgrowth of the sharing of like objects and circumstances—because they embody natural arrangements and natural affections. Thus prejudices, the Great Chain of Being itself, along with social conventions in general, are dependent upon a certain affection among the members of society. Bereft of affection, society will have only force to bind itself, and will disintegrate. Local affection—the attachment to "our little band"—is necessary if society is to exist because public affection forms from local attachments. And without public affection society becomes a mere collection of interests and powers, bereft of true authority and the ability to govern as a moral entity.

The good life grows from the locality upward, not only in terms of social structure, but in terms of social affection. This is why Burke placed such great emphasis upon the need for familial affection and deference. It is the family tie which is the most natural. It is the family tie which is the basis of affection, proper deference, and the structure of society. The family is the foundation of society, and familial affection is the natural basis of the good life, for one is not capable of real virtue if one is not capable of loving one's own.

It was his combination of vanity and lack of parental affection that made Rousseau ("a lover of his kind, but a hater of his kindred") Burke's archetype of the vicious man and of the viciousness of the French revolutionaries.[49] Rousseau's wish to be spoken of, and his conviction that his confessions would "pass at worst for openness and candor," led him to proclaim to the world his vulgar personal deeds.[50] Acknowledging his creator "only to brave him," Rousseau recorded a thoroughly vicious life, a life that the French revolutionaries then set up as an example for all to follow.

> To him they erect their first statue. From him they commence their series of honors and distinctions.
>
> It is that new-invented virtue which your masters canonize that led their moral hero constantly to exhaust the stores of his powerful rhetoric in the expression of universal benevolence, whilst his heart was incapable of harboring one spark of common parental affection. Benevolence to the whole species, and want of feeling for every individual with whom the professors come in contact, form the character of the new philosophy. Setting up for an unsocial independence, this their hero of vanity refuses the just price of common labor, as well as the tribute which opulence owes to gen-

ius, and which, when paid, honors the giver and the receiver; and then he pleads his beggary as an excuse for his crimes. He melts with tenderness for those only who touch him by the remotest relation, and then, without one natural pang, casts away, as a sort of offal and excrement, the spawn of his disgustful amours, and sends his children to the hospital of foundlings. The bear loves, licks, and forms her young: but bears are not philosophers. Vanity, however, finds its account in reversing the train of our natural feelings. Thousands admire the sentimental writer; the affectionate father is hardly known in his parish.[51]

Rousseau's vanity led him away from the natural basis of society and of all virtue. His attachment to general precepts and to rationalistic philosophy—an attachment shared by his Jacobin followers—led to the destruction of all true virtue and its replacement by the false virtue of "universal benevolence." Universal benevolence ignores the need for benevolence and affection at the much more local level—the level of those with whom one comes into intimate, daily contact.

Rousseau was without virtue because he broke the natural ties of the family—man's most natural hierarchy, which is based upon obedience to the Creator and upon recognition of the duty to care for one's young. The female bear knows better than Rousseau because she cares for her young, those for whom Providence has given her responsibility, those with whom she is intimately familiar. Parental affection is the basis of virtue because it is natural, local, and familiar. Parental affection is the basis of all relationships that are not formed solely by unfeeling abstract concepts, interest, or force. The virtuous man recognizes his responsibility to those who are dependent upon him. He recognizes that he is dependent upon others, particularly God and his society, and that he owes them respect and affection. He serves God, man, and society because it is natural and therefore proper for him to do so.

Virtue by nature is based in the family, and there is a natural progression of society and virtue from the family upward. "One's own" is a broad term that encompasses much. One owes allegiance to one's place in life—one's station—as well as to one's family. Those who do not defend the rightful position and prerogatives of their station are traitors. The French nobles who, during the revolution, failed to defend the established order of society from the leveling *philosophes* must necessarily have been vain, prideful men. "Turbulent, discontented men of quality, in proportion as they are puffed up with personal pride and arrogance, generally despise their own order." Furthermore, their pride, itself a vice that should be avoided through the virtue of acceptingness, also led these nobles to violate their trust, to fail to give to their fellow nobles the support due members of the same station in life. Such treacheries are committed only by bad men. "The interest of that portion of social arrangement is a trust in the hands of all those who compose it; and as none but bad men would justify it in abuse, none but traitors would barter it away for their own personal advantage."[52]

If one does not support one's group, one's "little platoon," one is a traitor. One has violated the requirement to support one's compatriots, and to support them *because* they are one's compatriots. The good man loves his neighbors and seeks to aid them, not because he agrees with their philosophy, not because he finds it convenient to support them, but because he by nature, unless this nature has been perverted, loves those with whom he shares experiences and circumstances.

BURKEAN VIRTUE AND THE CONSERVATIVE GOOD LIFE

For Burke, any good life is intimately concerned with the pursuit of virtue, and this pursuit is closely linked, not just with what one does, but with what one actively refrains from doing. One is virtuous because one defers to the wisdom of the ages and of the society in which one lives. One serves one's society because one loves it and feels that it is one's natural, God-given duty to serve it. Conservative virtue requires an awareness of the dictates of natural law, an awareness that is not subverted by corruption, idealized theory, or blind obedience. It calls for a recognition of man's limitations and of the goodness of society. Virtue requires that one acknowledge both that natural law dictates one's place in the social order and that the given social order is authoritative and good.

Those whose professions themselves are worthy of honor may achieve great honor because they are capable of great virtue or of vice. The Duke of Bedford was given a high position and a high responsibility. By betraying his responsibility, he betrayed his position and his nation—and thus committed extreme vice and folly, acting unvirtuously and deserving dishonor. Those with more humble callings are capable of less "august" virtue and less harmful vice. But those of humble station must accept their place in the Great Chain of Being and seek to provide service within its dictates. Although there is room in any good society for some proper mobility of station, virtue and honor, the virtue of those in lower stations is both less "heroic" and less honored than that of those in high station. But "lower" virtue is nonetheless real and is an integral part of any good social life.

One certainly may argue that the Burkean conception of virtue fails to recognize the full potential of man, his ability to forge a moral life for himself without destroying society. But it is this limited view of man that lies at the base of the conservative view of natural law and the good life. To dismiss conservative thought as merely hierarchical and therefore bad is to miss the rich variety of thought and possibility inherent in the accepting nature of conservative political philosophy.

The conservative is willing to accept many kinds of society. Be they the "Liberal/Democratic" society of America, the caste system of India, or the Catholic tradition in Ireland, Burke accepted the social order natural to a given society in its given circumstances, provided it allowed for the pursuit of virtue and the good life. And this good life, although it justifies a hierarchical order denying much in the way of material goods and social recognition to members of the lower classes, does allow these members to partake a great deal more in the good life than do other systems of virtue demanding great leisure, learning, and/or "great" civic and military deeds. The conservative good life is one of closeness and affection. This good life provides, not only the possibility of advancement through the provision of public service, but also the protection of tradition and prejudice against the moral enormities of those who would mold men to fit some idealized, corrupt, and hubristic vision of "true justice." The virtuous man is the man of public affection, the man who serves society because it is his society, familiar and so loved. The man who accepts the dictates of Providence and the modifications of collective reason—as justified by prejudice—is able to live at least some form of the good life, regardless of the place he has been given in society.

It is when society loses track of its conventional nature, its basis in history and circumstance as dictated by natural law, that Burke believed virtue becomes impossible. It becomes impossible because the intimate connections on which it is based are sundered by theories and practices that ignore man's limited, local nature and his need for familiarity if he is to love. Natural law is embodied in the natural relations of family, locality, and the platoon to which one belongs. These relations naturally produce outgrowths—traditions, prejudices, and manners—that allow for the good life so long as they remain unquestioned. By accepting the authority of society as it exists, one allows oneself the opportunity to partake of this society without perverting it. One is even able to serve society, and to do so out of affection is the essence of conservative virtue.

Such a life is worthy of honor because it is difficult (it may well place society before one's own interests) and (seemingly paradoxically) because it is natural. Yet God has willed that man's achievement of his nature shall be a difficult undertaking—one worthy of a creature, possessed of limited reason to be sure, but also possessed of a moral sense, of a free will, and of the capacity to recognize and to act upon the will of God.

Man's nature is not angelic; he is selfish and his reason is limited. Man's natural attachments and duties may be subverted by greed, attachment to idealized theories, pride, or simple weakness of character. Still, for Burke, the answer to the human predicament does not lie in the abandonment of our ability to act. Rather, the answer lies in the recognition that good or virtuous action is that which dedicates itself to the interests of the familiar, that which one loves out of habit. After all, virtue itself is no more (and no less) than a good habit.

4 • Tocqueville and the Conservation of Liberty in America

The Burkean good life provides all members of society with an opportunity to live a life of accepting virtue. It is, however, a life of limited horizons—its emphasis is on acceptance. It is certainly true that the conservative may accept many different societies, but man himself must accept that which the circumstances of history have given him. And this is not so broad and varied a prospect because for Burke human nature is severely limited and so must be man's opportunities to exercise his capacities independently. Man must be constrained by historical institutions, by that which he did not create but must still accept and support.

In practice, acceptance means that men with a certain lineage are given the right to judge, reward, and punish others. Men of talent and ability are assumed to be rewarded according to the extent of their service to the public and the inherited aristocracy is assumed to be capable of putting the public interest before its own. Yet, even assuming that men will act as Burke would have them act—virtuously, with independence from corruption but not from social norms—this notion of service to the public interest may appear inherently unfree to some observers. That is, Burke's notions of man's limited nature may be seen as leading him to provide a good life that is not terribly good for free men. If one serves only others, one is not serving oneself. On this reading society is the central object of affection and of effort in Burke's schema, not the individual.

It is not an original criticism to point out that Burke seems to value the existing society more than the individual. Moreover, such a criticism distorts the conservative program since the conservative believes that the individual can exist and be free and virtuous only within a calm, accepted society. But for those critics who believe that man is capable of tending to his own concerns and of independent, rational, and affectionate action without the need for substantial social constraints, the Burkean notion of virtue seems unnecessarily confining. Burkean conservatism may be seen as overemphasizing the limits of individuals' ability to form free and meaningful lives and underemphasizing the same limits for institutions.

Even the hairdresser may partake of the Burkean good life, but only in a limited way. He acts virtuously by accepting his subservient position in society and by following the orders of those placed above him in the Great Chain of Being without complaint or fundamental questioning. The hairdresser achieves virtue by stifling his desire to act independently, to claim public honor and respect for himself since, for Burke, he deserves none. One need not be an advocate of any notion of equality of condition to point out that such a good life provides very little in the way of "goods" where the "lower orders" are concerned. Burke's notion of human virtue assumes that one's occupation and social circumstances necessarily form the bulk of one's character. Certain occupations are beneath the possibility of honor; thus in practice certain men also are considered beneath that possibility.

Since human nature itself is so limited, it is largely formed by social circumstance. The mere fact of being human thus entitles one only "not to suffer oppression from the state."[1] This is no small right, and one that many regimes claiming to serve the interests and to respect the humanity of those men with undesirable occupations blatantly violate. But the Burkean notion of rights—what is reasonable and for the good of those involved—assumes that those bestowing rights will have the interest of those beneath them in mind. And, even if the powerful serve the interests of the weak, the entire notion of class-based guardianship does not allow individuals not in positions of power to act freely and to protect their own liberty. Class structure also prevents those in less esteemed positions from exercising and achieving their full capacities, and thus learning (through habituation) how to live independent lives.

The charge one may make against Burke then is relatively simple and is no doubt familiar: Men have the right to the position in life that their own abilities and efforts merit, not the position that the virtues of their ancestors earned them, not the position into which they were born and perhaps habituated, but the position their own efforts may achieve for them. And the requirement for just deserts is above all the rejection of

presumptive virtue and vice as passports to power and privilege or unquestioning service.

If the occupation and actions of one's father or ancestors entitle one
to the presumption of virtue and if one's worth is judged according to
one's occupation, then opportunities to rise and fall in occupation and
social estimation will be uncommon. Such opportunities will exist for
those with great talent (like Burke), but they will be relatively rare. Given
a strong class structure, there will be inherited presumptions of bad as
well as of good character. Men will not be judged according to their real
worth and will not be allowed to achieve their full potential since such
presumptions act as self-fulfilling prophecies. Men who are treated as incapable of independent action or reason will have little opportunity, and
therefore ability, to act independently and reasonably.

And it is not only government that may oppress members of the
"lower orders." Prejudice and the very notion of a Great Chain of Being
may produce a society in which certain men—such as the so-called un-
touchables of the caste system in India defended by Burke—are subject
to bad treatment and severely limited prospects, regardless of their own
merits and merely because of their parentage. Prejudice may not deserve
its present bad reputation, but one may argue that Burke went too far
in accepting existing beliefs, as well as existing institutions and practices,
that fail to recognize personal effort and worth.

The injustices of hierarchical presumptions may seem minor when one
is faced with the prospect of tyranny or anarchy. But tyranny and anarchy are not the only alternatives to hierarchy. The most powerful and
commonly noted alternative to hierarchy is of course equality. Tocqueville generally is regarded as one of the first and perhaps the greatest theorist and exponent of equality. An attachment to equality—and thus
Tocqueville himself—would seem, then, to be at odds with the conservative vision of human nature and the human good. But the nature
and extent of Tocqueville's attachment to equality serve to show that
conservatism is not obsolete in the age of equality.

Tocqueville accepted the spread of equality as a divinely ordered historical movement or circumstance. He sought to *promote* only an equality that was moderate and limited in its scope and application. Egalitarian
tyranny is unconservative. Well-ordered liberty, based on traditional attachments and a general acceptance of equality before the law is not.
And Tocqueville defended and sought to foster well-ordered liberty
wherever it was fitting. Facing radically different circumstances, living

amidst the unrest and the extremisms unleashed by the egalitarian revolution Burke fought, Tocqueville sought to apply the same principles
of natural law Burke used in pursuit of the same conservative good life.[2]
Opposing the schemes of rationalistic philosophers—now more appropriately termed social engineers—Tocqueville asserted man's need for
hierarchy and authority if he is to live a free and virtuous life in democratic times.

THE PROMISE AND DANGER OF LIBERALISM
AND DEMOCRACY

Tocqueville saw nineteenth-century America as a hopeful and instruc-
tive example of how the democratic revolution then sweeping the globe
might be dealt with successfully. Men might look to America in answering
the question of whether each nation now would have "an agitated or
tranquil republic, an orderly or a disorderly republic, pacific or warlike,
liberal or oppressive, a republic which threatens the sacred rights of property and of the family, or one which recognizes and honors them."[3]
    Tocqueville praised the United States and held it up to his country-
men as an example to be emulated because, in America,

> for sixty years that people who has made [the sovereignty of the major-
> ity] the common fount of all their laws has increased in population, ter-
> ritory, and wealth; and, let it be noted, throughout that period it has been
> not only the most prosperous but also the most stable of all the peoples
> in the world. While all the nations of Europe have been ravaged by war
> or torn by civil strife, the American people alone in the civilized world
> have remained pacific. Almost the whole of Europe has been convulsed
> by revolutions; America has not even suffered from riots. There the re-
> public, so far from disturbing them, has preserved all rights. Private prop-
> erty is better guaranteed there than in any other land on earth. Anarchy
> is as unknown as despotism.[4]

America was a successful democracy because it had shown that the sovereignty of the people might be made compatible with peaceful government, with prosperity, and with the enjoyment of the sacred rights
of the family and of private property.
    For Tocqueville the American form of democratic government was

intrinsically good. But neither democracy nor the particular government of the United States was the goal toward which Tocqueville sought to have all nations, and particularly his native France, strive. Indeed, near the end of the first volume of *Democracy*, Tocqueville argued that

> those who, having read this book, should imagine that in writing it I am urging all nations with a democratic social state to imitate the laws and mores of the Anglo-Americans would be making a great mistake; they must have paid more attention to the form than to the substance of my thought. My aim has been to show, by the American example, that laws and more especially mores can allow a democratic people to remain free. But I am very far from thinking that we should follow the example of American democracy and imitate the means that it has used to attain this end, for I am well aware of the influence of the nature of a country and of antecedent events on political constitutions, and I should regard it as a great misfortune for mankind if liberty were bound always and in all places to have the same features.[5]

The proper goal toward which nations must aim, whatever their given circumstances, is (well-ordered) liberty. A democratic social state is merely one circumstance among many to be taken into account in the ongoing struggle to obtain and to maintain liberty. Those men who would aid their own society must act in accordance with that society's prevailing characteristics, and, "if patient observation and sincere meditation have led men of the present day to recognize that both the past and the future of their history consist in the gradual and measured advance of equality, that discovery in itself gives this progress the sacred character of the will of the Sovereign Master. In that case effort to halt democracy appears as a fight against God Himself, and nations have no alternative but to acquiesce in the social state imposed by Providence."[6]

One must accept that which history, the tool of God, dictates. But must we accept *any* government, no matter how bad? Burke said no, but that the only governments against which he would lift his hand were those that were "absolutely incorrigible."[7] Necessity is the only excuse for attacks against established authority. Natural law establishes what is right, but to subvert an erring government that is not incorrigible, when inaction would not bring disaster to society, is itself wrong.

In proper conservative fashion, Tocqueville accepted what he saw as the inherent tendency toward equality in American society and then attempted to find the practice of virtue in that society. Finding virtue, particularly in America's voluntary associations,[8] Tocqueville saw his task as that of pointing out how virtue might be fostered in the given, egalitarian, circumstances. Democracy must be accepted and dealt with properly so that liberty may be established and maintained. Indeed, given the circumstances of the time, "if we [in France] do not succeed in gradually introducing democratic institutions among us, and if we despair of imparting to all citizens those ideas and sentiments which first prepare them for freedom and then allow them to enjoy it, there will be no independence left for anybody, neither for the middle classes nor for the nobility, neither for the poor nor for the rich, but only an equal tyranny for all; and I foresee that if the peaceful dominion of the majority is not established among us in good time, we shall sooner or later fall under the *unlimited* authority of a single man."[9] The danger most to be feared is that of tyranny. Given the inevitability of equality—the spirit of democracy—tyranny may be avoided only through the proper acceptance of moderated equality and democracy.

Tocqueville sought to promote human liberty. But it is important to note that for Tocqueville mere unfettered individualism was not the proper end for any society. Tocqueville's vision of liberty was specific and did not accept individualism as a good. As John P. Diggins points out, for Tocqueville individualism may be equated with narcissism. It is "the diminishing power of the individual who becomes preoccupied with the self."[10] Liberty can be used for good or ill, and individualism, the selfish devotion to home and family to the exclusion of all other concerns, is not good. For Tocqueville, individualism, if left unchecked, is a menace because it separates men from one another, leaving them too weak to prevent the rise of tyranny.[11] It is based on the "misguided judgment" that man's individual reason and his "circle of family and friends" are sufficent unto themselves,[12] that society and human perfection do not rest upon habit, prejudice, and a multiplicity of social attachments. Thus the very notion that the private sphere is the sole arena for right action was rejected explicitly by Tocqueville as a *danger* to liberty.

Independence and freedom of thought were important to Tocqueville. But our proper goal is not to maximize each man's liberty to enjoy the self-chosen pleasures of private life. Societies, be they democratic or aristocratic, must aim at something higher—the life of virtue. Tocqueville has been called "the greatest analyst of the problem of classical [i.e., republican] virtue in democratic America," attempting to reformulate ancient notions of virtuous action so that they might be perpetuated in a new world and time.[13] But Tocqueville explicitly linked virtue with nonrepublican notions of rights (and with the rule of law in particular). "Next to virtue as a general idea, nothing, I think, is so beautiful as that of rights, and indeed the two ideas are mingled. The idea of rights is nothing but the conception of virtue applied to the world of politics."[14]

Political rights are good and necessary, but they are not so beautiful as the idea of virtue, nor are rights necessarily democratic or egalitarian in nature. The "fairness" or equality of "rights" to governmental largesse now so often touted as the essence of any just order can play no part in any Tocquevillean order. Indeed, equality, and the democracy with which it is linked, brings a tendency toward individualism.[15] Individualism is an evil, however, that only freedom can combat. "For only freedom can deliver the members of a community from that isolation which is the lot of the individual left to his own devices and, compelling them to get in touch with each other, promote an active sense of fellowship. . . . It alone replaces at certain critical moments their natural love of material welfare by a loftier, more virile ideal; offers other objectives than that of getting rich; and sheds a light enabling all to see and appraise men's vices and their virtues as they truly are."[16] Liberty, like society itself, is good because it is necessary if man is to attain the life of virtue. Only by coming into contact with his fellows can man develop the desire to serve them. Only by choosing the ways in which he will interact with his fellows will man learn of the invigorating possibilities of the life of virtue—the many ways in which he and his fellow man can aid one another in their pursuit of a good life.

PUBLIC SPIRIT, ORDER AND THE TYRANNY OF THE MAJORITY

Tocqueville's attachment to public spirit has led some commentators to argue that his thought has republican leanings and goals.[17] Yet Burke was also attached to public spirit, and few would argue that his political philosophy is republican in nature. Conservative public spirit— Burke's and Tocqueville's public spirit—springs from a vision of the good of man and society quite unlike that of republicanism. Conservative public spirit must be orderly and based on the acceptance of tradition. After the French Revolution of 1848, Tocqueville, frightened and horrified by the socialist uprisings of the June Days, rescinded his support of economic and social reforms and opposed any amnesty for the insurgents, supporting only a military solution to the crisis.[18] Those men who had subverted the very bases of French society were to be shown no mercy; they were to be crushed in order to assure the survival of the nation.

It was in fact consensus rather than a specific form of regime—including the republican form—that Tocqueville sought in French political life. In an unpublished manifesto for a proposed journal, Tocqueville wrote, "If the free expression of the will of the nation returns the senior branch of the Bourbons to the throne, if a Restoration could take place that ensured the nation the rights due to it, the editors of the review would witness this event with pleasure. They would consider it a favorable omen for future social progress, but they do not want a Restoration except under these conditions, and if it were to come about in any other way and lead to contrary results, they would regard it as their duty to oppose it."[19] If the French were to accept their traditional form of government and if it were made consistent with the rights necessary for a good life, Tocqueville would be pleased. Traditional forms and practices would have gained the necessary consensus for their stability.

As Tocqueville himself stated, he never did believe "that the republican form of government is the best suited to the needs of France." Republican government, by which Tocqueville meant government dominated by an elected executive power, was too prone to produce revolutions among a people accustomed to administrative centralization. Far better, for Tocqueville, to have a constitutional monarchy capable of quieting the people's passions. But since the "old Dynasty was profoundly antipathetic to the majority of the country," Tocqueville himself took up the defense of the republic as the best available government in the given circumstances.[20]

Although Tocqueville defended his republic, he worried that democracy might destroy liberty, and with it the possibility of virtue. Relating his reaction to the events of the egalitarian Revolution of 1848, Tocqueville commented that "I had spent the best days of my youth amid a society which seemed to increase in greatness and prosperity as it increased in liberty; I had conceived the idea of a balanced, regulated liberty, held in check by religion, custom and law; the attractions of this liberty had touched me; it had become the passion of my life; I felt that

I could never be consoled for its loss, and that I must renounce all hope of its recovery."[21]

Greatness and prosperity are dependent upon a liberty that is well ordered. The good life cannot be had by men who are immoderate in their goals or their means. The heady action of politics is good only to the extent that it is aimed at and serves the interests of liberty. In the preface to *The Old Regime*, Tocqueville gave high praise to the spirit of the French Revolution: "Youth was at the helm in that age of fervid enthusiasm, of proud and generous aspirations, whose memory, despite its extravagances, men will forever cherish: a phase of history that for many years to come will trouble the sleep of all who seek to demoralize the nation and reduce it to a servile state."[22]

The early revolutionary spirit was not proud and generous merely because it opposed the despotism of the Bourbon monarchy, however. In outlining the unfinished sequel to *The Old Regime*, Tocqueville stated his plans to "begin by depicting [the revolutionaries] as they were in the hey-day of the Revolution; when the love of equality and the urge to freedom went hand in hand; when they wished to set up not merely a truly democratic government but free institutions, not only to do away with privileges but also to make good and stabilize the rights of man, the individual."[23] Clearly, then, the spirit of the revolutionaries was noble because, and only when, it aimed beyond equality toward freedom.

The love of reform was stronger and lived longer than the love of freedom, and the revolution soon became the tool of "men who carried audacity to the point of sheer insanity; who balked at no innovation and, unchecked by any scruples, acted with an unprecedented ruthlessness."[24] Because the spirit of freedom was so fleeting and that of hubristic reform so constant, the revolution was, for Tocqueville, a bad thing for France. Indeed, it would have been better if the reforms of the revolution had been imposed by an "enlightened autocrat," for this "might well have left us better fitted in due course to develop into a free nation."[25]

Tocqueville was opposed to both tyranny and revolution. In the anarchic aftermath of the Revolution of 1848—when old structures lay in ruins and new structures had yet to be erected in their place—Tocqueville and his compatriots sought to forge a middle path. "Our object was, if possible, to found the Republic, or at least to maintain it for some time, by governing it in a regular, moderate, *conservative* and absolutely constitutional way."[26] In describing his own views, Tocqueville claimed, "I belong neither to the revolutionary party nor to the conservative party, and when all is said and done I am more attached to the second than to the first. For I differ with the second concerning means but not their end, while I differ with the first concerning both their means and their end."[27]

The "conservative" (Monarchist) party was too intransigent and authoritarian, in Tocqueville's view. But the real enemy was the party advocating revolutionary democracy, the party that would sweep away liberty in the name of equality. Revolutionaries present a far greater danger to society and are much further from Tocqueville's own views and sentiments than are conservatives who seek peace and stability through improper means.

Tocqueville's particular political recommendations, whether deemed republican or (more accurately in light of his attachment to political rights) in some sense classically liberal, do not reflect an unconservative cast of mind or political philosophy. Since conservatism may encompass numerous political regimes—from the Indian caste system to the British mixed Constitution to traditional, semifeudal societies such as that of Burke's Ireland—there is no reason to believe that classically liberal (or constitutionally monarchical) regimes are somehow "unconservative" per se. What is important for the conservative—and for Tocqueville, as a conservative—is that the political regime be fitting, so that it may allow for the possibility of virtue.

Democracy itself, wherever it rules, could make any form of liberty, and thus virtue, altogether impossible. Tocqueville feared the French radicals because he believed that they would establish a tyranny of the majority. Already in his day Tocqueville observed that even the more moderate American democratic majority held excessive power. Public opinion, the legislature, the executive, the police, juries, and even judges were ruled by the majority, and they enforced its will.[28] As the majority enforces its will, it makes freedom of thought almost impossible. Indeed, "the majority is invested with both physical and moral authority, which acts as much upon the will as upon behavior and at the same moment prevents both the act and the desire to do it."[29] Those who still oppose the will and opinion of the majority may retain their official rights, but are cut off from the only social and political life available. Thus a society ruled by a tyranny of the majority will have little real diversity and almost no great writers and statesmen.[30]

Perhaps Tocqueville's fears are summed up best by his assessment of his own thought and disposition: "I have an intellectual taste for democratic institutions, but I am an aristocrat by instinct, that is I fear and scorn the mob."[31] There was at least a certain ambivalence on Tocqueville's part where equality was concerned. However, ambivalence may not be the proper term, here. Tocqueville's feelings may be placed more accurately within the context of a particular philosophy, which recognizes the need to accept the tenor of the times and the general prejudices of a people, or group of peoples, if one is to follow nature and God's will. For Tocqueville, equality was the trend of the times, the generally accepted good of European societies. And to question the judgment of entire societies would be to question the judgment of God Himself. Yet a mob—a motley collection of individuals held together only by unreasoning hatred—reflects only the will of the ungodly demagogue who would destroy in the name of his own glory.

For Tocqueville, as for Burke, institutions must be accepted in accordance with their ability to fit the societies they are to govern. There is no perfection on earth because human reason is severely limited. The best we can do is to deal with circumstances, such as the trend toward equality, as they arise. In this way we may defeat the demagogue—whatever his ideological program—and preserve the ability of societies to provide for their own survival and for the possibility of virtue.

THE LIMITS OF HUMAN REASON

Tocqueville, like Burke, emphasized the limits of human rationality, the extent to which man is a creature of nature, habit, and circumstance. Man himself, by himself, is weak—incapable of constructing anything lasting. Even the man who is brought up in society, if he chooses to leave the context of that society, can achieve little on his own. In *Democracy*, Tocqueville recounted the story of how he passed through an isolated area of New York State,

> coming to the shore of a lake surrounded by forest, as at the beginning of the world. A little island rose from the water, its banks completely hidden by the foliage of the trees that covered it. Nothing on the lake shore suggested the presence of man; only on the horizon could one see a column of smoke stretching perpendicularly above the treetops to the clouds as if hung from the sky instead of rising thither.
>
> Nature seemed completely left to herself, and it was far from my thoughts to suppose that the place had once been inhabited. But when I got to the

middle of the island I suddenly thought I noticed traces of man. Then, looking closely at everything around, I was soon convinced that a European had come to seek a refuge in this place. But how greatly his work had changed appearance! The logs he had hastily cut to build a shelter had sprouted afresh; his fences had become live hedges, and his cabin had been turned into a grove. Among the bushes were a few stones blackened by fire around a little heap of ashes; no doubt that was his hearth, covered with ruins of a fallen chimney. For some little time I silently contemplated the resources of nature and the feebleness of man; and when I did leave the enchanted spot, I kept saying sadly: "What! Ruins so soon!"[32]

Lacking the permanence of human cooperation—of a community—human endeavors come to nothing in the face of nature in all her power. In Tocqueville's view, purely independent efforts produce nothing that can last in the face of circumstance.

Men require society, and for Tocqueville society requires that men accept on faith the basic notions on which their lives and communities are based. Only within the context of shared, dogmatic beliefs can truly productive activity take place, for only in this context is civilization itself possible. "Without ideas in common, no common action would be possible, and without common action, men might exist, but there could be no body social."[33] With no body social, there can be nothing lasting or worthwhile.

According to Tocqueville, fundamental beliefs are constantly in danger of being called into question—both intentionally and unintentionally—by general ideas. General ideas are the stuff of theory. Tocqueville himself specialized in their use; his analysis of America in terms of its embodiment of the spirit of equality points this out. But general ideas, particularly those that are arrived at independently rather than accepted dogmatically, are dangerous ideas. General, abstract ideas call into question existing institutions and practices because institutions and practices are the products of circumstance and so cannot logically follow from any particular general principle. Since general ideas cannot take account of particular circumstances, they are centralizing forces. If one is to establish a system of government on a specific general principle, one must see to it that localities and subsidiary institutions meet the requirements of that general principle. Thus the central government must have the power to enforce uniformity on local governments and institutions. This, for Tocqueville, is the essence of tyranny. Centralization stifles variety, individual initiative, and the individual's ability to protect himself from the central government through appeals to local governments and institutions.

General ideas themselves are imperfect at best. For Tocqueville, "General ideas do not bear witness to the power of human intelligence but rather to its inadequacy, for there are no beings exactly alike in nature, no identical facts, no laws which can be applied indiscriminately in the same way to several objects at once. . . . General ideas have this excellent quality, that they permit human minds to pass judgment quickly on a great number of things; but the conceptions they convey are always incomplete, and what is gained in extent is always lost in exactitude."[34] This seemingly obvious point brings out that general ideas *by their very nature* ignore circumstance and particularity for Tocqueville; they impose conformity where none naturally exists. In a society seeking to be free, ideas that impose conformity are dangerous in the extreme because no existing order can stand up to the criteria set by any particular general idea.

General ideas are the products of intellectuals—would-be philosophers who have had more contact with ideas than with concrete reality. The *philosophes* who brought about the French Revolution were cut off from the people and more concerned with the elegance of their own theories than with the actual circumstances and personal characters of their society. It is a blindness to the realities of everyday life—to habit, character, and experience—that produces general theories, theories that do not take man as he is, in his given society. Thus champions of general ideas attempt to change man, succeeding only in destroying the coherence of society, and the lives of many men.

American practicality was conducive to a much more stable and peaceful democracy than that produced by French intellectualism: "The Americans are a democratic people which has always managed its own political affairs, whereas we are a democratic people which for a long time could only speculate on the best way to manage them. . . . Our state of society led us to conceive broad general ideas about ways of government at a time when our Constitution prevented us from correcting them by experience and gradually finding out their deficiencies. Whereas in America the two things naturally and constantly balance and correct each other."[35]

"True enlightenment is in the main born of experience."[36] Experience—familiarity with circumstance and the habits that develop from it—

allows us to deal properly with circumstance. General ideas ignore circumstance in favor of abstract notions of truth and therefore are often useless or worse in the face of concrete problems. Tocqueville lamented that in France "no writer, however second-rate, is satisfied with an essay revealing truths applicable to one great kingdom, and he remains dissatisfied with himself if his theme does not embrace the whole of mankind." French writers reflected and promoted "an increased taste for generalization which goes hand in hand with a weakening of the old constitution."[37]

The revolutionary French intellectuals were guilty of idealization; they formulated rationalistic philosophies based upon notions of human nature with no real basis in fact. Lacking experience in the actual affairs of men, these intellectuals propounded uncompromising, unrealistic theories that brought about the disaster of the French Revolution and its bloody aftermath. "A nation so unused to acting for itself was bound to begin by wholesale destruction when it launched into a program of wholesale reform."[38]

The violent anarchy and eventual tyranny of the majority produced by the French Revolution were all but inevitable because the intellectuals who produced it—*philosophes* and economists writing decades before its actual outbreak—were not interested in freedom but only in putting their (idealized) reforms into effect.[39] "According to the Economists the function of the State was not merely one of ruling the nation, but also that of recasting it in a given mold, of shaping the mentality of the population as a whole in accordance with a predetermined model and instilling the ideas and sentiments they thought desirable into the minds of all."[40] Out of hubris, the Economists cast aside the very real limits of human reason—limits that must be respected if society is to be protected and virtue promoted.

As Peter Augustine Lawler points out, for Tocqueville the project of the Economists—and of modern philosophy in general—is fundamentally misanthropic. It sacrifices the dignity of man to the pride of the philosopher. Although Platonic philosophy, for Tocqueville, was fundamentally misguided (because it posited the existence of a nonexistent truth), it nonetheless spoke to man's soul poetically, and not merely rationally, and therefore enriched it. Modern philosophers deny anything not rationally comprehensible and so treat men as mere inputs into deterministic systems. As Lawler puts it, "The Platonists and the early modern philosophers attempt to turn human beings into gods, either by word or by deed. The late modern or deterministic thinkers turn human beings into brutes. . . . The philosophers apparently can conceive clearly of angels or gods and beasts, but not of human beings. Their thought is that being human is unreasonable and undesirable."[41]

Failure to recognize man's necessarily intermediate position between angels and beasts—his possession of both soul and body—leads to philosophical corruption. The Platonists promised an illusory fulfillment of the human soul in this life. Replacing Christianity with faith in the philosopher's ability to "perfect" Creation, the modern philosophers promise an unobtainable earthly paradise, to be constructed by an unrealizable human reason. Seeking to convince man that this life is the only one available and that he therefore should content himself with the goods of material existence (and dispense with his "nonexistent" soul), modern philosophers replace Christianity with a crude, mystical pantheism and replace human virtue with the particularly degrading general idea of unreflecting, materialistic human selfishness.[42]

For Tocqueville, self-interest, which numerous commentators have seen as the centerpiece of his theory of human action, is neither infallible nor ennobling as a (supposedly universal and circumstantially unmitigated) general idea. His observation that "on all sides beliefs are giving way to arguments, and feelings to calculation," did lead him to argue that with the waning of faith societies must link the idea of rights to personal interest. If interest is not used to govern the world, all that will be left is fear.[43] But Tocqueville did not value self-interested action for its own sake. He sought prudently to combat, not foolishly to further, the increasing materialism and selfishness of the modern era. Modern nations must use self-interest if they are to be free. All forms of rational thought are severely limited in their utility and applicability, however, and self-interest is no cure-all. Indeed, "if remote advantages could prevail over the passions and needs of the moment, there would have been no tyrannical sovereigns or exclusive aristocracies."[44]

We cannot expect democratic masses to respect, out of mere self-interest, the ("sacred") right of the wealthy to their property.[45] And freedom itself must not be judged in material terms; it may not produce prosperity immediately, and even if it does, "the man who asks of freedom anything other than itself is born to be a slave."[46] Not only must the idea of rights be linked to personal interest, personal interest must be linked to the idea of rights. If this second link is not established in a manner and form appropriate to the particular given society and people, the individual character necessary for the exercise of freedom will not be forthcoming; "free" or not, men will be fit only for slavery.

Man is a social being; such is God's will. But there are no rational general theories of human nature and conduct—not even base self-interest—according to which we may safely construct and maintain our necessarily disparate societies. General ideas are tyrannical by nature because of the very fact that they ignore particular circumstances in favor of imagined uniformity. Given the natural limits of human reason, we must look to the factors that modify and shape human behavior if we are to maintain virtue—and society itself.

NATIONAL CHARACTER: CIRCUMSTANCE, MORES, AND FITTINGNESS

For Tocqueville, the trend toward equality is a circumstance that must be dealt with; the French Revolution swept away all effective opposition to it. Each society must treat with equality in such a way as to preserve its own basic coherence and allow for the continued practice of virtue. Since societies vary, the trend toward equality must be moderated in a manner appropriate to a given people's specific national character: a national character which is the product of mores, laws, and physical circumstances—in that order.[47] But there are definite principles upon which a free and virtuous society must rest, and these are given example in the United States: "The laws of the French republic can be and, in many cases, should be different from those prevailing in the United States. But the principles of order, balance of powers, true liberty, and sincere and deep respect for law, are indispensable for all republics."[48] And it is "true liberty"—limited by the rule of law and by the dictates of preexisting institutions, beliefs, and practices—that for Tocqueville is the essence of a good and virtuous society.

Preceding circumstances—embodied in mores and laws—combine with existing circumstances to determine the particular nature of a people. Human nature and national character are natural only in the sense that they are formed by circumstance and the spontaneous connections of political association.[49] More specifically, with reference to the United States, "when, after careful study of the history of America, we turn with equal care to the political and social state there, we find ourselves deeply convinced of this truth, that there is not an opinion, custom or law, nor, one might add, an event, which the point of departure will not easily explain."[50] The point of departure—the customs, traditions, and circumstances with which the American colonies were founded—had determined the current nature of the United States. Thus the New England states might be defined by their foundation—or by their departure from England—upon the Puritan ideal.

The Puritan ideal shared in many respects "the most absolute democratic and republican theories." It also led the men who left their homes in England to do so with the intention of finding a place in which they and their families might live "in their own way and pray to God in freedom."[51] The New England colonies were founded upon *"the spirit of religion* and *the spirit of freedom."* Because of these founding principles, "two distinct but not contradictory tendencies plainly show their traces everywhere, in mores and in laws."[52] In the moral world of the United States, all was predecided. In its political world all was negotiable and subject to change. By the same token, "Slavery, combined with the English character, explains the mores and social condition of the South."[53] Having brought the evils of a slave society with them, the adventurers who settled the southern colonies condemned their progeny to its evils as well. "The social state is commonly the result of circumstances, sometimes of laws, but most often of a combination of the two. But once it has come into being, it may itself be considered as the prime cause of most of the laws, customs, and ideas which control the nation's behavior; it modifies even those things which it does not cause."[54]

"Laws are the children of custom."[55] The particular forms and institutions of a society are the result of experience, of the interaction between circumstance and already existing institutions and mores. And, for Tocqueville as for Burke and Aristotle, customs grow from the locality upward. "The township is the only association so well rooted in nature that wherever men assemble it forms itself. . . . Communal society therefore exists among all peoples, whatever be their customs and their laws; man creates kingdoms and republics, but townships seem to spring directly from the hand of God."[56] The nature of small communities—their physical circumstances and the way their people deal with these circumstances—determines the nature of the nation of which they are a part. As for Burke and Aristotle, so for Tocqueville: The more local an institution, the more natural; the more distant, the more conventional. "The sovereignty of the Union is a work of art. That of the states is natural; it exists on its own, without striving, like the authority of the father in a family."[57]

Although America was far from perfect, it was a successful democratic republic because "American legislation, taken as a whole, is well adapted to the genius of the people ruled thereby and to the nature of the country."[58] American mores were based in localities whose relative independence was recognized by the comparatively weak central government of the United States. Thus local circumstances were taken into account and the appropriate fit between the character of the people and of their institutions was maintained.

Because Tocqueville considered local mores and circumstances so important, he studied England as well as the United States from the locality upward—from the most local and natural associations to the man-created nation. For him, the parish was the fundamental unit of public participation in England, as the local community was in America. Thus he "accounted for England's aristocratic and democratic constituents in terms of 'Saxon' and 'Norman' institutions . . . the Saxon principle [being] basically the democratic principle."[59]

Ancient institutions, or more properly ancient mores, continue to dominate a nation's character long after the ancient community itself ceases to exist. History, and above all habit, controls the context in which societies exist and relate to new circumstances. Only by recognizing the proper role of habit and by acting according to the dictates of fittingness, which never countenance the blind application of idealized general ideas, may disaster be avoided. And, just as the man who would discard habitual relations in order to apply his own general ideas to an existing society is doomed to failure, so too is the man who ignores the need to maintain the fittingness of a given society in the face of changing circumstances.

> In France we regard simple tastes, quiet mores, family feeling, and love of one's birthplace as great guarantees for the tranquility and happiness of the state. But in America nothing seems more prejudicial to society than virtues of that sort. The French of Canada, who loyally preserve the tradition of their ancient mores, are already finding it difficult to live on their land, and this small nation which has only just come to birth will soon be a prey to all the afflictions of old nations. The most enlightened, patriotic, and humane men in Canada make extraordinary efforts to render people dissatisfied with the simple happiness that still contents them. They

extol the advantages of wealth in much the same way as, perhaps, in France they would have praised the charms of a moderate competence, and are at greater pains to goad human passions than others elsewhere to calm them.[60]

French mores were inappropriate in the circumstances of the New World. And it was as difficult a task as it was a noble one to attempt to change them so that the offspring of the French nation in Canada—whose point of departure had not suited them for their new circumstances—might have the chance to survive. If a given set of mores do not fit the given circumstances, they must be changed or the people in question may perish. The character of a people is the result of years of interaction among that people, their institutions, and their particular circumstances. The results of this interaction, for Tocqueville, are not self-justifying; they can be either good or bad. In the cases of both the American Indians and the slaves (and slave owners) of the South, the effects of the historical interaction between a people and their circumstances resulted, for Tocqueville, in mores that were unquestionably bad.

Blacks in America were stripped of the forces that naturally form the human character. Their mores, their religion, their language, their very families were taken from them.[61] In the face of this, they were at the mercy of their masters; their very natures were the result of their treatment by those who brought them forcibly to the New World, and the effects were anything but beneficial. Often born into slavery, the black's "first notions of existence teach him that he is the property of another who has an interest in preserving his life; he sees that care for his own fate has not devolved on him; the very use of thought seems to him an unprofitable gift of Providence." Even if he were made free, according to Tocqueville, the black man would remain a slave because he had been given the nature of a slave through the habits of a lifetime.[62] With the protection of ancient mores—his historical nature—lost to him, the black man was thoroughly degraded by slavery and would recover from its effects neither easily nor soon.

But the black man was not the only one degraded by the institution of slavery. Slavery, and the mores it creates, degraded southern whites as well: "From his birth the American of the South is invested with a sort of domestic dictatorship; the first notions he receives in life teach him that he is born to command, and the first habit he contracts is that of effortless domination. So education has a powerful influence in making the southerner a haughty, hasty, irascible man, ardent in his desires and impatient of obstacles; but he is easy to discourage if he cannot triumph at the first effort."[63] The southerner was habituated into a bad-tempered, lazy, and unprofitable tyrant. His neighbor to the North, not having the superfluity of slaves and the bad effects that total dominion over them engenders, according to Tocqueville was a better man, as well as a better tradesman or practitioner of any craft.[64]

Mores are the very nature of a people; mores are not just the result of but in their essence *are* "habits, opinions, usages, and beliefs."[65] Habits, opinions, usages, and beliefs grow over time; they develop according to the mesh between preexisting mores and the events, physical circumstances, and institutions of a given people.

As the habits of servitude degraded the American black, according to Tocqueville, so the habits of excessive freedom—the lack of moral or institutional restraints—degraded the American Indian. His degraded state condemned the Indian to defeat at the hands of the civilized white American. The black man had reached the limits of servitude, but the Indian "lives on the extreme edge of freedom."[66] And the one condition proved as fatal as the other. While the black man was in a state of complete dependence, "the savage is his own master as soon as he is capable of action. Even his family had hardly any authority over him, and he has never bent his will to that of any of his fellows; no one has taught him to regard voluntary obedience as an honorable subjection, and law is unknown to him even as a word."[67] Tocqueville believed this to be the tragedy of the Indian: His love of excessive freedom, his refusal to cooperate in a civilized, social setting, degraded the Indian and condemned him to defeat by the white man's arts and designs.[68] The mores, habits, and social institutions of a people must fit its particular circumstances, but these may create mores that are bad in and of themselves. Indian mores were the product of and suited life only within the uncivilized wilderness; blacks were thoroughly degraded by the circumstances forced upon them in America. The one set of mores produced degraded barbarism, and the other degraded servility.

Because of its degrading and lasting effects, Tocqueville condemned slavery but urged caution in dealing with it since "all those who formerly accepted this terrible principle are not now equally free to get rid of it."[69] This "terrible principle" resulted in a grim dichotomy of choices: "If freedom is refused to the Negroes in the South, in the end they will seize it themselves; if it is granted to them, they will not be slow to abuse it."[70]

Burke also viewed slavery as a great evil, best abolished if possible. But, so long as slavery exists anywhere, according to Burke, "It is better to allow the evil, in order to correct it, than, by endeavoring to forbid what we cannot be able wholly to prevent, to leave it under an illegal, and therefore an unreformed existence."[71] No ready cure exists for the consequences of slavery. An entirely evil and unnatural institution, slavery produced an unnatural and dangerous human nature, one that defied easy modification and whose consequences defied easy solution.

A well-ordered character, like well-ordered liberty, cannot simply be imposed, for it is based upon a proper reading of and response to circumstance and especially to preexisting institutions, beliefs, and practices. A heated reformism is much less likely to foster good character than is respect for tradition. This is why, for Tocqueville, the English legal system, whether in England itself or as applied in America, provided such good protection for liberty. "When the American people let themselves get intoxicated by their passions or carried away by their ideas, the lawyers apply an almost invisible brake which slows them down and halts them. Their aristocratic inclinations are secretly opposed to the instincts of democracy, their superstitious respect for all that is old to its love of novelty, their narrow views to its grandiose designs, their taste for formalities to its scorn of regulations, and their habit of advancing slowly to its impetuosity."[72] Their shared habits and social position formed lawyers in America, as in England, into a separate class from the mass of the people, one able to use its social esteem to enforce the inherently conservative use of precedent upon the impetuosity of the people.

"The English lawyer values laws not because they are good but because they are old." He has an instinctive aversion to innovation and thus changes laws only when he must in order to maintain their effectiveness in the face of changed circumstances. Further, he does not justify these changes on the grounds of any abstract principle, preferring to believe "that in adding something to the work of his fathers he has only developed their thought and completed their work."[73] As Burke praised the lawyers' view of the Glorious Revolution for its concern with the appearance of continuity, so Tocqueville praised the general aversion of English lawyers to innovation because it restrained the excesses of the democratic spirit and so preserved true liberty.

The rule of law—upon which well-ordered liberty depends—was protected by the Americans' respect for precedent and also by the particularity of American judicial rulings. "Moreover, the law thus censured is not abolished; its moral force is diminished, but its physical effect is not suspended. It is only gradually, under repeated judicial blows, that it finally succumbs."[74] American judges could examine laws only when a specific case was brought before them, involving the rights of particular individuals. Because of their exclusive concern with specifics, American judges were not made parties to political debates, as were their French counterparts, over grand theories of law and rights—theories that called the rule of law itself into question in France.

Legal gradualism and specificity kept the people's attention focused upon particular cases and away from general, political ideas. The project of striking down a law was too difficult to be taken up lightly in Tocqueville's time, and the effects of any particular case were too limited to be dangerous. Given the backward-looking and incremental nature of the judicial system, Tocqueville wondered "if this way in which American courts behave is not both the best way of preserving public order and the best way of favoring liberty."[75]

For Tocqueville, law, especially that based on precedent, becomes a form of habit. We do things a particular way because we have done so in the past—in the legal sphere as well as in our private pursuits. And proper habits protect well-ordered liberty. Indeed, Tocqueville was "convinced that if despotism ever came to be established in the United States it would find it even more difficult to overcome the habits that have sprung from freedom than to conquer the love of freedom itself."[76]

RELIGION, GOVERNMENT, AND INTERVENING INSTITUTIONS

Liberty requires that even elected officials be subjected to the judicial power. "The courts are the only possible intermediary between the central power and an elective administrative body. They alone can force the elected official to obey the law without infringing the voter's rights."[77] The law is an intermediary between officials and the people; it may force elected officials to carry out their duties and respect the rights of the citizens without itself violating those rights.[78] Judicial proceedings are one method by which governmental power is checked, and this was of primary importance for Tocqueville. "The great object of justice is to sub-stitute the idea of right for that of violence, to put intermediaries be-tween the government and the use of its physical force."[79]

It is the desire to place intermediaries between government and the use of force—to prevent tyranny—that dictates limits upon, and more important, counterweights to the central government. Indeed, although "provincial institutions are useful for all peoples, . . . none have a more real need of them than those whose society is democratic."[80] An aris-tocracy's great families provide counterweights to the central govern-ment, but democratic republics are run, in all their social aspects, by the majority. Thus the majority must be broken up geographically so that the individual may ally himself with others who share his interests. Fur-ther, institutions and practices as well as attachments must be placed be-tween the individual and the central authority. Even formalities—matters more of manners than of substance—take on great importance in a democracy. "For their chief merit is to serve as a barrier between the strong and the weak, the government and the governed, and to hold back the one while the other has time to take his bearings."[81]

Localism and legalism serve to interpose protective forces between the individual and the central government and so serve the interest of lib-erty. But liberty requires more than just institutional protection.

> There is hardly any human action, . . . which does not result from some very general conception men have of God, of His relations with the human race, of the nature of their soul, and of their duties to their fel-lows. Nothing can prevent such ideas from being the common spring from which all else originates.
>
> It is therefore of immense importance to men to have fixed ideas about God, their souls, and their duties toward their Creator and their fellows, for doubt about these first principles would leave all their actions to chance and condemn them, more or less, to anarchy and impotence.[82]

Like other dogmatic beliefs, those concerning religion must be fixed lest men be immobilized. Most men have neither the time nor the ability to consider religious questions independently and so should accept the traditional beliefs of their community. As long as a religion provides fixed explanations concerning relations between God and man, it fulfills its central temporal function—the protection of liberty. "When there is no authority in religion or in politics, men are soon frightened by the limitless independence with which they are faced. They are worried and worn out by the constant restlessness of everything. With everything on the move in the realm of the mind, they want the material order at least to be firm and stable, and as they cannot accept their ancient beliefs again, they hand themselves over to a master."[83]

Liberty requires that horizons be drawn—that boundaries be maintained to limit men's view of the universe. If the religious world is not properly and dogmatically ordered, the material world will degenerate because men cannot function without limits. "One cannot establish the reign of liberty without that of mores, and mores cannot be firmly founded without beliefs."[84] If men are left without faith—and without controlling thoughts and institutions—they will fall prey to the first tyrant to come along who is willing and able to mold them into his slaves.

Tocqueville did not see religion as mere dogmatic belief—purely the creature of habit and circumstance. The religious instinct is natural, for Tocqueville; "So long as a religion derives its strength from sentiments, instincts, and passions, which are reborn in like fashion in all periods of history, it can brave the assaults of time, or at least it can only be destroyed by another religion."[85] Furthermore, Tocqueville's own attachment to Christianity, and to Catholicism in particular, led him to value a particular view of God and the soul over all others, not just as proper for his own society but as the best and most true religion available to man.[86] Man is a religious animal; he cannot understand how to order his life unless he believes in the goodness of God's will. But while Catholicism, for Tocqueville, is the most natural of religions, the proper limits of reason and government dictate that we *demand* from the institution of religion only that it make society and virtue possible. Religion is natural; it is good, and it is useful in securing another great good: liberty. Religion promotes liberty by providing a firm context within which mores may form and operate. It provides the possibility for and some of the means of proper habituation. And in the end proper habits, or mores, are what prevent anarchy and tyranny and make virtue possible.

By teaching its citizens from their youth the habits of well-ordered liberty—within the context of religious certitude—America protected its liberty.

The inhabitant of the United States learns from birth that he must rely on himself to combat the ills and trials of life; he is restless and defiant in his outlook toward the authority of society and appeals to its power only when he cannot do without it. The beginnings of this attitude first appear at school, where the children, even in their games, submit to rules settled by themselves and punish offenses which they have defined themselves. The same attitude turns up again in all the affairs of social life. If some obstacle blocks the public road halting the circulation of traffic, the neighbors at once form a deliberative body; this improvised assembly produces an executive authority which remedies the trouble before anyone has thought of the possibility of some previously constituted authority beyond that of those concerned.[87]

Liberty—independence from governmental authority—is taught through practice. And it is taught through practice, not at the individual level, but at the level of the local community. Children, as a group, show their liberty by subjecting themselves to their own rule. Local neighbors show their liberty as a group by removing an obstruction from the public road without calling on the government. Liberty is learned through social interaction, but its practice is not strictly political in the republican sense. In organizing repairs to a public road, a man exercises a form of authority, but it is a *social* authority. Indeed, liberty begins only when *governmental* authority is absent or excluded.

Liberty is a form of social participation rather than of individual, private pursuits. Thus it must be learned through participation. "Local institutions are to liberty what primary schools are to science; they put it within the people's reach; they teach people to appreciate its peaceful enjoyment and accustom them to make use of it."[88] If a nation has no local communities, it may have free institutions, but it cannot have the spirit of liberty. Such a nation is still possessed of a "despotic spirit" that, although it may be held in check for a time by interest or by circumstance, will sooner or later destroy liberty.[89]

Tocqueville's liberty requires practice, and practice requires time. This is why, for Tocqueville, the eastern part of the United States was so much more orderly and truly free than was the West of that time. In the East, men "had the longest experience of democratic government" and so had developed proper democratic habits. "Their customs, opinions, and forms of behavior have been gradually penetrated by democracy, and this shows in every detail of social life, as much as in the laws."[90] Habits of thought and behavior—of mind and heart—naturally form the human character. One becomes a free man, spiritually as well as physically, by acquiring the character of a free man, and one acquires a free character by practicing freedom.

True liberty depends upon forms of behavior—shaped by social institutions such as religion and local associations—rather than upon a particular political structure. If liberty is to be preserved, however, men must not only have free characters; they must have the goodness of character necessary to recognize that liberty itself must be temperate and well ordered. American liberty was possible, in large measure, because true liberty—local participation—counteracted individualism, as well as the effects and power of the central government.

But Tocqueville also praised a more explicitly conservative tendency within the American character, one produced by juries. "Juries, especially civil juries, instill some of the habits of the judicial mind into every citizen, and just those habits are the very best way of preparing people to be free."[91] The judicial mind—the backward-looking respect for history and continuity—is the proper internal check to the spirit of unlimited liberty; it forms habits that themselves keep the habits of liberty from running amok. Judicial habits teach man to concern himself with specifics and with the good of continuing practices rather than with constant change and general ideas. Juries instill judicial habits, and therefore the judicial mind, by putting men in a situation in which they must act judicially. Faced with the same particular cases and circumstances with which lawyers and judges deal, acting within the same judicial system, those men serving on juries form the same habits of mind. And it is the judicial habit of mind which tempers the desire for unlimited liberty and so makes true liberty possible.

THE GREAT END

Institutions, practices, and beliefs form the character of the individual. If they are not constructed (or rather allowed to operate) so as to give proper mores to the people in question, the people will suffer the evils of barbarian "freedom" or the servitude of the slave. Peoples always must choose between the natural formation of character—the recognition of natural law—and the degradation of character. For Tocqueville, the slave and the Indian provide paradigms of the effects produced by improper mores, mores formed by the lack of proper intervening social institutions. The Indian's character was not shaped by social institutions; thus he was left to his whims and remained uncivilized. The natural socializing forces of the black in America were stripped from him; thus his character was formed and degraded by the tyranny of slavery.

True liberty requires that the natural character-forming institutions of religion, family, and local association be allowed to operate and habituate men to the proper forms of behavior and therefore of mind. It is in the nature of man to seek association with those socializing forces that in turn principally form his civilized character; the lack of such forces degrades man.

The United States as a whole avoided the degradations of anarchy and tyranny. Still, democratic social institutions have their own dangers. The majority may take over all socializing functions and so make independence impossible. The individual, feeling insignificant in the face of the majority and of his religious doubts, may seek relief from his troubles by turning himself over to a tyrant. And the search for wealth so common in a democratic society, though in moderation not a bad thing, may limit the human mind to something less than full humanity requires. Intent on achieving prosperity, "bent on improving everything around him, [man] may at length degrade himself." Because man's pursuit of wealth may blind him to the importance of higher, more important pursuits, "in a democracy . . . it is ever the duty of lawgivers and of all upright educated men to raise up the souls of their fellow citizens and turn their attention toward heaven." More than any other, democratic man requires "an appreciation of greatness, and a love of spiritual pleasures."[92] Democratic conditions do not preclude human greatness, and the influence and prestige of the legal class may help protect the desire for it. Moreover, in a well-ordered democratic society, a natural aristocracy will arise and, freed from material want, may foster higher pursuits.[93] But man's greatness *requires* that equality itself not be allowed full sway.

If each man is given equal "enlightenment and independence," men of wealth will arise in democratic societies. And, while wealthy men will not form as cohesive or as powerful and stable a class as that of the nobility, "they will be infinitely more numerous than any aristocracy could be. These persons will . . . devote themselves to the labors and pleasures of the mind. In those pleasures they will indulge, for though one part of the human mind inclines to the banal, the material, and the useful, there is another side which is naturally drawn toward the infinite, the spiritual, and the beautiful. Physical needs hold it to the earth, but when these are relaxed it rises of its own accord.[94]

Furthermore, given the existence of a natural aristocracy, interest in intellectual and spiritual pursuits will expand even to the masses since "when there is no more hereditary wealth, class privilege, or prerogatives of birth, and when every man derives his strength from himself alone, it becomes clear that the chief source of disparity between the fortunes of men lies in the mind. Whatever tends to invigorate, expand, or adorn the mind rises instantly to a high value."[95]

Presumptive virtue gives way to an aristocracy of talent. Class no longer is to be based on heredity. But class must remain a central organizing feature of society if the stupefying effects of the tyranny of the majority are to be avoided or even lessened. And, though classes are based on economic distinctions, their members must not limit themselves to economic pursuits. That way lies an "aristocracy of manufactures"—tyranny and the degradation of the human spirit.[96] Upper classes, freed from the constraints of pure materialism, must be fostered, protected, and properly directed so that man may pursue goals beyond a purely material existence—so that he may fulfill his nature.

The Great Chain of Being, which connects all men in society, must be acknowledged even more explicitly in democratic than in aristocratic times. Love of one's own must not be defined and practiced so narrowly that individualism is allowed to reign. Members of the upper classes must be made to recognize their duty to care for the lives and especially for the spirits of those around them, lest the lives and spirits of all men be degraded. If man is to be fully human in democratic times, he must be taught to rise above mere individual pursuits in order to pursue greatness, the life of the spirit, the life of virtue.

Tocqueville's own faith was shaken at times by the anarchy of his era. The seemingly endless cycles of revolution and counterrevolution that plagued France led him to exclaim, "I do not know when this long voyage will be ended; I am weary of seeing the shore in each successive mirage, and I often ask myself whether the *terra firma* we are seeking does really exist, and whether we are not doomed to rove upon the seas for ever!"[97] A virtuous life for a people is unobtainable without stability, but virtue is also unobtainable without the spirit. The search for mere stability, for peace, well-being, and contentment is degrading. The socialist revolutions of nineteenth-century France were caused largely by the turmoil of "an epoch when our view into another world has become dimmer, and the miseries of this world become more visible and seem more intolerable."[98] In times of materialism and the decline of faith, those men who wish their people well will seek to foster higher pursuits than mere material contentment. The God who willed that man seek society willed also that he seek the life of virtue.

5 • Virtue Properly Understood: Tocqueville and the End of Self-Interest

India. A great position, from which England dominates all Asia. A glory which revives the entire English nation. What a sense of grandeur and power this possession creates in every part of that people. The value of a conquest ought not to be calculated only in terms of financial and commercial considerations.
—Alexis de Tocqueville

The value of a conquest should be calculated in terms of the honor and glory it brings to the conquering people. Tocqueville's approval of both French and British colonialism is often condemned as inconsistent with his generally "liberal" and "humanitarian" views and policies.[1] But Tocqueville advocated colonialism as a means to a higher goal: the conservation of accepting virtue. In a letter to John Stuart Mill, he wrote,

> I do not need to tell you, my dear Mill, that the greatest illness that menaces a country such as [France] is the gradual weakening of its mores, the degradation of its spirit, the mediocrity of tastes. . . . Thus it is not this nation which ought to be allowed to develop the habit of sacrificing its grandeur to repose, of subordinating great matters to petty ones. . . . It is unhealthy to allow France to believe that although its place in the world is smaller than that bequeathed to it by our ancestors, it can be consoled by adding to the well-being of every individual by a prosperity based on peace, regardless of how that peace is obtained. Those who march at the head of such a nation must always maintain an attitude of pride, or else they will degrade its mores.[2]

A people must pursue glory if it is to survive. If men no longer strive after greatness, then their mores will decay and their society will disintegrate. Mere self-interest, the single-minded pursuit of material gain, is not only spiritually unsatisfying, it is insufficient for the survival of a people. The spirit of a people, its mores, its self-awareness and acceptance of its own value, is its lifeblood. And spirit requires a certain grandeur and a certain pride.

Clearly, one could condemn colonialism as simply and inherently unjust because it involves the theft of others' land and also the murder of those men who resist this theft. Yet for the conservative the moral problem of colonialism is rather complex. The life of accepting virtue requires a government limited in its purpose and activities to the support of the natural and traditional institutions that form the nature of a people. Colonialism would seem contradictory to the very notion of limited government. It may serve the interests of the conquering conservative by helping in the maintenance of his society's virtue—its concern with honor, glory, and service to the community. However, the conqueror necessarily disrupts the society he conquers. A society's subjugation necessarily entails the subversion of its preexisting institutions and practices. The advocate of colonialism may also be accused of valuing the glory and interests of his own nation above the survival of the nation conquered.

This last accusation is dispensed with fairly easily. To charge a conservative with provincialism is to shower him with flowers. Conservatism is based, after all, on the idea that it is a positive good to value one's own—that with which one is familiar—above that which one does not know and to which one has no habitual attachment. The conservative is allowed, by his own lights, to consider his own society to be superior to and more important than that of others, even if he believes the other society is virtuous and so worthy of conservation.

The larger, moral problem of colonialism for the conservative arises from its disruption of preexisting societies. Tocqueville defended both colonialism and the notion that some people's mores (such as those of the French Canadians) should be changed in order to fit new circumstances. If conservation must bow to circumstance, and if circumstance may include armed invasion, then Tocqueville's notion of conservation would seem almost meaningless. Further, one who advocates the subjugation of one people by another logically must argue that the conquering society is the best under which all men could live (in one capacity or another) *regardless* of history or circumstance. The only other alternative would seem to be that of viewing "inferior" peoples as subhuman—cattle to be used in whatever way the victor desires, regardless of their own interests and wishes. Tocqueville expressly rejected this latter view.[3]

Tocqueville championed "the European spirit of movement pitted against Chinese immobility."[4] The decadence of the Chinese, along with that of seemingly most of the rest of the peoples of the world, made them rightful targets, in Tocqueville's view, for European conquest and subjugation. But, for Tocqueville, colonial subjugation should take a particular, almost a conservative, form. Colonialism should entail the oversight, but not the overtaking, of preexisting institutions. The institutions already existing in a colonized area should be retained and left to their own devices wherever possible—consistent with the grandeur and interest of the colonial power. Colonial government should be decentralized, and the institutions of the natives should be used by the colonial power whenever possible.[5] Of course, Tocqueville was not willing to sacrifice French interests in order to conserve French-dominated Algerian institutions. He quite seriously considered the Algerians to be backward and "half civilized," and such peoples should be reformed and improved by their colonial overlords.[6] Still, Tocqueville did see the need to treat with preexisting institutions in the interests of both conqueror and conquered.

Tocqueville's view of the proper treatment of conquered peoples is not in conflict with his attitude toward the treatment of "followers"—those not fit to rule—in any society. The democratic party in England was good, according to Tocqueville, because of its endeavor to make the people *fit* to govern.[7] Governing, like all activities, requires certain habits. And habits cannot be achieved spontaneously; they must be taught and inculcated over time through the use of properly constituted—but largely natural—intervening institutions. The task of society's leaders is to preserve existing institutions and practices while allowing for the development of self-governing habits.

Unless everything is a historically determined circumstance (and this certainly was not Tocqueville's view), colonialism is unconservative. It is a violent circumstance impinging upon a preexisting society from outside that society's realm of experience. Yet, even with the interests of his own nation making him ignore those of others, Tocqueville attempted to place a conservative veneer on colonialism. Colonialism and war itself are good, for Tocqueville, only if used appropriately and for proper ends. In his March 1841 letter to Mill, Tocqueville stated his opposition to those who valued war "either for its own sake or for the revolutions to which it can give birth."[8] Conquest is the kind of grand exploit, like other great projects, that is needed, in nonrevolutionary moderation, to maintain the citizenry's concern with honor. Faced with the increasing enervation of the French spirit (brought about by egalitarian materialism), Tocqueville sought to reinvigorate his people's natural desire to achieve virtue. His means were immoderate—perhaps colonialism even called for a *virtue* that was unconservatively immoderate—but Tocqueville's goal, like Burke's, was the maintenance of a moderate, virtuous society.

Honor is the vital force of a people. There exist universal laws which declare some actions to be good and others to be bad. Yet the variation in circumstances of particular peoples dictates that there be other more specific criteria for the judgment of good and bad action within given communities. Killing a man is a universally bad act, but the demands of a particular code of honor may make certain kinds of killing, under certain circumstances (such as war), good. And it is a code of honor, with its basis clearly to be found in natural law, that makes coherent the lives of a particular people. Members of a given society are able to order their lives only because they know what actions are right and what actions are wrong, and the particular outlines of these rights and wrongs depend largely on history and circumstance.[9] Each society must have its own different but nonetheless active and authoritative concept of honor if it is to survive.

Without great deeds to bring into sharp focus the issues of right and wrong action, without the motivation of glory and honor to stir the spirit of the people and make them strive to provide virtuous public service, the mores of a people—their accepted rules of right and wrong—will degenerate. If a people's mores degenerate, so will the people themselves. Even with colonialism, the goal is not the hubristic virtue of the founder but the accepting virtue of an honorable people.

ACCEPTINGNESS: HUMILITY IN A PRIDEFUL COMMUNITY

Tocqueville's America had no single established religion, its press was free and willing to publish vastly divergent views, and its people's attachment to equality made the very idea of aristocracy appear unbearable. Such a society would not seem likely to foster the humble acceptance so valued by Burke, and Tocqueville joined Burke in praising the accepting attitude fostered by *aristocratic* society. Before the philosophy and tyranny of the Old Regime's last days made it impossible, according to Tocqueville, the French subject's submission to royal authority was in its own way noble. The Frenchman "did not know what it was to bend the knee to an illegitimate or dubious authority, a government little honored and sometimes heartily despised, which it is well to truckle to because it has power to help or harm. . . . The King's subjects felt towards him *both the natural love of children for their father and the awe properly due to God alone.* Their compliance with his orders, even the most arbitrary, was a matter far less of compulsion than of affection, so that even when the royal yoke pressed on them most heavily, they felt they still could call their souls their own."[10]

Whatever their station in life, members of aristocratic society recognized the legitimacy of the existing order. "Because it never entered the noble's head that anyone wanted to snatch away privileges which he regarded as legitimate, and since the serf considered his inferiority as an effect of the immutable order of nature, one can see that a sort of goodwill could be established between these two classes so differently favored by fortune. At that time one found inequality and wretchedness in society, but men's souls were not degraded thereby."[11] Inequalities of condition were neither unbearable nor degrading so long as general acceptance of the existing chain of being made good will, the basis of mutual affection, possible.

Americans also accepted the structures of their own society, but democratic acceptance had a much less spiritual cast than its aristocratic counterpart. It is ironic, given virtue's spiritual nature, that it was possible in the United States only because of Americans' practicality and their pursuit of material well-being. Their practical materialism prevented Americans from engaging in idealized theorizing and also caused them to accept on faith the results of a society in which individual effort was rewarded. Americans' concern with wealth thus allowed for a natural aristocracy, a natural hierarchy among men, and the accepting attitude that is the essence of virtue.

In democracies, men are continually and passionately involved with the work of their daily lives. Their constant movement leaves them little leisure to consider great theories and little interest in such theories in any case. Hence, according to Tocqueville, "It is an arduous undertaking to excite the enthusiasm of a democratic nation for any theory which does not have a visible, direct, and immediate bearing on the occupations of their daily lives. Such a people does not easily give up its ancient beliefs. For it is enthusiasm which makes men's minds leap off the beaten track and brings about great intellectual, as well as political, revolutions."[12] Self-interest focuses attention upon the specific rather than on the general. The pursuit of one's daily occupation, itself intimately concerned with the pursuit of wealth, leaves one with neither the time nor the inclination to question the fundamental bases of society.[13]

Although practically motivated acceptance seems useful for any attempt to conserve existing ideas and practices, it does not seem especially virtuous. To say that Americans were too busy scrambling after money to become socialist theoreticians is hardly to say that they were good and virtuous men. However, American self-interest allowed accepted, particularly religious, beliefs to hold full sway. Because of self-interest, there was little in the way of idealized, abstract theory in America. Thus existing notions of good and of God were accepted without question. Self-interest served to protect the virtuous acceptance of proper, preexisting ideas and institutions.

Purely material self-interest is not good. In *The Old Regime and the French Revolution*, Tocqueville argued that the "craving for material well-being . . . leads the way to servitude."[14] But Tocqueville did not present self-interest as the proper goal of American society. Self-interest is the proper and fitting tool, within democratic society, for the maintenance of accepting virtue. It helps democratic citizens maintain an accepting attitude by focusing their thoughts on more specific and less dangerous subjects than the inconsistencies and injustices of society's guiding ideas and institutions.

Self-interest also provided for virtue by producing a fitting hierarchy in American society. In the United States, the concern with material well-being and the acceptance of existing structures of rights assured that the natural hierarchy, which inevitably results from open competition, would remain respected and safe. Property rights were respected because so many Americans owned property they did not wish to put at risk. And the social status of those who had been successful in the search for wealth, though not nearly so great as that of hereditary aristocrats, was sufficient to lend them power and influence.[15]

Self-interest is a strong force in the formation and maintenance of American values and of the values of peoples in general. After all, even a people's code of honor has its basis in their particular needs.[16] But it is not merely self-interest that motivates men—even Americans. A role is also played "by the disinterested, spontaneous impulses natural to man." And a significant role also is played by faithful acceptance of things as they exist—as the will of God.[17] Americans accepted as good the society, the beliefs, and the hierarchy within which they lived. They accepted existing institutions, beliefs, and practices because they saw them as just and because to do otherwise would mean taking time away from what they saw as their proper and primary pursuits. The dogmatic belief in self-interest served to promote virtue by allowing appropriate social institutions to hold full sway and by showing Americans the justice and beneficiality—the goodness and authoritativeness—of their existng institutions and practices.

Neither freedom nor nobility comes from a particular set of institutions. Both come from a particular set of mind and habits allowing for affectionate acceptance of given institutions. Both require that what is given be accepted as good rather than acquiesced in or truckled to as inevitable or merely beneficial. As the French monarchy was served reverently by subjects who thereby attained their own nobility, so the American natural aristocracy could elevate the minds of those beneath it without any risk to its own position. For Tocqueville, the democratic chain of being, though not so great as in aristocratic society, exists nonetheless. It is the product of a belief that the free pursuit of self-interest will raise some who are naturally more able to high places. And the existence of high places, open to all, is accepted not just out of self-interest, but out of the belief that it is just. Given the justice of the free and open pursuit of self-interest, the results of this pursuit are also accepted as just. To rise to a higher place requires success in the material world, or success in providing for the (not merely material) good of all.

PUBLIC SERVICE: SELF-INTEREST FOR THE COMMUNITY

Conservative public service may take many forms—most of them explicitly nonpolitical. Indeed, it is an irony of conservative thought that the two greatest proponents of a society in which politics plays a very small role were both statesmen. But both Burke and Tocqueville were particular *kinds* of statesmen—ones concerned primarily with protecting their accustomed social forms rather than with inventing new ones.

Burke's political career was taken up with combating corruption and incursions of one branch of government upon another and, in his later years, with combating the expansionist, radically egalitarian French Revolution. Tocqueville's political career was devoted to fighting the anarchy and degradation he saw swallowing up his beloved homeland.

Tocqueville was convinced that "the effective reason which causes men to lose political power, is that they have become unworthy to retain it. . . . If it is right to have this patriotic prejudice at all times, how much more is it not right to have it in our own? Do you not feel, by some intuitive instinct which is not capable of analysis, but which is undeniable, that the earth is quaking once again in Europe? . . . Well then, my firm and profound conviction is this: that public morality is being degraded, and that the degradation of public morality will shortly, very shortly perhaps, bring down upon you new revolutions."[18] To prevent the horrors of revolution, Tocqueville sought to recall the rulers of his day to the pursuit of virtue. He attempted to protect the "sacred rights of property and of the family" because he recognized them as "the foundation of our social order." He tried to defend the social forms he knew and loved from the corruptions brought about by philosophical hubris and selfish materialism.[19] Political service is neither transitory nor dispensable. If not confronted with dispatch and in their proper (political) realm, political discontents will become deeper, more fundamental and, as Tocqueville himself put it, dangerously "social."[20] Thus the statesman constantly must be prepared to confront new circumstances in order to defend his given order.

Furthermore, as political writers, both Burke and Tocqueville powerfully defended the dignity of their own calling. Defense of one's calling, like defense of one's family, locality, or class, is itself virtuous, but the conservative good life, though it requires the services of the statesman, does not elevate him to the commanding heights of the republican founder. The focus of accepting virtue is social rather than political. Thus the powers of the government, and of "great" statesmen, should be limited. In particular, the powers of the *central* government should be limited so that virtue may be fostered in the localities. Because its government was decentralized, "in the United States the motherland's presence is felt everywhere. It is a subject of concern to the village and to the whole Union. The inhabitants care about each of their country's interests as if it were their own. Each man takes pride in the nation; the successes it gains seem his own work, and he becomes elated; he rejoices in the general prosperity from which he profits. He has much the same feeling for his country as one has for one's family, and a sort of selfishness makes him care for the state."[21] Because of local autonomy, the American could see and profit from the results of his own contributions to the public good. The natural growth of human affection and attachment from the locality upward, the natural growth of public spirit, was aided by a local autonomy that brought Americans into constant contact with one another on the basis of mutual interest.

Although for Aristotle social attachments are formed beginning with the family (which Tocqueville also recognized as natural and fundamental), Tocqueville's chain of attachments begins one step further back—with the individual. Social attachments begin, not with the community of the family, but with the interests of man himself. Further and more distant attachments can and must grow out of the primary attachment to the self. Tocqueville did not propound a philosophy of selfishness. Rather, he recognized that the golden rule commands us to "love your neighbor as yourself" and not to "love your neighbor and forget yourself." Even the saint loves his soul. And, for most of us, to love one's neighbor requires that we first learn how to love ourselves *properly*.

Self-interest means taking care of one's own interests, but it also means taking care of those with whom one is intimately connected—those whose interests one takes for one's own. The growth of community from the locality upward is largely the result of the self-interested desire to take care of one's own, one's family, one's friends—all those with whom one feels an intimate connection. It was by appealing to this attachment to the self that local American institutions inculcated ideas and practices of public service. And the attachments thus formed went beyond mere self-interest to "self-interest properly understood" and even a kind of virtuous and benevolent sacrificing of one's own for the public good.

Man naturally seeks and forms social attachments. By keeping social and political attachments local, the Americans allowed man to see how his efforts affected both himself and his community. The American was able to see how his own interests were served and also to take a certain accepting pride in his ability to aid his community. His feelings for his community came to resemble those one has for one's family—the primordial social group in whose interests sacrifice is natural and habitual.

American localism and liberty made public service possible in democratic society. "The Americans have used liberty to combat the individualism born of equality, and they have won."[22] The individual citizen, seeing his own interest and that of his neighbors at stake in local affairs, gained the habit of cooperating with those around him.

> The free institutions of the United States and the political rights enjoyed there provide a thousand continual reminders to every citizen that he lives in society. At every moment they bring his mind back to this idea, that it is the duty as well as the interest of men to be useful to their fellows. Having no particular reason to hate others, since he is neither their slave nor their master, the American's heart easily inclines toward benevolence. At first it is of necessity that men attend to the public interest, afterward by choice. What had been calculation becomes instinct. By dint of working for the good of his fellow citizens, he in the end acquires a habit and taste for serving them.[23]

Mutual interest and reliance become mutual affection and form the habits of public service. One acts in the interests of the public because one has come to feel that it is intrinsically good to do so. Interest and habit foster a taste for and a sense of duty to provide public service.

Public service is good for society and for the soul of the individual because "feelings and ideas are renewed, the heart enlarged, and the understanding developed only by the reciprocal action of men one upon another."[24] Such interaction may be achieved only through local liberty, in voluntary associations that do not have the inherently authoritarian character of governmental decrees. Voluntary associations bring men into *reciprocal* contact; they involve mutual compromise in the interest of a greater whole. In contrast, where governmental action is concerned men have no choice but to obey, and this servility is hardly ennobling. The road improvement instigated and carried out by concerned citizens is a sign and a reinforcement of their virtue. The road improvement resulting from governmental decrees is a sign and a reinforcement of their servility.[25]

While politics is the primary realm of neither liberty nor virtue, political *associations* are necessary for both. Where there are no political associations civil associations will be rare because it is in political associations that men are taught "the general theory of association."[26] Unlike other associations, political associations involve no monetary risk and so are most likely to attract members in materialistic democratic society. If they are not taught to associate where their money is not at risk, democratic men will not form voluntary associations—and the habits of virtue—at all. The government must allow for, and foster through decentralization, voluntary political associations so that their citizens will "learn to submit their own will to that of all the rest and to make their own exertions subordinate to the common action."[27] Thus political associations serve the crucial but rather limited purpose of training men to participate in the more fundamental voluntary associations in which the bulk of public service takes place.

Liberty makes possible—and is possible because of—the virtue of public service. Men, having been shown the extent to which their well-being is dependent one upon another, acquire the habit of providing for the public interest—in the absence of governmental action. The habits of mutual assistance transcend mere self-interest, however, because man is an inherently social being. He values the affection of his neighbors and is capable of benevolence when properly habituated. The natural aristocrats of America provided public service through political, intellectual, and practical leadership in the local community. They acted as statesmen, patrons of the arts, and leaders of local voluntary associations. Since America was a democratic society, those not of the natural aristocracy provided public service in much the same ways, through numerous professions and activities. They were frequently not leaders, but this did not make their service unimportant.

One's place gives one particular means and duties of service, and a society is bound together by its code of duties or honor. The Old Regime attempted to "humanize" feudal society by replacing requirements that local lords see to their peasants' needs with public welfare measures. The government succeeded only in severing the natural ties binding the classes, to the spiritual and often material impoverishment of all.[28] Thus, "not only was the peasant almost entirely deprived of any contacts with the upper classes; he was also separated even from those of his own class who might have been able to befriend and to advise him. For once such persons had achieved a certain culture or prosperity they turned their backs on him. He was, in fact, cold-shouldered on all sides and treated like a being of a peculiar species. . . . The fourteenth-century peasants had been at once more oppressed and better cared for; the great seigneurs may have sometimes treated them harshly, but they never abandoned them to their own resources."[29]

The replacement of local feudal duties with centralized governmental programs eliminated the *feelings* of obligation that lay at the heart of social connections. No longer obligated in fact, the nobles (and well-off commoners) were no longer obligated in their own minds to associate with their "lessers" and so chose not to associate with them—with disastrous results for the souls and the society of all involved.

Men will subordinate their own interests to those of the public in a properly ordered society. The virtue of public service is open to all men who are willing to exert themselves in serving the public. But the aristocratic code of honor, the appeal to and of greatness that produced public spirit in aristocratic society before it was destroyed by centralization, must be replaced in democratic society. New habits of public service must be formed through the attachments of local voluntary associations if public spirit is to survive. Human sociability—the attachments of affection and benevolent action—must be fostered with the tools appropriate to the new situation.

PRUDENCE: THE MODERATION OF SELF-INTERESTED DEMOCRACY

> Do you not notice how on all sides beliefs are giving way to arguments, and feelings to calculations? If amid this universal collapse you do not succeed in linking the idea of rights to personal interest, which provides the only stable point in the human heart, what other means will be left to you to govern the world, if not fear?[30]

With the collapse of old beliefs, self-interest is the only belief upon which liberty might be built. It is important to note, here, what Tocqueville was *not* saying about self-interest. He was not claiming that self-interest is the only motivating factor of human action in democratic times—let alone of human action in general. Self-interest is "the only stable point in the human heart"; that is, the only firm and *unchanging* aspect of human nature is man's concern with his own well-being. Self-interest provides a firm and well-known basis upon which to build something which transcends self-interest—virtue. Tocqueville also was not saying that self-interest is the only *proper* motivating factor of human action or that it is good to act only in one's own interest, however well understood. Self-interest is a fact, not a goal. It must be used as a tool, not pursued as an end.

Tocqueville was asserting that self-interest is the proper tool in democratic times for the establishment and protection of rights—of liberty.

He valued benevolent action in the public interest, and for him liberty both requires and makes possible the virtue of public service. The use of self-interest in the pursuit of liberty and virtue is prudent. It is based upon a proper reading of the natural order, a recognition that our tools must fit society's changed circumstances if we are to maintain the life of virtue.

Because Americans recognized the need for calm judgment and moderation, they chose great rather than popular leaders to form their government. Because these great men were calm and moderate, they were able to discern the dictates of natural law and so found a democratic polity that was moderate and decentralized.[31] Their moderation made the American republics capable of producing virtue: "What is meant by 're-public' in the United States is the slow and quiet action of society upon itself. It is an orderly state really founded on the enlightened will of the people. It is a conciliatory government under which resolutions have time to ripen, being discussed with deliberation and executed only when mature."[32] Natural law was followed in the United States because decisions were made calmly, with moderation and decorum. Mature discussion in an atmosphere of conciliation led over time to truly natural decisions that took into account both current circumstance and the abiding (democratic) nature of the people.

Europeans could not discern the true character of democracy and the dictates of natural law in regard to it because the passions engendered by the conflict there between democracy and aristocracy obscured both principles and circumstances.[33] Men were too agitated to consider calmly the dictates of natural law; their reason was clouded by the conflict between general beliefs.[34] And the European conflict could not be settled through moderate compromise between the democratic and aristocratic principles since mixed government of this sort is impossible.[35] But while the aristocratic *principle* (the denial of universal rights) cannot be maintained in democratic regimes, prudence dictates that democracy be moderated through aristocratic means, that is, by checks on the majority's unguided will. Accepting the universality of rights, American lawyers and judges nonetheless must fulfill the aristocratic function of moderating the people by holding their passions in check through the application of precedent. And founders, where they must exist, must establish moderate republics, which in turn will moderate the will of the majority.

In Tocqueville's time, the bicameral legislature of the United States included a Senate that was not directly elected. Since these men were chosen by state legislators, who in turn were chosen by the people, the senators

> represent the result, albeit the indirect result, of universal suffrage, for the legislature which appoints the senators is no aristocratic or privileged body deriving its electoral right from itself; it essentially depends on the totality of citizens; it is generally annually elected by them, and they can always control its choice by giving it new members. But it is enough that the popular will has passed through this elected assembly for it to have become in some sense refined and to come out clothed in nobler and more beautiful shape. Thus the men elected always represent exactly the ruling majority of the nation, but they represent only the lofty thoughts current there and the generous instincts animating it, not the petty passions which often trouble or the vices that disgrace it.[36]

The refining process of indirect election produced a Senate capable of moderating American democracy. One step removed from the will of the majority, the Senate was able to act with calm decorum and so transcend vice and petty passions. Senators, chosen for their good character, were willing and able to find and follow the dictates of natural law. A prudent choice of governmental forms thus allowed for prudent government. As a result, America was not, like France, led by imprudent and hubristic would-be founders into the lethargic barbarism of centralized tyranny and the subservient craving for mere material well-being.

This does not mean that Tocqueville did not see very real problems with American democracy. The instability of American laws was "a great ill."[37] Moreover, the prudent management of American government, the moderate leadership of good men, was constantly endangered by an excess of democracy and equality. The tyranny of the majority and the soft despotism of paternalistic government (which the majority itself demanded) always threatened to destroy prudence and good government by chaining men to a will and a judgment not their own.

INDEPENDENCE IN THE SERVICE OF THE MAJORITY

> Over this kind of men stands an immense, protective power which is alone responsible for securing their enjoyment and watching over their fate. That

power is absolute, thoughtful of detail, orderly, provident, and gentle. It would resemble parental authority if, father-like, it tried to prepare its charges for a man's life, but on the contrary, it only tries to keep them in perpetual childhood. It likes to see the citizens enjoy themselves, provided that they think of nothing but enjoyment. It gladly works for their happiness but wants to be sole agent and judge of it. It provides for their security, foresees and supplies their necessities, facilitates their pleasures, manages their principal concerns, directs their industry, makes rules for their testaments, and divides their inheritances. Why should it not entirely relieve them from the trouble of thinking and all the cares of living?[38]

What is most striking about this stirring condemnation of soft despotism is that the "kind of men" who make this despotism possible, in Tocqueville's view, are those who have fallen under the spell of *individualism*. Despotism that cares for its people like the father of perpetual children is made possible when men become too interested in their individual affairs to pay attention to public affairs. Men lose their liberty when they become too concerned with making money to consider more important social matters. Abandoning public life in pursuit of material wealth, men increasingly leave public matters to the government until they become too isolated, too small and frightened to oppose the governors who are destroying the last vestiges of true liberty.

By doing for its citizens what they should do for themselves, a government takes away the very humanity of its subjects. Only men who have learned to see to their own needs—and to combine with their neighbors to see to their community's needs—can prevent the majority from chaining all men to its will. The tyranny of the majority stifles independent thought and action as it imposes a kind of mob rule—the rule of its own petty interests and passions of the moment.

Democratic peoples are unreasonably shortsighted and are ruled by their passions. If unguided by men independent of its will, the majority is incapable of looking after its own interests in a calm, prudential manner. In a democracy, "the people, surrounded by flatterers, find it hard to master themselves. Whenever anyone tries to persuade them to accept a privation or a discomfort, even for an aim that their reason approves, they always begin by refusing."[39] If given full sway, the majority will destroy its own liberty, its own society, itself.

Because equality makes each individual see himself as a small and weak creature confronting a faceless, all-encompassing majority, this majority is difficult to moderate. Rather than oppose its political will, democratic man will withdraw from contact with the majority into his private affairs. Such habits are spiritually debilitating. Thus Tocqueville lamented that

> among the immense thrusting crowd of American political aspirants I saw very few men who showed that virile candor and manly independence of thought which often marked the Americans of an earlier generation and which, wherever found, is the most salient feature in men of great character. At first glance one might suppose that all American minds had been fashioned after the same model, so exactly do they follow along the same paths. A foreigner does, it is true, sometimes meet Americans who are not strict slaves of slogans; such men may deplore the defects of the laws and the unenlightened mutability of democracy; often they even go as far as to point out the defects which are changing the national character and suggest means by which this tendency could be corrected, but no one, except yourself, listens to them, and you, to whom they confide these secret thoughts, are only a stranger and will pass on.[40]

The Americans' desire to avoid going against the will and general thoughts of the majority led to two great evils: the loss of men of great character and the loss of the good such men may do for democratic society. Because so few were willing to oppose majority opinion—because there was so little independent thought—there were few men willing and able to provide the sort of public service a democratic people requires. There were no great *leaders* of public opinion capable of moderating the will of the majority, pointing out and causing it to follow its own long-term interests. Public men of great character, virtuous men, can arrive at independent, considered conclusions concerning the dictates of natural law in their particular circumstances. They discern for themselves how they may best serve the interests of their community's preexisting institutions and practices. They moderate the power and the passions of democracy itself.

But the majority is not the only source of dangers to independence. The search for money, which fosters individualism, also promotes corruption and the inherently corrupt practice of place hunting—actions that stifle virtuous and independent public service. Tocqueville thought this point obvious: "There is no need for me to say that this universal and uncontrolled desire for official appointments is a great social evil, that it undermines every citizen's sense of independence and spreads a venal and servile temper throughout the nation, that it stifles manly virtues; nor need I note that such a trade only leads to unproductive activity and unsettles the country without adding to its resources."[41]

Corruption, the search for material gain through public office, destroys independence and manhood, whatever the form of government. Corruption destroys independence because a corrupt man cannot act on his prudent assessment of the public interest, for this would conflict with his pursuit of wealth.[42] It destroys manhood because a man who is not independent is a servile wretch.

Tocqueville had strong words for those who choose not to serve the public interest. Corruption was all the worse, for Tocqueville, because it was not only bad and unvirtuous, but also unnecessary and avoidable. The structure of American society, and the corresponding nature of the American people, made independent public service possible as well as desirable.

Despite the problem of majority tyranny, independence remained a part of both American character and American practice. The frontier had habituated Americans to self-reliance, and the decentralization of the American system made despotism almost impossible.

> However far the national majority may be carried away by its passions in its ardor for its projects, it cannot make all the citizens everywhere bow to its will in the same way and at the same time. The sovereign commands of its representative, the central government, have to be carried out by agents who often do not depend upon it and cannot be given directions every minute. Municipal bodies and county administrations are like so many hidden reefs retarding or dividing the flood of the popular will. If the law were oppressive, liberty would still find some shelter from the way the law is carried into execution, and the majority would not know how to enter into the details and, if I dare call them so, the puerilities of administrative tyranny.[43]

The decentralization of the American political system allowed for many governments rather than just one. Thus the decisions of the national majority could not be carried into practice without the cooperation of naturally uncooperative—naturally free and independent—localities. And it was in these localities that habits were inculcated whereby individualism might be overcome.

The American system contrasted sharply with the zealous, centralizing programs begun under the French Old Regime. Instigated by national administrators, these "improvements" had cast the government in "the part of an indefatigable mentor . . . keeping the nation in quasi-paternal tutelage."[44] It was this tutelage that broke up the French nation into uniform but self-interested and hostile subgroups lacking the honor, cohesion, and mutual affection of a properly constituted society.[45] This tutelage destroyed the virtue and—what is much the same thing—the ability for self-government of the French people and particularly of the proper, historical French ruling class: the aristocracy.

By the late days of the Old Regime, French aristocrats had been stripped of their power by the king's administrators and left as arrogant, frivolous, and pampered royal playthings. In uprooting the aristocratic class rather than forcing it to submit to its proper obligations and the rule of law, however, the French revolutionaries commited a great sin against the nation. "When a class has taken the lead in public affairs for centuries, it develops as a result of this long, unchallenged habit of pre-eminence a certain proper pride and confidence in its strength, leading it to be the point of maximum resistance in the social organism. And it not only has itself the manly virtues; by dint of its example it quickens them in other classes. When such an element of the body politic is forcibly excised, even those most hostile to it suffer a diminution of strength. Nothing can ever replace it completely, it can never come to life again; a deposed ruling class may recover its titles and possessions but nevermore the spirit of its forebears."[46]

The French "social organism" once possessed, indeed consisted of, classes with their own proper pride and manly virtues, but centralization and revolution destroyed the training grounds and the leading practitioners of independent self-government. Thus France was left with a collection of squabbling, self-interested, and materialistic groups concerned only with the rewards that their servile activities might garner them from the central, paternal authority.

Independence is made possible by public service, itself made possible by local autonomy. Frenchmen became servile because the government did for them what it thereby made them incapable of doing for themselves. In contrast, American federal and state governments left to the people, or at most to *local*, township governments, the many everyday tasks making up civil life. Through experience they developed independent judgment and the desire to serve their neighbors.

LOCAL AFFECTION: VIRTUE IN THE
AMERICAN COMMUNITY

> [The American] has conceived an opinion of himself which is often ex-
> aggerated but almost always salutary. He trusts fearlessly in his own pow-
> ers, which seem to him sufficient for everything. Suppose that an individual
> thinks of some enterprise, and that enterprise has a direct bearing on the
> welfare of society; it does not come into his head to appeal to public au-
> thority for its help. He publishes his plan, offers to carry it out, summons
> other individuals to aid his efforts, and personally struggles against all ob-
> stacles. No doubt he is often less successful than the state would have been
> in his place, but in the long run the sum of all private undertakings far
> surpasses anything the government might have done.[47]

Confident of their own abilities, Americans independently conceived
and carried out projects in the public interest. Knowing that the government would not see to all their needs, Americans learned to arrange
their own lives, combining (when needed) with their neighbors to tend
to community affairs.

Thus, for Tocqueville, independence and public service are related intimately, and the glue holding these two virtues together is affection.
Men naturally are capable of affection, but they must be habituated to
it. Naturally social beings, men will nonetheless resign from the public
sphere, particularly in times of equality, in favor of the enjoyments of
the most local of attachments—themselves, their own interests, and the
affairs of their families—if society does not foster common action. Only
by combining one's will and interests with those of one's neighbors can
one learn affection and so become virtuous. The realm within which common action takes place is the same one in which character itself is
formed: the local community.

The character of New England and the New Englanders differed from
that of the South because of their dissimilar historical circumstances and
mores, just as the people of one township in New England differed from
those in another. The central government did not interfere unduly with
local circumstances—with the mode of life as played out in varying institutions, beliefs, and practices. Allowed their full influence, differing
circumstances fostered close communities in which citizens shared basic
characteristics and a common way of life.

America's traditional decentralization permitted its states to form into essentially separate republics with their own political lives and individual characters.[48] The conservation of these separate institutions and (both individual and community) characters fostered virtue by fostering independent, affectionate communities. Sharing circumstances and a basic character, Americans learned affection for their neighbors. Sharing circumstances, men come to share activities. They face the same situations in the same basic way. In recognizing this, the American Founders, in their fight against individualism, gave "each part of the land its own political life so that there should be an infinite number of occasions for the citizens to act together and so that every day they should feel that they depended on one another."[49]

Citizens of local communities come into constant contact with one another because their daily lives are naturally intertwined. This interaction helps citizens in these communities to recognize that they depend on one another, and mutual dependence and interaction lead to mutual affection. As Tocqueville wrote, "The general business of a country keeps only the leading citizens occupied. It is only occasionally that they come together in the same places, and since they often lose sight of one another, no lasting bonds form between them. But when the people who live there have to look after the particular affairs of a district, the same people are always meeting, and they are forced, in a manner, to know and adapt themselves to one another."[50]

The business of a large nation is too impersonal to form lasting bonds of affection. Only daily interaction in the common business of the community can teach men to take one another into account. In the local community one must look to the interests of one's neighbors as well as oneself because only then may the common interest be served. Self-interest itself dictates cooperation, and naturally one will try to make such cooperation pleasant. All men desire the esteem of those around them. "Local liberties, then, which induce a great number of citizens to value the affection of their kindred and neighbors, bring men constantly into contact, despite the instincts which separate them, and force them to help one another." By rendering this help, men learn virtue: "To gain the affection and respect of your immediate neighbors, a long succession of little services rendered and of obscure good deeds, a constant habit of kindness and an established reputation for disinterestedness, are required."[51] Since one achieves esteem and affection through affectionate and disinterested public action, one will acquire both the habit and the desire to act virtuously. One acts benevolently because one has grown to love one's neighbors, to value their affection and their interests as one's own. The familiarity of locality breeds, not contempt, but affection.

The most tragic and important casualty of the Old Regime's administrative centralization was the affectionate character of ancient local communities. Government programs and the lifting of obligations from the aristocracy destroyed the affections and thus the very character of the French locality.

> Now that [the aristocrat] had ceased to hold a dominant position he no longer was at pains . . . to help "his" peasants, to further their interests, and to give them good advice. . . . This led to what might be called a spiritual estrangement more prevalent and more pernicious in its way than mere physical absenteeism. For in his dealings with his tenants the landowner who lived on his estate often developed sentiments and views that would, were he an absentee, have been those of his agent. Like an agent he came to regard his tenants as mere rent-payers and exacted from them the uttermost farthing to which the law, or ancient usage, still entitled him, the result being that the collection of such feudal dues as still existed was apt to seem even more galling to the peasants than it had been in the heyday of feudalism.[52]

The natural relations between French aristocrats and peasants were formed by shared feelings and obligations. Anxious to secure the nobles' services for the king and blind to the effects of estranging them from their peasants, the Old Regime's administrators usurped the traditional, local role of the aristocracy and so destroyed the ties that held their nation together. Tocqueville sardonically noted the disapproval that the seventeenth-century intendant for the province of Anjou expressed over the behavior of his district's nobles. Anjou's nobles, complained the intendant, actually preferred "living among their peasants in the country to fulfilling their duties toward the King." This disapproval was "particularly interesting" since these "were the only nobles who subsequently took up arms in defense of the monarchy and died fighting for it. And what made it feasible to put up this heroic resistance was the fact that they had always been on close and friendly terms with those same peasants for living amongst whom this short-sighted Intendant reproached them!"[53] Common living had produced common feeling and common affection in Anjou and allowed for a heroic if futile defense of the Old

Regime. This defense was based on a set of relations that were not unique in France but that had become seemingly anachronistic because they had been destroyed almost everywhere by administrative centralization.

No less than Burke, Tocqueville recognized that man requires local attachments (or little platoons) if his affections are to proceed from himself toward the nation and mankind. In a passage strikingly reminiscent of Burke, Tocqueville argued that nationalism is necessary for virtue because

> man has been created by God (I do not know why) in such a way that the larger the object of his love the less directly attached he is to it. His heart needs particular passions; he needs limited objects for his affections to keep these firm and enduring. There are but few who will burn with ardent love for the entire human species. For the most part, the sole means by which Providence (man taken as he is) lets each of us work for the general good of humanity is to divide this great object into many smaller parts, making each of these fragments a worthy object of love to those who compose it. If everyone fulfills his duties in that way (and within these limits such duties are not beyond anyone's natural capacities if properly directed by morals and reason), the general good of humanity would be produced by the many, despite the absence of more direct efforts except by a few.[54]

Man cannot love and serve the human species taken as a whole—that way lies Rousseauean hypocrisy. Yet man can come to value and serve those around him and so join with them in the formation of a viable, affectionate, and truly good community.

The local communities of feudal France were not the servile creatures they had become by the time of the French Revolution. In combing through administrative records and correspondence, Tocqueville "found much evidence in support of the view that during the Middle Ages the inhabitants of each French village formed a commonality independent in many ways of the seigneur. No doubt he requisitioned their services, watched over and governed them; but the village held property in common and had exclusive ownership of it. The villagers elected their own officials and governed themselves on democratic lines."[55]

Tocqueville did not see France's feudal past as a world apart from the American democratic community. Instead he saw in these seemingly incompatible political systems a common local community with common features and a common origin.

Neither had permanent representatives, that is to say a town council in the strict sense of the term, and both were administered by officials acting separately, under instructions from the whole community. General assemblies were convened from time to time in both and at these the townsfolk, acting in concert, elected their own officials and passed orders on matters affecting the interests of the community. In short, the [later] French and the American systems resembled each other in so far as a dead creature can be said to resemble one that is very much alive.

For these two systems of local government, though their ways soon parted, had in fact a common origin. Transported overseas from feudal Europe and free to develop in total independence, the rural parish of the Middle Ages became the township of New England.[56]

These two systems of local government had much more in common than mere political structures. The rural parish and the New England township shared the proper way of life, which made possible the local affection that is the life force of accepting virtue. In the rural parish the authority of the local nobility was accepted and reinforced by the carrying out of aristocratic obligations in daily life: the fulfillment of ceremonial functions, the giving of advice and charity. The natural aristocrat fulfilled the same basic functions in America. Where political leadership resided in the hereditary aristocracy in France, deference, if more limited and subject to questioning, was also given to the natural aristocrat—the successful man and virtuous citizen—in America.

The important aspects of life are not embodied in a particular political system but in the freedom to maintain fitting local communities. In Tocqueville's view, free local communities by nature foster liberty and a certain democratic spirit—extensive participation in public matters, a certain equality before the law, and a mutual acceptance of personal worth. These factors in turn bind citizens together with the habits of local affections.

THE DEMOCRATIC GOOD LIFE

Democracy was successful in America. Despite the problems of majority tyranny and the dangers of soft despotism, American democracy provided for a good life. Virtue was possible and was even fostered in the American republics because of the local differentiation and the liberty afforded by the history and circumstances of American society. Participating in the local community, Americans came to value the esteem and affection of those with whom they came into constant contact and with whom they shared a common character and circumstances. Pursuing their esteem and affection, Americans learned to love their neighbors and to seek to benefit them.

Well-ordered liberty produced an independent character, a self-reliance born of free action in the local community. Americans decided on their own how best to serve the interests of their neighbors. And, being prudent men, they recognized that the moderation of democracy was in the best interests of all. The American republics were moderate because the rule of law was respected and the natural aristocracy was allowed to rule. This aristocracy was accepted and respected as such because it was seen as just and natural that those men who are most capable should rise to high positions within the hierarchy natural even in democratic times. Thus equality was moderated and made both bearable and virtuous.

As he was no uncritical democrat, Tocqueville also was no extreme classical Liberal seeking to free all aspects of human character from the constraints of the state and the community. Tocqueville was not even an unhesitating proponent of Liberal economics. He did not value the idea of the free market, unimpeded by any public interference, as an absolute good. Indeed, Tocqueville praised the New England colonies for having bequeathed to the United States a significant amount of public intervention.

> Clearly they had a higher and more comprehensive conception of the duties of society toward its members than had the lawgivers of Europe at that time, and they imposed obligations upon it which were still shirked elsewhere. There was provision for the poor from the beginning in the states of New England; there were strict regulations for the maintenance of roads, with officials appointed to supervise them; the townships had public registers recording the conclusions of public deliberations and the births, deaths, and marriages of the citizens; there were clerks whose duty it was to keep these records; officials were appointed, some to look after intestate property, others to determine the boundaries of inherited lands, and many more whose chief function was to maintain public order.
>
> The law anticipates and provides in great detail for a multitude of social needs of which in France we are still now but vaguely conscious.[57]

Tocqueville's goal was not the elimination of the public sphere—far from it—the public sphere was primary for him. Indeed, there is no proper separation between the public and private sphere. Individualism, the single-minded pursuit of private life, destroys liberty as well as virtue. As for Aristotle and for Burke, so for Tocqueville man is a social being, able to live as he should—to achieve his nature—only in society.[58]

It was good that Americans had taken it upon themselves to care for their poor and had assumed a number of other public (though not necessarily political) tasks. American public action was good because it was not undertaken by a central government but by local communities that provided for public needs in a manner consistent with liberty and virtue. If public goods are formulated and distributed within local communities, the independence and the public service—the virtue—of the citizens remain necessary, are called upon, and are made habitual by public action.

As Tocqueville would have it, man is made virtuous through social interaction. Social interaction is natural, and it is necessary if man is to achieve his end. Particularly in an era of misanthropic "philosophers" and rampant egalitarian materialism, virtue must be the goal of democratic society if democracy is to ennoble rather than debase those whom it governs.

6 · The Dilemma of Contemporary Conservative Horizons

Providence did not make mankind entirely free or completely enslaved. Providence has, in truth, drawn a predestined circle around each man beyond which he cannot pass; but within those vast limits man is strong and free, and so are peoples.

The nations of our day cannot prevent conditions of equality from spreading in their midst. But it depends upon themselves whether equality is to lead to servitude or freedom, knowledge or barbarism, prosperity or wretchedness.
—Alexis de Tocqueville, *Democracy in America*

CONSERVATIVE LIMITATIONS

Tocqueville saw both hope and danger in the great, democratic crisis of our time. The search for equality may bring liberty and its essential guarantor: the rule of law. The search for equality also may breed materialism, conformity, and an unquenchable thirst for ever greater equality at all costs—even at the cost of our liberty.

In the face of the crisis of equality, conservatism has lessons to teach us, lessons concerning the limitations, and the promise, of man. For the conservative it is when we accept the limitations of our reason, of our capacity for independent thought and affection, that virtue becomes possible. Bereft of the limited horizons of our accustomed surroundings—our locality, our neighbors, our accepted beliefs—we are left languishing in a sea of uncertainty. No longer able to determine what is good and what is bad, we will abandon the pursuit of virtue in favor of the pursuit of comfort.

The quest for equality of condition is the quest for uniformity. It is

144

the attempt to make others like ourselves, whether they wish to be so or not. When pursued for its own sake, equality destroys variety. It tears asunder the little platoons that shape human nature in accord with local circumstances and preexisting norms. For both Burke and Tocqueville, we are all equal in that we ought not to be oppressed (we should be allowed to live under the rule of law and tradition) and in that we need varying intervening institutions in order to prevent tyranny and to shape our character in accordance with our particular circumstances. The quest for mere equality tears the fabric of society by destroying the institutions, beliefs, and practices that give us the character necessary to live a good life.

Tocqueville was not sanguine about the prospects for virtue in an era of equality. Egalitarian materialism is a particularly corrupting and degrading idealized notion. Thus Tocqueville at times despaired at the apparent victory of the same corruption against which Burke had urged a holy war decades earlier. But the conservative recognizes that Providence, the will of God, must be accepted if humanity itself is to be possible. Those who, like Nietzsche, reject Providence and attempt to free themselves from its dictates, become slaves to their own delusions. Seeking to take the place of God, he who rejects faith and attempts to go "beyond" good and evil succeeds only in sinking beneath humanity into the madness of bestial self-worship.

An important goal of the conservative is to show us the virtue of limited horizons. Having accepted the goodness of that which exists, we may get on with the important business of serving it to the best of our abilities, within its own dictates and rationale. For Tocqueville no less than for Burke, liberty is the ability to serve one's society in a way that is not fully predetermined. We are necessarily limited by our own natures and by the nature of society; this is dictated by Providence—by natural law. To ignore our limits is to imperil our society and ourselves. Thus to accept our limitations is not to abandon hope, but to abandon hubris. Acceptance leads, not to despair, but to virtue.

The writings of Burke and Tocqueville differ in many ways. Tocqueville was more open than Burke to changes in existing mores—in the characters of peoples. This may be because Tocqueville was faced with the success of the democratic revolution Burke opposed. Unlike Tocqueville, Burke was much more concerned with political than with social tyranny. This may be because Burke was opposing France's democratic revolution in its political beginnings, rather than studying the successful democratic revolution's social effects in America and France. Despite their differences, Burke and Tocqueville were both convinced that only limits upon man's hubris can make true liberty possible. One can be truly free only by living a good life. And in a good life one follows the dictates and serves the interests of a good society—a society capable of commanding affectionate obedience. Wherever they found it, and they found it in many places, Burke and Tocqueville praised and sought to defend this life of accepting virtue.

The good man serves that which is, to the best of his abilities, because it is familiar and therefore loved. He willingly follows the dictates of natural law because he believes that they are good. He separates himself from the mass of his brethren to the extent necessary to determine best how he may serve them. He has affection for his family, neighbors, and people and serves their interests within the confines of his place in society. He may perhaps be able to improve his place in society, but the virtuous man would do so only if it were consistent with, and in the service of, preexisting institutions, beliefs, and practices.

The virtuous man personifies the mores of his own people. He lives up to his potential by fulfilling and furthering his society's standards. He holds himself up to a standard of behavior conceived by no individual, but developed in his society over the course of history, through the interaction of existing and new circumstances. The conservative standard of behavior calls for accepting and dedicated, affectionate, and disinterested service. No conservative would have a society, let alone a government, demand such service, but the conservative nonetheless would expect the truly virtuous man to provide it.

Only the recognition that we are not entirely free allows us to exercise the freedom we have. For the conservative, our need for preexisting institutions, beliefs, and practices ensures that our society will contain many forms of "preexisting," or presumed, virtue. As Burke's nobleman is presumed virtuous because he has an aristocratic title, so Tocqueville's rich man—the member of the natural aristocracy—is presumed virtuous because of his success in the marketplace of life. Virtue in one sphere is to translate into presumed virtue in all spheres. The rich man is given a prominent place in society as a leader of opinion and culture because he is good at making money. The nobleman is given power and prestige because his ancestor committed some act (virtuous or not) that resulted in his ennoblement.

One certainly may argue, without denying their rightful rewards, that the rich man and the nobleman do not deserve unearned power and prestige. But it is precisely this sort of ascription of goodness, on the grounds of something other than actual virtue, that is necessary if conservative horizons (acceptance of society's essential bases) are to be maintained. Thus the notion of presumed virtue presents one of conservatism's central tensions. To value the assumption of virtue is at times to value appearance over reality. One rewards what appears good in the name of maintaining the general good, and in the process one rewards much that is bad and overlooks much that is good and virtuous.

No society may test every man for virtue. It is impossible to maintain social stability of any kind, let alone conservative, accepting virtue, if each man's virtue must be judged every time he acts or fails to act. Some men, by necessity, gain power and leadership on grounds other than their own clear virtue. Unfortunately, the result of this presumption of virtue is a certain amount of injustice (rewards do not equal and are not constantly awarded to merit) and an ever-present problem of power. Presumptions of virtue allow those men presumed virtuous to violate the interests of the community with relative impunity. Thus these men may come to assert a claim that both Burke and Tocqueville explicitly denied—that they have an inherent right to rule others as they in their hubris see fit, regardless of the standards of virtue and natural law itself.

Natural law places limits on those in high as well as those in low places. It also accords to each man, regardless of his position in life and of the source of that position, standards and means of virtue. The conservative good life is not reserved for members of any given class. All men may do God's will and so attain virtue, or ignore His will and be lost. Only when society's given horizons, its preexisting institutions, beliefs, and practices, are believed to be good—not merely necessary or inevitable but *good* —can this good life be attained.

Conservatism entails a certain skepticism. Misplaced faith in man's supposedly unlimited powers of human reason and morality does not allow for accepting virtue. But when skepticism is applied to existing institutions and beliefs, when it is used to question the moral status of the very society that it is the conservative's duty to defend, this defense and the conservative good life itself become impossible. For the conservative, attacks on tradition are based on the mistaken notion that individual reason is superior to the wisdom of the ages. Yet modern man's evisceration of traditional standards has not, as many had hoped, left him as the creator of his own morality. Attacks on society's traditional standards did and continue to appeal to a common criterion: material well-being. This standard has done more to enslave man than could all the chains on this earth.

The standard of goodness combated by both Burke and Tocqueville was egalitarian materialism. For the Jacobins and for many Americans, equality, measured in material terms, is the ideal toward which all societies must strive, whatever their history and circumstance. Thus the doctrine Burke and Tocqueville both sought to defeat—formulated most powerfully by Hobbes but increasing in scope and power to this day—has come to dominate political and moral debates, to the detriment of human society and the human soul. Burke and Tocqueville each showed that conservative skepticism concerning man's ability to act rationally and morally can be coupled with a recognition of his dignity and his capacity for virtue. Man is limited. But then it is only within proper limits—the limits dictated by God—that he may attain his true potential.

We may choose to judge societies solely on their provision of egalitarian material well-being. That is, we are free to degrade ourselves and our society by abandoning our pursuit of the good life in favor of a pursuit of the comfortable life. However, such a project is based on the assumption that man is capable of building a peaceful material paradise and, just as important, that man is such a pathetically small and limited creature that he will be made happy by trading his soul for his comfort.

If man's independent abilities and morality are exaggerated, he becomes a slave to idealized projects. If man's moral and rational capacities are denigrated, he may become the self-enslaved thrall of forces supposedly outside his control. Belief in the goodness of the variety of fitting social arrangements dictated by true natural law may give way to belief in the arbitrary and hence morally unfounded nature of all horizons—of all "products of historical circumstance." If we reject the dictates of natural law, we are left with only one possible "objective" criterion by which to judge existing societies: egalitarian well-being. And this criterion can lead only to the degradation of societies and of man himself.

If conservatives themselves come to judge societies according to materialistic criteria, if they, for example, defend economic liberty only on the grounds that capitalism is more productive than socialism, then virtue has lost its greatest defenders. If they lose sight of the good life, conservatives are left with no moral basis on which to construct effective opposition to destructive, idealized projects. They are left with no moral argument as to why man *should* not strive to create an earthly paradise. Thus the way is left open for would-be founders to subvert in the name of recreating the fundamental structures of society.

Bereft of faith in natural law, man is left with only resigned acquiescence in an inevitably tragic fate. Unlike acceptance, which declares the goodness of what is, acquiescence provides no defense against would-be founders. Acquiescence can show that those who would destroy existing arrangements are likely to produce nothing coherent, prudent, or reasonable. It cannot show why the products of such tamperings should be recognized as the abominations they are rather than valued because they serve some arbitrary and self-involved end. Particularly if would-be founders promise (whether or not they deliver) material equality and well-being, they can only be aided by conservative abandonment of natural law.

THE CONTEMPORARY DILEMMA

Both Burke and Tocqueville have been criticized for their supposedly worldly and materialistic views. Strauss praised Burke for his attacks on Jacobin dismissals of the virtues. The virtues Burke was defending, according to Strauss, restrained human appetites and allowed man's higher sentiments to function.[1] Yet Burke himself supposedly was engaged in the modern "attempt to integrate the eternal into a temporal context."[2] According to Strauss, Burke's identification of accident with Providence—his rejection of human (philosophical) wisdom in favor of circumstance as the proper molder of political life—constitutes a damaging identification of the good with the existing.[3]

Likewise, the Straussian Marvin Zetterbaum argues that Tocqueville failed in his attempt to reconcile religion with liberty. Instead, "Tocqueville manages only to reconcile spiritualistic myths with a drive for freedom so distorted by materialistic overtones that it is incompatible with freedom's usual meaning."[4] For Zetterbaum, Tocqueville's appeal to the practical benefits of religion and his reliance on self-interest cannot support a good society because they are materialistic. And Tocqueville's espousal of patriotism (based on local affections) is paradoxical for Zetterbaum because it contradicts the natural fact of human equality.[5] According to Zetterbaum, Tocqueville attempted the impossible: to create spirit out of mere matter—or worse, to create virtue out of selfishness. That Zetterbaum's criticism, if accepted, would apply with equal force to Burke's defense of existing human relations seems clear.

Straussian charges of mythmaking constitute, at base, a charge of insincerity: Strauss (and Zetterbaum) assume that Burke and Tocqueville were not sincere when they claimed that a spiritual life may result from attachments formed in everyday, practical, and terrestrial pursuits. They assume that Burke and Tocqueville *used* religion and habitual attachments for utilitarian ends—that conservatives seek to achieve terrestrial goals (principally political stability) by convincing men to act in an irrationally public-spirited manner.[6] In the end, the argument that Burke and Tocqueville were materialists boils down to the assertion that God is not in fact a necessary part of their natural law arguments.

It would seem odd that one would base his own system of morals and politics on a self-acknowledged myth. Hubristic mythmaking seems much more a strategy of contemporary materialists than of the more traditional notions of human nature tied up with the idea of a conservative good life. For the conservative, religion orders this world by shaping our character. Transcendent laws concerning right action must be followed because to follow them is good (that is, in accordance with God's will) and not merely because virtue is necessary for our material well-being.

To argue that our self-interest leads us into communities in which mutual affection is fostered (provided idealized philosophy and governmental policy do not destroy the practical bases of these natural relations) is not to argue that materialism is a good thing. We all desire a good life, and any good life requires certain material goods—from the requirements for Aristotle's life of leisure to the barest of necessities for a monastic existence. It is inevitable that men will pursue material goods. The task of any political philosophy is to see to it that material pursuits are circumscribed and directed by rules that recognize and are conducive to a good and not merely to a comfortable life. Tocqueville recognized that most free men inevitably seek their own comfort. Still, daily activities are seldom heroic in any society. Tocqueville's genius was to see that the calm, considerate relations of democratic men (if proper habituating institutions, beliefs, and practices were maintained) *could* contain the same affectionate, virtuous spirit Burke saw in more stringently class-based societies.

Virtue is possible in democratic as well as in aristocratic society because both may allow for affectionate attachments born of familiarity, respect, and humility. Virtue is possible wherever the dictates of natural law are accepted, respected, and followed. The pride of those whom Voegelin criticized for trying to bring heaven to earth, as well as thinkers such as Hobbes who opposed utopian violence with pictures of an earthly material paradise, may—indeed must—be combated by those who seek to follow God by acting rightly and by accepting the dominant circumstances of this life as God's will.

The problem faced by Burke and Tocqueville, the rise of egalitarian materialism, has worsened rather than abated. But to call materialistic—or, more damning, perpetrators of religious and materialistic myths—those men who fought most vigorously against egalitarian materialism is to call into question any resistance to the projects that corrupt our lives. For it is only by emphasizing the goodness and the God-willed nature of what exists that we may counter spurious, idealized promises. And to appeal to the worldly importance of belief is, if the belief is sincere, no more antispiritual than to point out that the good man as well as the saint may lead a good life. It is natural to seek happiness. It is virtuous to seek happiness by acting properly—by doing unto others as you would have them do unto you. Not all of us can be holy, but for the conservative all of us, if allowed, are capable of being good.

Tocqueville saw self-interest as a proper basis for right action because men are not merely materialistic beings: we value affection as well as wealth. Burke sought to build upon habitual attachments because men are capable of loving what is familiar for its own sake, and not just for its "utility." The dilemma of contemporary conservatism arises from the fact that the very institutions and practices within which men operate now are judged in purely materialistic terms. If "social justice" means an equal distribution of material goods and opportunities, justice is no longer a transcendent value according to which we may order our lives while retaining—let alone enriching—our souls.

Contemporary conservatives are faced with a dilemma: The society they seek to defend by and large does not value virtue. Instead our "social consensus," such as it is, rests upon the promise of egalitarian well-being. In the face of the contemporary dilemma, conservatives have a choice; they may treat with material self-interest so as to reinvigorate institutions, beliefs, and practices conducive to a life of virtue (they may seek to combat egalitarian materialism through appeals to man's higher self as manifested in daily life), or they may eschew appeals to transcendent standards in favor of practical arguments pointing out the material failures of materialistic utopianism. The former course is difficult and promises only a long struggle to make clear what is missing in our lives and how we must use the means at our disposal to reconstruct the good life. But the latter course, practical as it may appear, can bring only acquiescence in a life that denies that man is made for more than mere gratification—that he is made to live a good and proper life and so become worthy of receiving Grace and approaching God.

The skeptical pessimism of many contemporary conservatives prevents them from accepting the full vision of the conservative good life set forth by Burke and Tocqueville. But prominent contemporary conservatives share the bulk of the philosophical vision and the moral desire of these two giants of conservative thought. And only the vision of a conservative good life may complete and give hope and purpose to conservative thought today.

In the next two chapters I shall focus upon the thought of three prominent twentieth-century conservatives: Michael Oakeshott, Irving Kristol, and Russell Kirk. Each of these thinkers is recognized as a leader of at least a significant part of the contemporary conservative movement: Oakeshott as a philosophical guide for (particularly "libertarian" or free market) conservatism,[7] Kristol as the journalistic/intellectual spokesman for "welfare state" or neo-conservatism, and Russell Kirk as the spiritual and intellectual leader of "traditional" or "cultural" conservatism. Because each of these thinkers is clearly a member of the conservative movement and because, just as clearly, each represents a position far different from that of the other two, Oakeshott, Kristol, and Kirk will serve, in contemporary jargon, to "test the hypothesis" that conservatives in general share a commitment to the life of accepting virtue.[8]

Oakeshott, Kristol, and Kirk do not present a single, unified philosophical vision. The skepticism of Oakeshott and Kristol precludes recognition of a transcendent natural law dictating and allowing for the practice of conservative virtue. Clearly alienated from and pessimistic about much contemporary practice, Kirk nonetheless explicitly bases his view of man and society on the eternal norms of natural law. But these thinkers share the conviction that prudence must take precedence over any particular substantive goals. Oakeshott, Kristol, and Kirk see the need for limits on centralized governmental power. All see the need for, and in some sense value, the role of tradition in shaping our lives. They recognize the dangers of abstract theorizing and attempts to attain human perfection. Excessive skepticism has done much to reduce their ability to recognize, let alone reconstruct, the conservative good life. For it is the notion that our contemporary society is without virtue or the possibility of virtue—that life within our existing horizons is inherently impoverished—that renders the conservative good life unattainable. Despite their understandable skepticism, and caution, as well as their rejection of utopian prescriptions, however, Oakeshott, Kristol, and Kirk each argue in more or less finished form for a mode of conduct that, if defined and defended in more complete terms, would constitute a conservative good life.

OAKESHOTT: THE LIMITS OF REASON, POLITICS, AND MAN

British political philosopher Michael Oakeshott (perhaps the only twentieth-century conservative generally seen as deserving of the title philosopher) was, until his death in 1991, the guiding force behind much American as well as British conservative thought.[9] His attacks against abstract theorizing and attempts to apply such theorizing to practical life—particularly in the political sphere—have been influential among conservatives, as has been the philosophical skepticism at their base. Yet, despite his prominence as a self-declared conservative, some recent commentators have asserted that he is actually either a particularly cautious and thoughtful liberal[10] or even an intellectual cast in the mold of French neo-Marxist Michel Foucault, attempting to open up "the maximum amount of space for criticism" of society's existing and potential norms.[11] These claims stem from misreadings, first, of Oakeshott's hostility toward the view that the state must have a substantive purpose beyond the promotion of peace and, second, of Oakeshott's failure to acknowledge openly the existence of a transcendent natural law (what contemporary jargon dubs his "anti-foundationalism").

In both cases, the commentators overlook Oakeshott's emphasis on the essential role of tradition in any coherent, properly led life. Oakeshott's statement that man "has a history but no 'nature'"[12] renders him neither a Foucaultian nor a liberal. It does not denote a denial that there are fixed limits on man's capacity to "create" meaning (let alone morality).[13] Nor does it denote a denial of the fundamental role of preexisting institutions, beliefs, and practices in forming man's proper character.[14] Oakeshott does reject the notion that there is any "ultimate or perfect man" or Marxian "species being" that mankind must realize.[15] But standards of proper conduct—*conservative* standards emphasizing the need to learn how best to make our behavior fit the nature of our society's inheritance—are necessary if we are to make the most of ourselves.[16] Indeed, if there is a flaw in Oakeshott's conservatism it is that his inability or unwillingness to formulate a coherent vision of the natural, transcendent norms prescribing our limitations and our proper behavior leaves man too small and limited, too dependent upon historical presuppositions and practices, to understand *why* he should follow tradition and maintain the coherence of society. Clearly for Oakeshott, man is extremely limited in his ability to act properly outside the realm of preexisting norms—particularly when he seeks to act through the state. What is less clear is why man should respect his proper limits rather than act incoherently, according to his selfish, hubristic whims of the moment.

Civil Association

> Governing is a specific and limited activity, namely the provision and custody of general rules of conduct, which are understood, not as plans for imposing substantive activities, but as instruments enabling people to pursue the activities of their own choice with the minimum frustration.[17]

Oakeshott opposed the imposition of any particular conception of the proper form of society. Government may properly do no more than provide peace by maintaining the authority of given rules of behavior. Our own various activities are made possible by the peace of civil association, but government has no further end in and of itself. Oakeshott opposed all attempts to describe, let alone guide, political action in terms of any substantive goal. Instead he recommended—on prudential and epistemological grounds—formal, rule-based political associations ("civil associations") that derive their stability from an adherence to tradition and authority by their members. Politics itself properly is concerned only with seeing to it that the "conditions or terms of association shall be acceptably authoritative or acceptably prudent and that what they require of the associates shall be recognizably desirable."[18] So long as men are satisfied with their political apparatus and so long as this apparatus does not enforce purposive action, politics has no role save to allow for rational participation in other idioms of activity.

Like Burke and Tocqueville, Oakeshott emphasized that the purpose of government is to protect the various, more or less voluntary activities and associations making up man's social life. But Oakeshott's opposition to particular, substantive political ends goes much further than this. Burke and Tocqueville recognized the objective truth of natural law—a truth according to which all good societies must be governed—yet for Oakeshott seemingly all that matters is that the members of a civil association accept the authority of its rules.

Politics, for Burke and Tocqueville, must protect the fundamental institutions, beliefs, and practices of a society. This duty may at times necessitate substantive political action in the name of prudent government—for example, colonizing so that French honor will not die, or restricting unorthodox religious practices in order to protect Britain's religious consensus. For Oakeshott, however, the validity of a rule does not relate one way or another "to its aptitude for achieving a substantive end." Such considerations are simply irrelevant since the concern is not with wise but with authoritative rule.[19]

There is a curious tension in Oakeshott's argument between his insistence that the only proper criterion according to which a rule may be judged is its acceptance by members of the civil association and his insistence that all substantive political activities are inherently wrong. Governing has no proper end save to allow individuals to pursue their own chosen ends. This insistence on individual autonomy, while one certainly may find it attractive and logically compelling, does not seem in keeping with the protection and fostering of traditional practices because it sets up an absolute standard according to which most societies would be judged bad.

Oakeshott's view of associations with specific purposes, particularly those at the level of the state, seems quite clear. He argues that attempts have and will be made to turn states into purposive associations. At all times,

> agents whose slavish concern for benefits makes them fit subjects of such an imposition are not wholly absent. But it is an indispensable condition of this kind of association that each and every associate shall have expressly chosen to be joined in its enterprise or shall have otherwise acknowledged its purpose as his own and that he be permitted to contract out of the association if and when he no longer wishes to be thus associated; . . . consequently, the undertaking to impose this character upon a state whose membership is compulsory constitutes a moral enormity, and it is the attempt and not the deed which convicts it of moral enormity.[20]

This passage argues, not that an involuntary purposive association (a state pursuing substantive ends) would be bad in Great Britain because it would not adhere to the precepts of the preexisting English libertarian tradition, but that such associations are *bad*, period. His unqualified condemnation of involuntary purposive associations, combined with his pointed refusal to weaken the meaning of the word "freedom" through attempts to make it relevant to, "say, a Russian or a Turk who has never enjoyed the experience"[21] indicates an attachment on Oakeshott's part to nonpurposive associations that is absolute. Substantive ends destroy civil association; they turn an association of independent-rule observers into a group of slaves pursuing collectively determined, coerced goals.

Thus, according to Oakeshott, societies in which substantive ends are and traditionally have been pursued are inherently slavish. But Oakeshott himself clearly did not seek to establish a political association in which liberty, the ability to do as one independently chooses, is paramount. Indeed, Oakeshott's extremely limited view of the power of human reason not only makes established practice the only possible arbiter of conduct but also calls into question the very idea of independent human moral choice.

"Rationalism" and Rational Conduct

Best known for his stirring attacks against the "category mistake" of "Rationalism," Oakeshott sought to point out the limited nature of knowledge and of our access to experience. For Oakeshott, the philosopher's proper task is to explain existing modes (realms of activity, "modifications of the whole of experience") in terms of their presuppositions. The philosopher seeks to show the explanatory limits of different ways of organizing experience since all such organizations fall short of the "unity of experience."[22]

The whole of experience is just that for Oakeshott: an entirety that, because it is an entirety, is without shape or form. Knowledge is inherently contextual and can come only from contact with experience. And experience itself may be shaped so as to make sense and allow us to carry out the particular projects of our lives only through the habituated forms of action—Oakeshott's "modes"—that we practice in our daily encounters with the world around us.[23] When we engage in a particular activity, be it scientific inquiry, painting, or cooking, we are in fact engaged in a tradition of conduct, a practice that has grown up over time and that we learn more from practical engagement than from any type of "recipe" book.

Because modes of experience are made up of habits of conduct, Rationalism—"Rational" or noncontextual thought and action—is by nature incongruous and so fundamentally mistaken.

> All actual conduct, all specific activity springs up within an already existing idiom of activity. And by an "idiom of activity" I mean a knowledge of how to behave appropriately in the circumstances. Scientific activity is the exploration of the knowledge scientists have of how to go about asking and answering scientific questions; moral activity is the exploration of the knowlege we have of how to behave well. The questions and the problems in each case spring from the knowledge we have of how to solve them, spring from the activity itself. And we come to penetrate an idiom of activity in no other way than by practising the activity. . . . Gradually, and by a variety of means, we improve and extend our first knowledge of how to pursue the activity. Among such means . . . is the analysis of the activity, the definition of the rules and principles which seem to inhere in it and in reflection upon these rules and principles. But these rules and principles are mere abridgments of the activity itself; they do not exist in advance of the activity, they cannot properly be said to govern it and they cannot provide the impetus of the activity.[24]

Activity *by its very nature* takes place within and depends upon the knowledge embodied in an existing idiom. And truly rational conduct is defined in terms of the idiom in which it takes place. Philosophy itself ("the definition of the rules and principles which seem to inhere" in an idiom) is only one very limited method by which we may improve our ability to follow an idiom of activity—that is, to act coherently. A kind of practical prudence, a reading of the dictates of existing practice (as opposed to the fittingness dictated by an eternal natural law) is the proper guide of human conduct.[25]

Furthermore, an idiom such as scientific activity appears itself to be self-sustaining in that "its coherence lies nowhere but in the way the scientist goes about his investigation, in the traditions of scientific inquiry."[26] For Oakeshott, Rationalism is inherently dangerous and misguided because it is the process by which the totality of experience is reduced to abstract (and therefore unreal and unrealizable) rules and notions. "Activity springing from and governed by an independently pre-meditated purpose is impossible; the power of premeditating purpose, of formulating rules of conduct and standards of behaviour in advance of the conduct and activity itself is not available to us."[27] The belief that independent activity is possible is a dangerous "illusion" arising from the fact that "no man engaged in a particular task has in the forefront of his attention the whole context and implications of that engagement."[28] In the heat of activity, men will forget that "it is the activity itself which defines the questions as well as the manner in which they are answered."[29] Activity, properly speaking, is nonreflective, and it is the nonreflective nature of activity that renders abstract reflection both possible and dangerous.

Since Rational or noncontextual prescriptions are inherently mistaken, "social achievement is to perceive the next step dictated or suggested by the character of the society in contact with changing conditions and to take it in such a manner that the society is not disrupted and that the prerogatives of future generations are not grossly impaired. In place of a preconceived purpose, then, such a society will find its guide in a principle of *continuity* . . . and in a principle of *consensus*."[30] For Oakeshott, Rationalism is bad because it confuses activity, it brings about further mistakes that render activity and society incoherent. Continuity and consensus must be sought and achieved if coercion and the anarchy of irrational social "choices" are to be avoided. "The practical danger of an erroneous theory is not that it may persuade people to act in an undesirable manner, but that it may confuse activity by putting it on a false scent."[31] Although man cannot act according to an abstract theory, his attempts to do so will interfere with the (natural) following of existing modes.

This point brings into view the cornerstone of Oakeshott's argument: his view of the natural limitations of human rationality and independent action. For Oakeshott, truly "'rational' conduct is acting in such a way that the coherence of the idiom of activity to which the conduct belongs is preserved and possibly enhanced." It is not truly rational merely to follow existing rules since rules themselves are simply abridgments of idioms. But rationality may *only* be determined through constant reference to the particular idiom within which one is acting.[32]

The origins of existing practices lie outside the reach of rational cognition; they must be accepted and practiced unquestioningly because the activity determines its own coherence. Reason follows action and is subservient to it. Man may not have an abstract nature, but he does have a history. And his history bequeaths to him habits, both intellectual and practical, that form his character and actions.[33] To attempt to act or to reason in contradiction to habit is thus unreasonable; it is to attempt to contradict the very nature of things.

For Oakeshott, it is not truly rational to depend on one's own faculties of reason because they are inadequate to the task of making sense of the world. Reason, and not just Rationalism, is a very limited faculty. Reason must be supplemented by habit (the following of modes) and, what is not the same thing, unquestioning acceptance if it is to serve its most basic function of allowing us to act rationally. Burke and Tocqueville both emphasized the habitual nature of much human action, the extent to which right action is determined in accordance with existing circumstances and practices. But in Oakeshott's work existing circumstances and practices become themselves the arbiters of right action rather than the embodiment of any transcendent moral truth. To act in contradiction to existing modes, for Oakeshott, is not "merely" evil, it is nonsensical.

Man acts, and may act, only within the confines of a particular idiom or mode of activity that provides both issues and answers. The idiom or mode of activity supplies us with the ability to act and with an understanding of the way to act (i.e., in accordance with the established mode). The idiom determines the nature of our actions and the thoughts that are a part of these actions. It is only through the carelessness to be expected of men engaged in particular activities that the pervasive nature of the idiom is forgotten. "Both the problems and the course of investigation leading up to their solution are already hidden in the activity, and are drawn out only by a process of abstraction."[34]

Indeed, it is apparently only through our inadequacies in properly carrying out the process of abstraction that deviations from the proper flow of the idiom's coherence, caused by mistakes such as Rationalism, arise. In the heat of culinary creation, the cook may forget that he is doing much more than following a given set of rules or a recipe. In actuality he is utilizing a skill gained from observation and, more importantly, experience and habituation in the following of an established tradition of activity.

Oakeshott powerfully points out the moral enormity of attempts to enforce particular, idealized visions of the proper arrangements of society (and of human wants and goals). But his argument is based, not on the inherent dignity of man and the power of human choice, but on the

limits of human reason. Burke, the man who considered the French revolutionaries and their regime to be hubristic philosophical abominations,
was no unthinking proponent of the powers of human reason. Tocqueville, the man who insisted that general beliefs must remain unquestioned
if civilization is to be possible, was no flatterer of philosophers and their
Rationalism. But unreflecting habit and contextual examination of the
presuppositions of habitual practices cannot provide reasons to value the
coherence, continuity, and liberty that Oakeshott advocates. For both
Burke and Tocqueville, tradition and the liberty of local variety (which
Oakeshott also seems to endorse since modes develop differently in different areas) are the products of and therefore are morally endorsed by
natural law. God wills that we follow preexisting practices and recognize the proper role of local intervening institutions because failure to
do so would prevent us from fulfilling our natures.

For Oakeshott, human activity has no particular end; our conduct is
not teleological. The most we can hope for, according to Oakeshott (self-
consciously following Hobbes), is felicity or the continual achievement
of the particular goals of the moment we set for ourselves.[35] There is no
overt religious or moral basis to Oakeshott's schema; he seems to reject
the role of transcendent as well as Rationalistic goals for human action.
Oakeshott claims to be presenting us only with clear, prudential arguments aimed at explaining the nature of truly rational conduct. Given
the limits of all types of human reason, it is difficult to see why, on
Oakeshott's account, we should not simply abandon reason altogether
and revel in the Dionysian anarchy of hubristic projects or in the slavish pleasures of material, substantive associations. Oakeshott shows us
that Rationalism is incoherent; he goes on to argue that substantive politics is slavish. Yet he cannot tell us how or why this moral judgment
can be justified. Oakeshott does not show us, according to his own system he cannot show us, why rational conduct—why acceptance of existing horizons—is good.

KRISTOL: COMMONALITY AND THE
REJECTION OF TRANSCENDENCE

Irving Kristol's work as journalist, policy analyst, and editor of the neoconservative journal *The Public Interest* has been aimed largely at combating the corrupting effects of the inherently adversarial class of

intellectuals spawned by what he calls (following Max Weber) "bourgeois capitalism." But Kristol does not claim to be a philosopher himself. He argues that practical, material concerns both do and ought to dominate our lives. On this view abstractions themselves, and not only idealized, Rationalistic meddling with existing practices, are inherently misguided and dangerous.

According to Kristol, the American political tradition is informed by the proposition that the best national government is mild government. "You can only achieve mild government if you have a solid bedrock of local self-government, so that the responsibilities of national government are limited in scope. And a corollary of this premise is that such a bedrock of local self-government can only be achieved by a people who—through the shaping influence of religion, education, and their own daily experience—are capable of governing themselves in those small and petty matters which are the stuff of local politics."[36] Thus good government requires good character, and good character requires habits formed by the local intervening institutions so valued by Burke and Tocqueville.

Our dilemma, for Kristol, is that the institutions that instill character in the people have themselves become corrupt. Man is an extremely malleable creature whose character is very much the product of his situation. And the situation of "late capitalist" man is corrupting. The rationalistic theorizing of our intellectual class has undermined the inherently precarious moral underpinnings of our society. Unfortunately, the only solution Kristol can offer to the dilemma he describes so persuasively is the dismissal of abstract as well as idealized theory. According to Kristol, we must dispense with intellectual theory in favor of commonly accepted notions and material self-interest. He thus recommends to us the very self-interest that has undermined the moral ethos we are in danger of losing. The result is, at best, a society that Kristol himself appears not to find terribly appealing.

Rationalism and Common Sense

For Kristol, as for Oakeshott, abstract (and not just idealized) theorizing is dangerous because it leads one to believe too much in one's own power and intelligence. Abstraction is dangerous, although sometimes necessary, because it constitutes an attempt to transcend the confines of existing modes of behavior. Thus the social sciences, and economics in particular, have overstepped their proper bounds by attempting to explain all human behavior (through abstractions such as "economic man") as if it were ruled by the "laws" of a particular academic discipline. "Those pretensions accumulated under the influence of a spirit of rationalism—a belief that a comprehensive understanding of all human affairs (i.e., of ourselves) can be achieved through the same methods, and with the same degree of success, as our understanding of physical processes in nature."[37] Believing in their own power and right to "improve" the world, social scientists and their followers have engaged in ideological attempts to change reality by changing the way it is perceived. That is, social scientists attempt to teach a particular, rationalistic view of reality so that they might turn it into a true, concrete reality.[38]

According to Kristol, we must defend our existing society against rationalistic attempts to improve it or its members. Kristol rejects the notion that social science has much to teach us about society itself—that social science has much useful information to impart on general, abstract issues. Instead, the people's accepted beliefs should be viewed as inherently correct.

> When you need an economist or a sociologist to bring you intelligence about inequalities of income or social class, that is in itself proof that neither issue is of serious concern to the citizenry. There are simply no "mysteries" to be elucidated about income inequality and social class, since there is no reason to think that common opinion, based on observation and experience and gossip, is likely to be self-deceiving about a matter of such interest to everyone. The very notion that such self-deception is probable derives from the Marxist idea—an ideological conception of the role of ideology—that bourgeois society is constantly at work instilling "false consciousness" into the populace.[39]

Men belong to the social and economic classes to which they think they belong. Social scientists' ideological attempts to teach us that this is not so are both wrong and dangerous. They are wrong because their views do not fit the existing reality. They are dangerous because they seek to change the existing reality.

The answer, for Kristol, to the problem of rationalistic meddling lies in the acceptance of common belief. Self-interest gives us the means necessary to perceive necessary truths. And the so-called truths of the intellectuals are not to be trusted because they are based on abstract thought rather than on concrete, self-interested experience and because they are the products of a class inherently hostile to the society that nurtures them. Unfortunately for Kristol and for society, commonly accepted beliefs may be both mistaken and dangerous—men may believe they deserve the material and social trappings of a class to which they do not actually belong. Egalitarian envy is thus allowed to run wild, particularly within horizons, such as those Kristol would establish and maintain, that are almost wholly materialistic in nature.

Adversary Intellectuals and Material Self-Interest

For Kristol, "bourgeois society" rejects the transcendent goals of earlier times. "It is a society organized for the convenience and comfort of common men and common women, not for the production of heroic, memorable figures. It is a society interested in making the best of this world, not in any kind of transfiguration, whether through tragedy or piety." Further, though it is true "that the pursuit of excellence by the few—whether defined in religious, moral, or intellectual terms—is neither prohibited nor inhibited, such an activity is merely interpreted as a special form of self-interest, which may be freely pursued but can claim no official status. Bourgeois society also assumes that the average individual's conception of his own self-interest will be sufficiently 'enlightened'—that is, sufficiently far-sighted and prudent—to permit other human passions (the desire for community, the sense of human sympathy, the moral conscience, etc.) to find expression, albeit always in a voluntarist form."[40]

Transcendent values, according to Kristol, are rejected by bourgeois society. Convenience and comfort, not transfiguration or the saving and uplifting power of personal sacrifice, are the purpose of the social structure. Indeed, self-interested prudence (and not any form of personal self-transcendence arising from love of family, neighbors, and community) is the proper and fitting guide for human action. It even will permit the fulfillment of other supposedly derivative human needs such as that for community. Material goods—the stuff of comfort and convenience—are the only real goals and bases of action Kristol believes can operate properly in society.

According to Kristol, "neoconservatives believe in the importance of economic growth, not out of any enthusiasm for the material goods of this world, but because they see economic growth as indispensable for social and political stability. It is the prospect of economic growth that has made it possible to think—against the grain of premodern political thought—of democracy as a viable and enduring sociopolitical system."[41] Although thinkers like himself may not value material goods for themselves, Kristol believes that the rest of us do, and that it is only by providing to the masses an ever-increasing supply of such goods that democracy can be maintained. Furthermore, though its particular forms should allow for as much individual choice as possible, Kristol identifies the compulsory welfare state with (an undefined) distributive justice and maintains that social insurance is both good and necessary for the survival of a modified liberal capitalism. Material goods are necessary for social stability, and their distribution by government is somehow just, even though their inherent value remains unclear.

There may be possible conservative defenses of a minimal welfare state.[42] But the search for mere material gain, unconnected to public service and affectionate attachment to the society and institutions that bestow rewards, appears most in line with the sorts of corruption the traditional conservative would find unacceptable in the man of independent virtue. That is, it would appear, given his notion of the primary role of self-interested materialism, that for Kristol right action should be neither called for nor encouraged. Instead, the greed and envy of the citizenry apparently are to be satisfied so that stability may be maintained.

For Tocqueville, self-interest must be enlightened by affectionate attachment to those with whom one shares one's life. Love of self must be transcended through love for those to whom one has become attached. Kristol minimizes this element of conservative thought to the point that it seems inoperative. The lower elements of human nature are to be appealed to, in the belief that the public interest may be served by so doing. And the aim is not to provide a virtuous good life, but to provide for the survival of society.

Bereft of virtue, however, even the survival of society seems in doubt. With the higher aspects of human nature ignored, many will remain unsatisfied with a society that attempts to quiet them through monetary rewards. Kristol notes that "it is not surprising that the bourgeois world view—placing the needs and desires of ordinary men and women at its center—was (and still is) also popular among the common people. Nor is it surprising that, almost from the beginning, it was an unstable world view, evoking active contempt in a minority, and a pervasive disquiet among those who, more successful than others in having bettered their condition, had the leisure to wonder if life did not, perhaps, have more interesting and more remote possibilities to offer."[43]

Kristol also points to the separation of "high" from "low" culture as both a symptom and the major cause of bourgeois society's conflicts. In all earlier societies the values of the high and low cultures were "basically homogeneous," but in our society, unfortunately, they are openly hostile.[44] This hostility between the culture "of the people" and the culture of the intellectuals puts society itself in danger. Its ideals are questioned by its own (high) culture. Thus the ability of the elite properly to lead the masses has been weakened. The result is a misguided, hubristic elite that attempts to radicalize the myopic masses but succeeds only in undermining society's legitimacy and all individual motivations beyond immediate self-gratification.[45]

The habits of thought and action governing our lives, according to Kristol, are under attack. "The culture that educates us—the patterns of perception and thought our children absorb in their schools, at every level—is unfriendly (at the least) to the commercial civilization, the bourgeois civilization, within which most of us live and work."[46] The institutions of socialization—those that mold human nature—have become hostile to the society that they by nature should support.

Kristol argues that one of the three great promises of capitalism, along with material well-being and increased personal freedom, was that "amidst this prosperity and liberty, the individual could satisfy his instinct for self-perfection—for leading a virtuous life that satisfied the demands of his spirit (or, as one used to say, his soul)—and that the free exercise of such individual virtue would aggregate into a just society."[47] Self-perfection and the just society were both subverted by the loss of the bourgeois ethos; thus, according to Kristol, society is in crisis. But Kristol seems to argue that we should merely acquiesce in our impoverished state, lest things get worse than they are already.[48] From a conservative standpoint, this solution seems problematic at best. Material goods do not provide a good life. According to Kristol, these goods *can* quiet the passions of the masses so that they will not disturb the peace, allowing bourgeois society to survive. But Kristol himself seems incapable of defending his society on any moral grounds.

Bourgeois society provides material goods but an impoverished life. And the only reason Kristol seems able to give for defending this society is that the alternatives are even worse. The (for Kristol necessarily collectivist) alternatives to liberal capitalism range "from the hideous to the merely squalid."[49] This condemnation of collectivism hardly constitutes a positive defense of contemporary bourgeois society. Apparently we are left, as with Oakeshott, with skepticism and disbelief as the sole foundations of contemporary conservatism.

Kristol effectively points out the self-satisfied hubris of intellectuals who would prescribe utopian projects for a society from which they are almost wholly alienated. His defense of local intervening institutions and personal choice within the confines of preexisting and changing structures clearly owes much to Tocqueville's analysis of human nature and the requirements for its fulfillment. But Kristol's view of contemporary society, imbued as it is with structural/scientific theories concerning the relationship between economics and morality, leaves out a vast portion of human nature and thus human society.[50] The transcendent nature of the human spirit, the role of natural law in determining proper action and the requirements for a good life, are dismissed almost entirely in favor of "practical" material issues. The result, not surprisingly, is an impoverished view of man and society, one that focuses on the poorest elements of human nature—greed and envy—and leaves out many of the noble elements allowing man to transcend his lower nature.

KIRK: VARIETY, BELIEF, AND NORMS

> A culture which abandons knowledge of God in the expectation of creature-comforts already is far gone in decadence.[51]

In stark opposition to Kristol's studied materialism and both Kristol's and Oakeshott's rejection of any temporal role for "dangerous" transcendent moral notions, Russell Kirk proclaims man's need to follow God and the rules he has set down in natural law. Writer, teacher, and leader of the often criticized but undeniably influential traditionalist wing of the conservative movement, Kirk seeks to reawaken us to the importance of our society's norms. "A norm means an enduring standard. It is a law of nature, which we ignore at our peril."[52] Bereft of standards—which can come only from the eternal order set by God—we are left with nothing worthwhile after which to strive. We are left with only our self-indulgent and ultimately empty pursuit of pleasures of the moment and with our bestial attempts to mold the world in our own misshapen image.

For Kirk ours is a sick, or decadent, society. We have fallen away from the eternal standards of natural law into the petty and destructive world of greed and self-love. But Kirk argues that we must reestablish rather than reject an adherence to eternal, transcendent norms so that our civilization may be made healthy again.

> The sanction for obedience to norms must come from a source higher than private speculation: men do not submit long to their own creations. Standards erected out of expediency will be hurled down, soon enough, also out of expediency. Either norms have a reality independent of immediate social utility, or they are mere fictions. If men assume that norms are no better than the pompous fabrications of their ancestors, got up to serve the interests of a faction or an age, then every rising generation will challenge the principles of personal and social order, and will learn wisdom only through agony. For half a century, we have been experiencing the consequences of moral and social neoterism: so, like the generation of Socrates and Thucydides in the fifth century, we begin to perceive that somehow we have acted on false assumptions. No, norms cannot be invented. All that we can do is to reawaken our consciousness of the existence of norms; to confess that there are enduring standards superior to our petty private stock of rationality.[53]

Like Oakeshott and Kristol, Kirk opposes rationalistic attempts to prescribe particular, uniform ends for society. But for Kirk attempts merely to stifle Rationalism, to defeat (through skeptical argument or economic production) the hubris of those who would destroy society in the name of an earthly paradise, are doomed to failure. Man requires transcendent, God-given standards if he is to act rightly. Bereft of natural law, skepticism and material benefits do not inspire the awe necessary to quell the hubris of the would-be founder.

Variety under Natural Law

Kirk's attachment to natural law does not prevent him from rejecting the notion of particular social ends. "Conservatism is not a fixed and immutable body of dogmata; conservatives inherit from Burke a talent for re-expressing their convictions to fit the time."[54] It is important to note, however, that Kirk speaks of "re-expressing" rather than "reinventing" convictions. Natural law is eternal; only its application varies in accordance with the rules of prudence and the requirements of circumstance.

Rejecting all plans for construction of any form of earthly paradise, Kirk argues that man's nature can be fulfilled only within the confines of preexisting institutions, beliefs, and practices. Despite his aversion to definitions or "bodies of dogmata," Kirk argues that "the essence of social conservatism is preservation of the ancient moral traditions of humanity. Conservatives respect the wisdom of their ancestors . . . they are dubious of wholesale alteration. They think society is a spiritual reality, possessing an eternal life but a delicate constitution; it cannot be scrapped and recast as if it were a machine."[55] Kirk then expands this essence into a list of six "canons of conservative thought." These canons emphasize the transcendent order established by natural law, proper affection for variety, and recognition of the need for orders and classes, as well as property rights, respect for custom and convention, and prudence (and a certain skepticism) concerning notions of human perfectibility, rationality, and the search for equality.[56]

As for Burke and Tocqueville, so for Kirk natural law does not dictate a specific, idealized vision according to which man and society must be shaped.

> Government is instituted to secure justice, order, and freedom, through respect for legitimate authority; and if we ask from government more than government can provide, we imperil government's primary functions. The notion that mere political manipulation can make all men happy is one of the sorriest illusions of the liberal era. But some forms of government can make men miserable.
>
> I think that we need to refer to two norms or principles. The first principle is that a good government allows the more energetic natures among a people to fulfill their promise, while ensuring that these persons shall not tyrannize over the mass of men. . . . The second principle is that in every state the best possible—or least baneful—form of government is one in accord with the traditions and prescriptive ways of its people. Beyond these two general norms, there is no invariable rule of politics which may be applied, uniformly, universally, and without qualification, to all societies in all ages.[57]

Tyranny violates natural law, but circumstances, especially those of particular preexisting traditions and practices, dictate variety in man's social and governmental forms. Government is to serve only the limited functions of preventing tyranny and protecting the primary institutions of society—the customary beliefs and practices that form the character of a people. In considering reforms to America's written Constitution, Kirk argues that "we must remind ourselves that beneath any formal constitution . . . lies an unwritten constitution much more difficult to define, but really more powerful: the body of institutions, customs, manners, conventions, and voluntary associations which may not even be mentioned in the formal constitution, but which nevertheless form the fabric of social reality and sustain the formal constitution."[58]

It may be seen as a weakness of Kirk's argument that he offers little in the way of discussion concerning the ways in which custom and manners form human character through habit. His primary concern is with the beliefs that allow for or impede the influence of proper norms of behavior. But, while his central focus is on our spiritual poverty (our declining belief in norms), Kirk recognizes that "our political tradition is rooted in two bodies of belief and custom: first, the Christian religion; second, the English and colonial historic experience in politics, with its fruits of representative institutions, local government, private rights, and the supremacy of Law."[59]

The American political tradition has its basis in practices and beliefs that have grown over time in accordance with circumstance or historic experience. Beliefs and practices are properly formed and modified over time, through interaction with the particular exigencies of particular peoples and locales rather than through the exercise of the petty rationality of individual men. Natural law dictates that we maintain the social fabric— a fabric that may be torn apart by those who do not respect and adhere to customary beliefs and practices.

Kirk's emphasis on the need for prudent responses to varied and changing circumstances leads him to follow Burke and Tocqueville in stressing the importance of local autonomy. Closely following and at times directly quoting Tocqueville, Kirk argues for what he calls (citing Orestes Brownson) "territorial democracy" in the face of "the unthinking centralizer." If the process of centralization goes far enough, according to Kirk, "political permanence in this country may be lost altogether, the American people being launched upon the rough sea of uncontrollable innovation."[60] If the local vigor and autonomy of federalism are destroyed, norms will give way completely to ideological projects against which there will be no defense.

Particularly in America, where there is no "class of men competent to rule wisely," the nation would be set adrift "once territorial democracy and the federal framework (both principal schools of national leadership) should be undone."[61] America is no longer in danger of falling into disunion. "Our peril lies altogether the other way: the triumph of the total centralized state, with the dwindling of local and private vitality, and the extinction of federal order and territorial democracy."[62]

Should Americans continue abandoning vigorous local government in favor of centralized planning, the means of federal leadership and the vital resource of local and private action would be extinguished. In place of local variety and the following of local prescription—customs and manners that have naturally grown and been modified over time— the centralizer would impose his own blueprint for the good society. He would attempt to force his idealized, equalizing scheme upon those unequal men now bereft of the powerful, natural, and local means necessary to oppose him. The result would be unnatural and unjust.

> A domination which confounds popular government with equality of moral worth, equality of intellect, or equality of condition is a bad government. For a good government respects the claims of extraordinary ability. It respects the right of the contemplative to his solitude. It respects the right of the practical leader to take an honest initiative in the affairs of the commonwealth. It respects the right of the inventor to his ingenuity's rewards, the rights of the manufacturer or the merchant to his decent gains, the right of the thrifty man to keep his savings and bequeath them to his heirs. It respects such rights and claims, this good government, because in the enjoyment of these rights, and in the performance of the duties to which these rights are joined, men fulfill themselves; and thus a considerable measure of justice—"to each his own"—is attained.[63]

If we are to fulfill our various natures, the particular circumstances, rights, and duties that make up our various forms of life must be recognized and allowed to flourish. Since our natures are not equal, neither are the rights or duties properly accorded the occupations and circumstances of our lives.

Excessive equality stifles man's natural variety. Yet variety itself requires order: "Until some tolerable political order is achieved, nothing else can be." Order cannot be imposed according to any abstract theory, however. "Order is the harmonious arrangement of classes and functions which guards justice and obtains willing consent to law and ensures that we shall be safe together. Order also signifies the honor or dignity of a rank in society, and it signifies those established usages which deserve veneration."[64] Order is achieved when the variety of natures and circumstances making up any society are accorded their rightful place and respect. Only when each is given his just deserts, only when leaders prudently allow the natural ranks of men to hold sway and find a natural equilibrium, can society exist as a unified whole in which mutual respect and honor are possible.

There remains, for Kirk, a Chain of Being. Our various occupations, circumstances, and ways of life dictate that we be treated in the various manners fitting our particular station. Honor and dignity come only from the performance of the duties belonging to our particular place, and this place is determined largely by venerated, established custom.

Knowledge and Belief

Even the most gifted of men, and always the mass of humanity, must fall back upon normative knowledge, upon tradition and prescription, if they are to act at all in this world. . . . If we are to accomplish anything in this life, we must take much for granted and settled. . . . This is even more true of moral and social first principles. Only through prescription and tradition, only by habitual acceptance of just and sound authority, only by conformity to norms, can men acquire knowledge of the permanent things. Authority tells us that murder is wrong; prescription immemorially has visited severe punishments upon murderers; tradition presents us with an ancient complex of tales of the evil consequences of murder. Now a man who thinks his private petty rationality superior to the wisdom of our ancestors may undertake experiments in murder, with a view to testing these old irrational scruples; but the results of such experiments are sure to be disagreeable for everyone concerned, including the researcher; and that experimenter has no right to be surprised if we hang him by the neck until he is quite dead. For if men flout norm and convention, life becomes intolerable. It is through respect for tradition and prescription, and recourse to those sources of normative understanding, that the mass of human beings acquire a tolerable knowledge of the rules by which private and social existence is made tolerable.[65]

We have both the need and the moral imperative to follow the rules laid down by the wisdom of the ages rather than to rely upon our own limited ability to judge right from wrong. Right and wrong themselves are determined in large part by adherence to preexisting norms as set forth in the beliefs and practices of a given society. We learn how to act properly by respecting and following the authority of existing practice.

Projects that ignore the dictates of prudence in favor of abstract principles are doomed to failure since they ignore the determining role of tradition and local circumstance.[66] But this does not mean that the prevailing opinion of the moment provides the proper standard of behavior. "Ethical normality is determined not by mass behavior at any particular moment, but rather by the custom and consensus of many civilized generations, and by reference to ethical standards long accepted by moralists, jurists, and religious teachers. Similarly, political normality depends upon conformity to long-observed phenomena and rules of the civil social order, not merely upon the conduct of a particular majority in a particular political community in a particular year or decade."[67] A particular majority at a particular time may act abnormally, casting aside the dictates of prudence and the wisdom of the ages in favor of innovation and idealized planning. Majorities, and each of their members, place their very existence in danger by going against the dictates of natural law.

If beliefs properly come from neither current practice nor rationalistic blueprints they must, of course, come from somewhere else. Kirk emphasizes the role of established practice rather than the practice of the moment. He also overtly recognizes the proper role of Burkean prejudice in making "a man's virtue his habit."[68] Yet prejudice, for Kirk, is only one means by which norms are perceived; they are also perceived by revelation and by the "insights of the seer."[69] It is with the role of the seer that Kirk seems most concerned. The seer provides society with its fundamental requirement if order is to be achieved: authority.

> A few men mysteriously endowed with a power of vision denied to the overwhelming majority of us have been the Hammurabis of our moral and political and literary codes. . . . We accept such men of genius as authorities because we recognize, however imperfectly, that they see farther than you or I see. . . . No one appointed them: their strength of mind and eloquence of expression conquered the mass of men. Their authority in part is vindicated by the immense influence which their words have exerted ever since those words were uttered; and in part by the fact that in-

telligent men in every age, upon reflection, have assented to the truths exerted by these prophets and poets and philosophers.[70]

These men of genius see the true nature of things, and we know this because the consensus of intelligent men over the ages tells us that it is so. Most of us, for Kirk, are followers of the few geniuses who have been able to recognize the permanent things, and whom intellectual prejudice—the wisdom of intelligent men over the ages—bids us follow as authorities. Belief is a central factor in our lives, in our perceptions, and in our actions. We must believe in the authority of seers, of the men who have given us the central beliefs of our society (its customs and the foundations of its practices) or we will fall away from the norms according to which any good society must be ordered.

Kirk is more concerned with spelling out the proper nature of our beliefs than with the habitual nature of character formation. Perhaps this is because we have, in his view, lost the beliefs necessary for good character. To obtain the character proper to a good life we must believe in the inherent goodness of the institutions that inculcate this character and in the transcendent, permanent things (most notably the existence of God's law) that give these institutions their ultimate legitimacy.

Kirk considers himself a scholar and a teacher. Thus his primary focus is on the explication of the teachings of the great seers of the past.

Men of letters and teachers of literature are entrusted with a social responsibility; they have no right to be nihilists or fantastic or neoterists, because the terms on which they hold their trust are conservative. Whatever the immediate political opinions of the guardian of the Word, his first duty is conservative in the larger sense of that adjective: his work, his end, is to shelter and promulgate an inherited body of learning and myth. The man of letters and the teacher of literature have no right to be irresponsible dilettantes or reckless iconoclasts; they are placed in their high dignity so that they may preserve the ideas which make all men one, not so that they may indulge an appetite for denigration and a taste for anarchic cleverness. In a time like ours, when the political and religious institutions which kept some continuity in civilization are weakened or broken, the responsibility of the writer and the teacher of literature is greater than ever; it is possible that the only tie with the past which will survive our century may be a literary continuity, just as in the ages which followed the collapse of the Roman state.[71]

Amid the ruins of our hubristic, self-indulgent century, the man of letters and the teacher of literature—all men of the word—must pass on the learning and the myths (by which Kirk means poetic truths and not noble lies) that are the embodiment of the mind of a civilization.

Our intervening institutions are crumbling largely because their legitimacy has been eroded by a self-satisfied, rationalistic skepticism that questions everything save the rational capacities of the questioner. Authority has fallen into disrepute. If the rationalistic attitude should dominate (or continue to dominate) among scholars, the very basis of any decent life would be destroyed. "The aim of great books is ethical: to teach what it means to be a man. Every major form of literary art has taken for its deeper themes what T. S. Eliot called 'the permanent things'— the norms of human nature. Until very recent years, men took it for granted that literature exists to form the normative consciousness: that is, to teach human beings their true nature, their dignity, and their rightful place in the scheme of things."[72] For Kirk, literature teaches us the dictates of natural law. Only through familiarity with the knowledge of our great seers (either firsthand or through the following of the customary beliefs and practices embodying their knowledge) may we learn the requirements for a good life.

Kirk, as well as Oakeshott and Kristol, faces a dilemma in the search for a conservative good life in contemporary society. Kirk finds current practice so abnormal, in such violation of the eternal norms of natural law, that he is left defending the very idea of a patrimony of ideas on which institutions and practices should be built. Rationalistic skepticism and hubris, belief in one's own petty rationality (and disbelief concerning the wisdom of the ages) have called into question, not only the fundamental institutions and practices of any good society, but the very beliefs on which any civilization must be based. The "death" of God at the hands of would-be human deities spells the death of any healthy civilization. Bereft of the transcendent norms of natural law, of belief in the inherent goodness of our given way of life, we are without the means to fulfill our natures. For Kirk, the struggle to reestablish the makings of a conservative good life begins, not with the deed, which seeks to make the world anew, but with the word, which may convince us to reform our own souls in line with the dictates of natural law.

Kirk, Kristol, and Oakeshott believe our society to be very sick. This is at least in part the dilemma of contemporary conservatism: It is difficult to find a conservative good life—a life in which acceptance of that which exists is the basis of right action—in a society that itself seems not to value virtue. For each of these thinkers materialism and selfish individualism, coupled with centralization and the search for ever greater equality, have impoverished our lives. And a spiritually impoverished life—regardless of its material conditions—is not a good life.

Kirk, Kristol, and Oakeshott each seek a way out of our current dilemma, to a community in which some form of accepting virtue is possible. Yet each man approaches our dilemma with different amounts of hope, skepticism, and belief in the power of natural intervening institutions to mold proper characters. Each of these thinkers hesitates to provide any overt guidance as to how we should live our lives. Centuries of idealized planning have made contemporary conservatives extremely reluctant to take upon themselves the task of prescribing particular actions, let alone ways of life. Still, only by arguing for a particular way of life may thinkers help to preserve it or bring it about. There must be a recognition that opposition to idealized programs does not preclude explication of the alternative life of accepting virtue if the conservative good life is to be possible in contemporary society.

7 • The Quest for Virtue

So long . . . as we consider finance, industry, trade, agriculture merely as competing interests to be reconciled from time to time as best they may, so long as we consider "education" as a good in itself of which everyone has a right to the utmost, without any idea of the good life for society or for the individual, we shall move from one uneasy compromise to another. To the quick and simple organization of society for ends which, being only material and worldly, must be as ephemeral as worldly success, there is only one alternative. As political philosophy derives its sanction from ethics, and ethics from the truth of religion, it is only by returning to the eternal source of truth that we can hope for any social organization which will not, to its ultimate destruction, ignore some essential aspect of reality. The term "democracy," as I have said again and again, does not contain enough positive content to stand alone against the forces that you dislike—it can easily be transformed by them. If you will not have God (and He is a jealous God) you should pay your respects to Hitler or Stalin.
—T. S. Eliot

Societies (democratic or not) must derive their legitimacy from the truth of God's law if they are to survive the circumstances of this world. Even the most prudent materialism can provide no defense against the passions and the whims of man. Whatever its political structure, no society can long survive if it substitutes man's will for God's as its guiding force. Bereft of a transcendent ethic by which to order its institutions and practices, democracy itself may well lead to the moral enormities— the tyranny and mass murder—of a Hitler or a Stalin.

Democratic politics are merely procedural. To live under a democratic government simply means that, if one is a citizen, one has the right to vote on major policy issues—or, if one lives in a representative democracy, to vote on who shall make decisions concerning major policy issues. When Tocqueville studied democracy in America, he in fact examined the institutions and practices making up a particular (democratic) society possessed of a democratic government. Other democracies such as France differed greatly from America because their nonpolitical institutions and practices made their democratic societies different.

Tocqueville showed how the democratic desire for equality may lead to tyranny. Tocqueville also showed that egalitarian desires can and must be tamed through the promotion of *proper* equality—equality before the law—and through the maintenance of natural aristocracy and the other structures of virtuous local communities. As for Burke, for Tocqueville men must believe that inequalities of condition have their basis in a higher order that is both just and good if they are to accept and serve their society. The people must accept that their society's inequalities are good lest idealized theories of political equality come to hold sway and lead to the destruction of all inequalities and any possibility for a good life.

For Kirk, "The American people remain, in some ways, the most conservative in the world—even though their conservatism is not so much the product of reflection as it is of habit, custom, material interests, and attachment to certain documents. . . . Our difficulty, indeed, is not just now the clutch of ideology, but rather complacency—the smug general assumption that the civil social order, in essence, always will be for our sons what it was for our fathers."[1]

Conservatives in the twentieth century have hardly been complacent concerning the moral state of the nation. Economic success aside, conservatives acknowledge that American society—and Western Civilization itself—is in very ill health. The influence of transcendent, religious belief has waned in our era of egalitarian materialism; this much has been recognized by conservatives from Oakeshott to Kristol to Kirk. It is this waning of belief—and with it true understanding—that has presented conservatives with perhaps the most difficult question they, as conservatives, may face: How are we to argue for a virtuous life in a society in which the imperative truth of natural law is no longer recognized?

Although Burke and Tocqueville could concentrate on the earthly implications of revelation—on the socializing role of religious habits and practices—conservatives no longer have this luxury. For conservatives today the question of how to accept unvirtuous horizons is very real. Possible solutions to our dilemma seem to be of three sorts: to attempt to construct a life of virtue on a nonreligious basis (Oakeshott), to accept the loss of transcendence and virtue and attempt to make the best of a life that is not truly good (Kristol), or to attempt a reconstruction of the tradition of thought and belief founded on God's law (Kirk). I shall examine each of these approaches in turn.

OAKESHOTT: PRIDE, MYTH, AND VIRTUOUS RESTRAINT

Oakeshott cannot give us any particular program of action for the reconstruction of the good life. Specific prescriptions smack of the unconservative in all circumstances. And Oakeshott's view of the extremely limited role of reason in our lives makes it imperative for him that those involved in practical action refrain from making claims to philosophic truth and that those who claim to be philosophers refrain from prescribing particular actions.

In true conservative fashion, Oakeshott distinguishes between the rules and responsibilities of the philosopher and those of the practical actor. The "theoretician" who ignores this distinction, who has deserted his "modest programme of investigation" and assumed "the office of tutor" to those concerned with practice is a "deplorable character" who

> has no respectable occupation. In virtue of being a theorist he purports to be concerned with the postulates of conduct, but he mistakes these postulates for principles from which "correct" performances may be deduced or somehow elicited. He understands it to be his business to umpire conduct, certifying performances to be "correct" or condemning them as "incorrect" inferences from the theorems of an alleged understanding of conduct in terms of its condition. But since such theorems are incapable of specifying performances, the engagement of the theoretician is a spurious engagement in conduct itself, an undertaking to direct the activities of map-makers, diagnosticians and agents by systematic deception.[2]

The theoretician is guilty of Rationalism. He forms theorems divorced from their proper, practical context and seeks to force practice to conform to his idealized notions. In the guise of theorizing, the theoretician attempts the moral enormity of changing practice (and thus man himself) according to abstract, and necessarily incomplete and faulty, reasoning.

It is important to note that although the theoretician is certainly making a category mistake (confusing philosophy with practice), he is also acting in a manner that is deplorable. The hubris of the Rationalist theoretician endangers the peace of society and threatens its very coherence. His overweening pride leads him to believe that he is capable of prescribing correct actions by virtue of his own reason. His pride leads him to step out of his proper, limited role, making him a bad man.

Refusing to distinguish between good and bad regimes and practices, Oakeshott showed little reluctance in differentiating between men of good and bad ("slavish" or "deplorable") character. It is the weakness of Oakeshott's argument that his extreme skepticism did not allow him to argue for the conservative good life, for the virtue of existing horizons. But he did seek to influence our views and actions through other, less philosophical means. His philosophical skepticism prevented him from appealing to natural law or ("Rationalistic") reason in attempting to argue that existing horizons should be accepted as good. The absence of God and human reason left Oakeshott with yet another means by which to justify accepting society as it exists: myth. Rationalism is the illusion that philosophical knowledge may produce constructive prescriptions for human action; the greatest illusion is the notion that it is possible to dispense with illusions.

Reason, Conversation, and Myth

> We are apt to think of a civilization as something solid and external, but at bottom it is a collective dream. "In so far as the soul is in the body," says Plotinus, "it lies in deep sleep." What a people dreams in this earthly sleep is its civilization. And the substance of this dream is a myth, an imaginative interpretation of human existence, the perception (not the solution) of the mystery of human life.[3]

According to Oakeshott, "The view dies hard that Babel was the occasion of a curse being laid upon mankind from which it is the business of the philosophers to deliver us, and a disposition remains to impose a single character upon significant human speech."[4] The philosophers' goal is very much an imposition, for they would make of human intercourse an inquiry when it is in fact a conversation among "diverse idioms of intercourse" in which "reasoning is neither sovereign nor alone."[5]

Oakeshott's human conversation denotes much more than an "ecological vision of society" in which "society and individual are . . . two aspects of a single reality."[6] True, the human conversation, which by nature has no conclusion, "gives place and character to every human activity and utterance."[7] However, it gives this character, not through some social infusion of personality, but through the exchange, the provocation, the adventure that is itself the conversation. Indeed, only if we have the independence of character to recognize that "it is with conversation as with gambling, its significance lies neither in winning nor in losing, but in wagering"[8] may we avoid the confusion of voices that was the curse of Babel.

Prominent as it has become in Western thought over the last several centuries, Rationalism is both mistaken and ignoble, both foolish and childish. Rationalist practitioners are too caught up in the twin sins of self-love—hubris and the desire for material satisfactions—to recognize that their method makes for neither sense nor the possibility of a truly good life. They lack the maturity to recognize their own natural and proper limitations. Reason itself is a limited faculty, one often incapable of grasping the mythical mystery of human life. We do not reason as a civilization; we dream. To attempt to understand our dream with reason is to misunderstand the nature of civilization. Reason must be kept in its proper place so that our nonrational faculties may take their own places in the conversation of mankind.

Oakeshott recognized that men must have a particular, proper character if they are to accept existing horizons and enter coherently into the conversation of mankind. They must transcend hubris, slavish materialism, and mere fear, for these may lead men to seek the safety, comfort, or false glory of Rationalist projects, and thereby corrupt both society and themselves. Men must have the proper pride necessary to disdain slavish attachments and the self-indulgence of both materialism and attempts to displace that which is with some new foundation.

Oakeshott's man of proper pride is certainly afraid of being publicly shamed, dishonored, and even killed.

> But let us also suppose that the preponderant passion of this man remains
> pride rather than fear; that he is a man who would find greater shame in

the meanness of settling for mere survival than in suffering the dishon-
our of being recognized a failure; a man whose disposition is to overcome
fear not by reason (that is, by seeking a secure condition of external
human circumstances) but by his own courage; . . . not exactly a hero, too
negligent for that, but perhaps with a touch of careless heroism about him.

Now, a man of this sort would not lack stimulus for the vital movement
of his heart, but he is in a high degree self-moved. His endeavour is for
peace; and if the peace he enjoys is largely his own unaided achievement
and is secure against the mishaps that may befall him, it is not in any way
unfriendly to the peace of other men of a different kind.[9]

This man of honor, this almost-hero, maintains his pride by maintaining his independence from the baser actions political life requires. He
achieves peace through his own courage and so provides an alternative
life better than that moved by rational, calculating fear. He transcends
mere reason as he transcends mere slavishness.

This man's independence is not the product of any particular political system or society but of his own ability to remain aloof from communal enterprises, his determination to rely on his own efforts to make
his own achievements. Such a man requires only to be left alone. He
requires nothing from politics save peace and knows this. What differentiates this man from the fearful calculator is his ability to control his
fear and achieve peace through self-restraint rather than mere contrac-
tual agreement. A courageous character provides all that is necessary for
a good (magnanimous and noble) as well as a peaceful life.

Oakeshott's man of good character clearly is not as attached to the
subdivision of humanity to which he belongs as Burke would have him
be. But this man's courage rests largely on his acceptance of existing horizons, allowing him to share in the community that is the conversation
of mankind. Civility is his watchword. He revels particularly in the joys
of art, friendship, and love, and his very detachment from particular purposes leaves him free to participate in calm conversation—the essence
of humanity.[10]

The prevention of philosophical hubris is necessary for the conduct
of the conversation of mankind. Only by recognizing the limits of our
reason may we live the unconfused life of adventure and exchange that
is proper to us. This life cannot be defended on rational grounds since
to do so would be to engage in Rationalism, to contradict both the philosophical and the moral bases of the conversation itself.

According to Oakeshott, the office of literature (including great po-litical literature such as Hobbes's *Leviathan*, for Oakeshott the greatest piece of literature in the English language) in a civilization is "not to break the dream [that is civilization], but perpetually to recall it, to recre-ate it in each generation, and even to make more articulate the dream-powers of a people. We, whose participation in the dream is imperfect and largely passive, are, in a sense, its slaves. But the comparative free-dom of the artist springs not from any faculty of wakefulness . . . but from his power to dream more profoundly; his genius is to dream that he is dreaming."[11] The task and the genius of the artist lie in his ability to en-rich the dream that is our civilization. While most of us are slaves to this dream (capable, at best, of maintaining its coherence), the artist may actually comprehend the dream, may go beyond the surface of limited modes to the moral essence of a people, their nonrational, spiritual being.

Oakeshott's artist at first may appear to be the embodiment of the hubris he purports to oppose, but this artist is no Nietzschean superman. The good artist recognizes that any coherent view of human experience will necessarily be arbitrary (will be true only so long as it is believed), but he will not use his interpretive power to mold experience to the needs of his self-chosen, heroic life—to use history and thus become free.[12] The Oakeshottean artist does not intend to create anything for (or out of) civilization. There is no commanding intentionality to his creation, and his story partly transcends but does not displace the essential, his-torical myth that he is in fact merely retelling in an original way.

The horizons of civilization—its very essence—are given; they are mod-ified through artistic endeavors within the conversation of mankind. Par-ticularly powerful retellings will have a profound effect on those of us who are slaves to the dream (and to the artist's dream within a dream). But historical intimations remain and are followed in most instances even by the artist. The myth itself remains, even if it has changed its course and character somewhat in its windings through the landscape of human history.[13]

The artist's genius is his ability to dream that he is dreaming. "And it is this that distinguishes him from the scientist, whose perverse gen-ius is to dream that he is awake. The project of science, as I understand it, is to solve the mystery, to wake us from our dream, to destroy the myth; and were this project fully achieved, not only should we find ourselves awake in a profound darkness, but a dreadful insomnia would settle upon mankind, not less intolerable for being only a nightmare."[14] Even science, a legitimate mode, is dangerous because of its rational nature. Scientific truth, unchecked, will not be the salvation, but the damnation of mankind. Only myth, the very substance of civilization, may maintain the dream that is the one reality we may know with peace.

According to Oakeshott, the myth of medieval Christianity (retold most powerfully in Hobbes's *Leviathan*) remains *the* myth of European peoples. It is the myth of mankind's fall "from happiness and peace" through the sin of pride, "the perverse exaltation of the creature, by which man became a god to himself."[15] This myth, told many times in many forms, is a perception of the ways in which human lives swing between the two extremes of "pride and sensuality, the too much and the too little."[16] If earlier tellings erred, it was in their partiality for pride; Hobbes, on the other hand, "recalls man to his littleness, his imperfection, his mortality, while at the same time recognizing his importance to himself."[17] Oakeshott sought to convince us of the danger and moral enormity resulting from man's sensuality and his hubristic pride. It is with the taming of human pride, the promotion of *proper* pride so that something noble can come from the prevention of catastrophe, that Oakeshott was most concerned in his own retellings of this greatest of human myths.

The Tower of Babel

It was with the nature and effects of both hubristic pride and slavish materialism that Oakeshott specifically was concerned in two essays, both entitled "The Tower of Babel," appearing in *Rationalism in Politics* and *On History*. In the *Rationalism* essay Oakeshott argued that "the pursuit of perfection as the crow flies is an activity both impious and unavoidable in human life. It involves the penalties of impiety (the anger of the gods and social isolation), and its reward is not that of achievement but that of having made the attempt. It is an activity, therefore, suitable for individuals, but not for societies." The pride involved in attempting a shortcut to heaven, in pursuing an inherently unrealizable perfection, may be noble in the individual. His attempts, though doomed to failure in the long run, constitute a way of life that is good and that is beneficial to society because it provides an example of (eccentric) moral conduct. Social isolation is no great penalty to the man of cultivated independence, and it is the attempt at noble deeds—not their achievement—in which the man of proper character revels. But society cannot afford to be eccentric. While the individual may fall back on society or on his own pride, society requires moral as well as political peace. The search for social perfection results in a "chaos of conflicting ideals" that society cannot survive.[18]

Oakeshott's goal was to point out the category mistake he saw being made by moral idealists. These idealists fail to recognize the poetic nature of human activity—the sense in which, because we only know what we intend by our acts when we have acted, our acts are necessarily nonreflective and habitual.[19] Since the loss of the habituated (affectionate and nonreflective) morality of the early Christians, the pursuit of moral ideals has characterized and confused moral activity in our civilization.[20] The result has been Rationalism and the moral enormities it brings.

The purpose of the myth of the Tower of Babel, as explicated by Oakeshott, is to "disclose the corrupt consciousness, the self-deception which reconciles us to our misfortune."[21] Our self-deception certainly entails the mistaken notion that ideals can prescribe behavior. But at the heart of our self-deception lies a curious though not unfamiliar blend of slavish concern with material benefits and hubristic pride in the powers of human reason. It is this blend of sensuality and improper pride that is the very essence of Oakeshott's chosen myth, a myth he himself retold in the immensely rich concluding story of *On History*.

In Oakeshott's (self-consciously fictional) retelling of the Tower of Babel, the Babelians "have no spectacular vices, and no heroic virtues." Babelians were a rather vulgar, greedy people marked by "an aimlessness and an absence of self-discipline. The Stoic and the martial virtues are notably absent from their character."[22] Their lack of virtue, their fickleness, dislike for authority, and greed—the characteristics of spoiled children—brought about the Babelians' demise. The young Babelian duke, Nimrod —as spoiled and demanding as his subjects—also wanted to have all his needs met. Out of this desire by ruler and ruled to have their limitless demands satisfied arose the duke's grandiose scheme.

Babelians believed that God was the powerful though not "narrow-mindedly righteous" proprietor of a limitless estate, located above the sky, of all that is desirable. Seizing upon this belief, Nimrod asked the Babelians if their frustrations were not the results "of a cosmic conspiracy? Or, if not this, then at least of a criminal distributive injustice?" The duke then proposed that a tower be built that would reach up to this unjust God's great estate so that the Babelians might take by force what God refused to give. God would be ousted, and the Babelians would take his place in a paradise of limitless satisfactions. Now, Babelians having always "preferred to arrive rather than to travel," such a grand, hubristic task might well have been considered by them to be, not unthinkable as evil, but too good to be true. Nonetheless, the project gained their approval. "Some would say that greed had defeated both indolence and sense; others that they had at last found a purpose in life to contain their waywardness and had raised themselves to the status of priests of an ideal."[23] For Oakeshott both statements might be true, the second being no less damning than the first—making Babelians as much the slaves as the priests of their ideal. In Babel, slavish desires and hubristic attachment to an impious social ideal combined to produce a moral enormity.

The building of the tower began in earnest and soon changed the character of Babel and Babelian association. Private convenience was officially declared dispensable in the face of this great project of public good. "And this confirmation of the sovereignty of the *utilitas publica* terminated the civil history of Babel." Everything was sacrificed to the great enterprise of the tower. Education became nothing more than training in tower-building, thus changing conceptions of good and evil to denote relative service to the project. Theology and history were rewritten in accordance with the demands of the undertaking. The military were prepared and the populace polled and researched so as to reflect the importance of the enterprise. Everything private was sacrificed for the sake of the tower, including both public and private buildings torn down for their brick. In short, Babel was changed from a civil association to one whose sole purpose was to achieve the substantive (if illusory) end of storming and stealing heaven.[24]

The one great fear of the Babelians was that their leader was secretly planning to betray them. This suspicion grew until one evening Nimrod was late coming down from his daily sojourn into the tower. Panic spread through the Babelians. "The slogan 'Take the Waiting out of Wanting' had bitten deep into their consciousness. . . . In a moment the entrance to the Tower was filled with running men, women and children. Pounding up the stairway, . . . the entire population of Babel rushed on to snatch the reward of their labours from the hands of a man who they were now convinced was at this moment sneaking into paradise without them, having made a personal arrangement with its proprietor."[25] This mindless, headlong rush resulted, not merely in the destruction of the tower, but in the destruction of the people who had made themselves its slaves. The tower fell to earth, and everyone who was in it—everyone who was a Babelian—died in the crash.[26]

> Many centuries later, when the site of this city, . . . became the object of archaeological curiosity, an excavator . . . came upon an inscription: one of those pathetic messages that sometimes greet us from the past. Evidently it had been composed and incised by a Babelian poet who had lived in the early years of the city's obsession with the bottomless abundance of paradise. It foreboded nothing; it was not a premonition of disaster, but a forlorn comment on the engagement itself. On being deciphered it read:
>
> > Those who in fields Elysian would dwell
> > Do but extend the boundaries of hell.[27]

It is the attempt and not the deed that convicts projects like that of the Babelians of moral enormity. The Babelian project was born of sensuality and hubristic pride. It was motivated by undisciplined desire and by a marked absence of proper, self-regarding, rational fear. Their project resulted in their demise, but Babelian civil association ended the moment the enterprise became the project of the community. The tower, or rather the desire to build a tower and so steal heaven, destroyed Babel long before it fell. It brought to ruin everything that is civilization and put in its place a group of cave dwellers obsessed with the social project that would save them from the unavoidable lot of man. It is man's lot, the impossibility of the satisfaction of limitless human wants, that makes the travel and not the arriving both more noble and more rewarding for those with the reason and the character to recognize this truth.

Oakeshott's story, his retelling of the Hobbesian (Christian, Moslem, *human*) myth of pride and sensuality, is intended to show the fearsome consequences of both of man's great polar sins. Significantly, Oakeshott repeatedly pointed to the character of the Babelians and their leader as that of spoiled children, lacking the maturity and self-regard necessary for moderate forbearance. The need to have everything now, to "take the Waiting out of Wanting," motivated the truly petulant enterprise that consumed Babel.

Only through the self-restraint born of pride, of the desire not to be enslaved by one's passions or possessions but to enjoy the travel rather than the arriving, may Babelian projects be avoided or ended. Only through our acceptance of the meaning (and not merely the logic) of Oakeshott's myth may his lesson be learned. Only by taming our passions and convincing us of the superiority of a prudent, moderate pride may Oakeshott's story teach us the forbearance that is the basis of civil association.

Oakeshott's (poetic) concern was with a moral teaching, one that may convince us where (and that) reason fails to provide either coherence or comprehension, one that seeks to convince us not merely that it is unreasonable to act so as to disturb the peace of civil association but that it is *better* not to do so, one that would have us emulate the man of proper, magnanimous, and horizon-accepting pride for the sake of the life and the peace such emulation provides. The morality of Oakeshott's man of good character is based on acceptance of human limitations and the proper horizons set by the myth in which he believed we live. This acceptance allows the man of proper pride to pursue his own ends without worry or doubt, molesting no one and even achieving personal virtue in the social interactions in which he chooses to engage.[28]

Thus Oakeshott argued through myth for a kind of conservative good life. For him, the man of good character accepts society as it is and tries to maintain its coherence. He seeks this coherence through a life of self-restraint, by not questioning and by not attempting to harness for material ends the beliefs and practices of his people. He is less passionately attached to society as it exists than Burke's and Tocqueville's man of conservative virtue, but he remains attached to it and seeks to serve it in his given capacities, according to the rules and dictates of his particular profession.[29]

Oakeshott's moral prescription, real as it is, is not founded on any argument from objective moral truth or transcendent natural law, however. His argument addresses the passions because he believes that those of us who can and should be enthralled to belief in the myth of our civilization are incapable of recognizing that this myth—this dream—is necessary if the civilization it embodies is to survive. For Oakeshott, reason tells us that there is no objective truth and that dreams must be accepted as if they were true, at least by those who are not artist/philosophers.

This position is logically tenable within Oakeshott's schema: For him, chaos is a disruptive evil that must be combated with myth if independent action is to be possible. Yet the motive force of such an argument is questionable. The modern Rationalist project began with the questioning of the word of God by the reasoning of man. Increasingly since the time of Hobbes—the materialist philosopher on whom Oakeshott's work relies so heavily—intellectuals have dismissed revealed religion as a mere story. But the biblical "myth" succeeded century after century in providing the ordering system of life in the West precisely because it was not seen as a myth but as the word of God. The word of God, for those who believe, is both objective and passionate, true and good. The given way of life may be justified both rationally and morally, for the believer, as the will of God. Lacking a real belief (or faith) in God, it is difficult to see how disbelief in His word and will could be considered sin; such disbelief could at most be criticized as foolish.

Oakeshott wanted most of us to retain—or more properly to regain—belief in what he self-consciously described as a myth while the artist/philosophers who recognize the myth for what it is would enrich it without destroying it. Oakeshott, perhaps somewhat unrealistically, called for a moderate superman. His position rests on the assumption that those who are rational enough to understand his philosophical system are also rational enough to be convinced by his argument that the myth of civilization must be maintained. Oakeshott sought to convince potential artist/philosophers that the good life is one in which the independent man disregards the doings of communal life and engages in the practice of living, reveling in the freedom of action provided by the self-conscious acceptance of mythical horizons. He urged the artist/philosopher not to sully himself with the second-rate activity of politics or to brave the untamed, shapeless whole of experience in order to create what must necessarily be an abomination.

But there is no conservative substitute for the habits of communal affection and the faith on which they rest. Ideal reason may be sufficient to show the propriety of the character of proper pride, but the artist/philosopher clearly has passions at least as strong as the rest of us. By Oakeshott's own account, hubristic, Rationalist passions have been stronger over the last several centuries than have the tame passions his work seeks to promote. The temptation to play God has been difficult to resist for those who do not believe that such play is a sin the true God will punish.

Truth, and perhaps especially the truth that there is no truth (whether or not this is in fact a truth), is a dangerous thing. If the truth of philosophical disbelief becomes dominant, it is difficult to see how Oakeshott's vision of a good life could survive. The beliefs allowing men to be moderate could not operate effectively if they were dismissed as lies. It would seem odd that a philosopher of Oakeshott's skeptical insight should place such faith in the self-restraint of artist/philosophers as well as in their ability to defend as true to the rest of us what they themselves "know" to be a myth. Perhaps, just perhaps, this is why Oakeshott gives us his truth in the form of a myth; something only those who feel myths are important will understand. But then it is not necessary to understand something in order to destroy it.

All this does not necessarily establish that Oakeshott merely sought to "fool" the masses into quiescence so that "great men" such as himself might enjoy the philosophical life of adventure, divorced from the practical needs of the everyday world. Nor is it to say that Oakeshott, as most believe his model Hobbes to have been, was too enamored of the pursuit of particular wants of the moment to give any significant thought to the life of the spirit. As Timothy Fuller has noted, for Oakeshott, "We are caught between contemplation and delight, on the one hand, and the 'deadliness of doing,' 'the *danse macabre* of wants and satisfactions,' on the other."[30] The character and the life that Oakeshott sought to promote were as divorced as possible from the slavish pursuit of material comforts and power.[31] More to the point, man achieves his highest nature neither in material pursuits nor in mere detachment and self-contemplation but in faith.

As Fuller points out, there is no full and coherent religious element to Oakeshott's philosophy, but this does not render his thought irreligious. "His outlook is suffused with a religious character that yields no easy doctrinal formulation because its motive is not to construct propositions."[32] As with all else, so with religion; Oakeshott opposed the notion that man's pursuits may produce particular, practical prescriptions. What religion can produce, however, is the highest form of human experience. "Religious faith is the evocation of a sentiment (the love, the glory, or the honour of God, for example, or even a humble *caritas*), to be added to all others as the motive of all motives in terms of which the fugitive adventures of human conduct, without being released from their mortal and their moral conditions, are graced with an intimation of immortality." The "intimation of immortality" or "encounter with eternity" experienced through religious faith neither changes this world nor, for Oakeshott, enlightens us concerning the world to come.[33] Yet it is the motive behind all human motivations. It is the most important of human wants and desires. It guides our lives because it is their proper goal.

But the source, and the very nature of this motivation and goal, remains in doubt. Oakeshott, writing late in life to a personal friend, expressed his wish that he had begun, before it was "too late," an essay on Christianity, "in which . . . 'salvation,' being 'saved,' is recognized as [having] nothing whatever to do with the *future*."[34] Apparently salvation, like faith, takes place only in the here and now. Thus it would appear that Oakeshott refused to recognize any necessary separation between the spiritual and the material. Fuller argues, in fact, that Oakeshott sought "to grasp historical existence—the meeting of time and eternity" as the essence of human experience. "This is a project, ultimately theological in nature, which Oakeshott always thought of pursuing but never undertook."[35]

The fact that Oakeshott never undertook his theological project, indeed, that religion plays so small a role in his thought that it is only through the remembrances of his friends and his correspondence with them that one can grasp its importance to him, may indicate that he had his own doubts concerning its wisdom or its practicality. If Oakeshott truly rejected differentiation between the eternal and the material, then he was engaged in the immanentization Voegelin condemned, in the rejection of transcendent for merely historical standards for which conservatives are often unfairly criticized.

Oakeshott does argue for a particular human character and for the enduring standards of conduct by which this character is to be judged. It may be the ultimate expression of the spiritual poverty of our age that he could not bring himself to examine thoroughly, in print, the suppositions on which his prescriptions of right conduct are based. Oakeshott, rightly horrified by the results of political prescriptions, was unable to set forth the overt moral prescriptions necessary for the good life because he himself could not recognize the eternal, transcendent truth of natural law. Thus his scattered ruminations upon religion and religious experience point to a love of what is eternal, combined with a refusal to attempt to understand what provides the grace that alone may bless mankind. God's will is made known in this world through revelation and natural law, and if one cannot accept the rule of these transhistorical commandments, one cannot understand the proper nature and goal of man.

KRISTOL'S ACQUIESCENCE AND THE POSSIBILITY OF NEOCONSERVATIVE ACCEPTANCE

Conservatism's central problem today is not that its adherents no longer believe that virtue is good and necessary but that many of them no longer believe that virtue is possible. Kristol has given up the quest for virtue. He has abandoned even the attempt to formulate fully a conception of the good life. According to Kristol, we must accept our unvirtuous horizons so that we may avoid their "hideous" or "squalid" alternatives. Our only course of action, beyond tending to existing arrangements and defending them against their ideological enemies, is to wait and hope for the best. We must wait for some virtuous philosophical "savior" to reconstruct the good life for us. Kristol's vision is truly tragic, for he recognizes that a people bereft of virtue is less than fully human. And an unvirtuous, subhuman people makes for an impoverished, unstable society for which even prudence can provide no reliable guidance.

Acquiescence and Hope

> Liberal capitalism survives and staggers on. It survives because the market economics of capitalism does work—does promote economic growth and permit the individual to better his condition while enjoying an unprecedented degree of individual freedom. But there is something joyless, even somnambulistic, about this survival.[36]

Kristol recognizes and laments the emptiness of a society without virtue. He argues that there is no evident purpose to the survival of liberal capitalism. The bourgeois society he would preserve has no real meaning. Like sleepwalkers, we blindly follow our own self-interest, achieving material well-being and the impoverishment of our souls. Capitalism provides freedom and prosperity even as it undermines the values that make such freedom and prosperity worthwhile.[37]

The question remains: How can one defend a society one does not believe to be good? Kristol is attached to and deeply wishes for a society with meaning. He asks, "Is it possible to restore the spiritual base of bourgeois society to something approaching a healthy condition?"[38]

The hoped for answer is, of course, yes. For Kristol, men cannot "live in a free society if they have no reason to believe it is also a just society."[39] The members of a society must believe that its institutions and practices are right—not just useful and beneficial but morally *right*—if they are to accept and defend that society.

Kristol is not certain, however, that the spiritual basis of bourgeois society may be restored. He merely notes that "all we can say with some certainty, at this time, is that the future of liberal capitalism may be more significantly shaped by the ideas now germinating in the mind of some young, unknown philosopher or theologian than by any vagaries in annual GNP statistics. Those statistics are not unimportant, but to think they are all-important is to indulge in the silly kind of capitalist idolatry that is subversive of capitalism itself. It is the ethos of capitalism that is in gross disrepair, not the economics of capitalism—which is, indeed, its saving grace. But salvation through this grace alone will not suffice."[40]

The society that Kristol would conserve and defend is in fact in need of salvation and not merely preservation. By his own reckoning, Kristol's good society is not good. Bourgeois society is merely the least of possible evils, one that is sustained through economic self-interest but that provides little beyond material goods. Kristol explicitly states that he wishes for more. Salvation must come from a philosopher or a theologian, not from an economist or a sociologist. It must be founded upon notions of what constitutes a truly good life, and this good life requires something more than economic well-being.

A number of problems seem to arise from Kristol's method of defending society as it exists. Egalitarian materialism leaves little room for the natural socializing forces—family, church, locality, and profession—that traditional conservatism values and that teach the virtue whose loss Kristol laments. The welfare state Kristol defends as good and just makes charity (the giving of goods to those in need by those better off) both mandatory and anonymous (a matter of filling out tax forms). The welfare state thus undermines any sense of community and local attachment, as well as the beliefs and practices of local affection at the heart of the good life.

Furthermore, despite his opposition to abstract philosophy, Kristol's materialistic and egalitarian notions seem unconservatively abstract and idealized. They do not grow naturally from the locality upward. Instead, materialism and egalitarianism are pervasive notions that may motivate men regardless of their particular circumstances and that may thereby destroy the customary, localized training grounds of accepting virtue. Materialism and egalitarianism make irrelevant and impotent the natural intervening institutions, intimately connected with circumstance, familiarity, and natural affection, necessary for the teaching of virtue.[41] Moreover, if bourgeois society deprives us of the life of the spirit, leaving us mere sleepwalking survivors, it would seem clear that our nature demands something more than the material prosperity and equality Kristol offers.

Kristol acquiesces in society as it exists, but he does not accept it as good. He wishes us to refrain from questioning our existing horizons even though within them virtue has lost her loveliness. Our duty, for Kristol, is to fend off disaster—squalor and hideousness—while waiting for a philosophical or theological savior to awaken our virtue and end our sleepwalking existence. There is a certain nobility to Kristol's tragic acquiescence, but the hope it offers is rather passive and forlorn.

Kristol's is not the only neoconservative response to the contemporary conservative dilemma, however. Influential as he is, and predominant as is the Weberian view of our society's inherently contradictory nature (with our "economic system" undermining our necessary "cultural values"), at least one neoconservative sees his duty as that of reasserting the transcendent worth of our existing arrangements.

Novak and Corporative Virtue

Neoconservative Catholic theologian Michael Novak seeks to reconstruct the transcendent bases for a life of conservative, accepting virtue. Novak's status as a neo- or welfare-state conservative is beyond question. Accepting the moral as well as the practical claim of poverty to some relief from society at large, Novak states that "social welfare programs fit the logic of democratic capitalism and have a legitimate claim on it."[42] But Novak is much more concerned with defending the virtue of the corporation and of contemporary "Democratic Capitalism" as a whole than with defending the (for him significantly restricted) claims of "social welfare."

Novak is anxious to point out the communal nature of democratic capitalism and of the corporation that is one of its major elements. For Novak the corporation, founded by a community of mutually interested investors to promote their common benefit, is itself a form of local community. "Because a corporation is not an instrument of the state, it does not follow that it lacks social form and social function."[43] Corporations are based on the principles of interdependency and subsidiarity—the making of concrete decisions "on the level closest to the concrete reality."[44] The self-interest of the corporation—even of the chief executive officer of a corporation—must be enlightened if that corporation is to succeed. Immediate self-interest must give way to the interests of the community; it must involve habitual service to others, lest it be self-defeating.

> Consider the life of the chief executive officer of a large corporation. A high proportion of his time is spent in making decisions about personnel and in conveying a spirit of unity, coordination, and morale throughout a farflung organization. Many of the decisions to be reached involve kinds of expertise beyond his own. These become, necessarily, team decisions. Such a manager can scarcely be an autocrat. He must have the trust of many and must inspire many. The more his actions are inspired by all the moral virtues, not excluding all that is intended by the Christian concept of *caritas,* the better his relations with others will be. He depends heavily on such relations, for he is relatively easily replaced. The average tenure in his office is about six years.[45]

As Tocqueville argued that the requirements of local life foster public spirit, so Novak argues that the needs of corporations habituate even their "rulers" to act virtuously, and even charitably. The corporation, for Novak, acts as an intervening institution and so teaches virtue to all its participants. The life of communal affection is available to all who participate in the life of democratic capitalism.

> The ideal of a democratic capitalist society is to guarantee the right of each person to pursue happiness. . . . Thus the system as a whole must be open to enormous variety. It must afford satisfactions at work as well as in free time. Since it is in the nature of humans to be social, the ideal is also to build decent and even affectionate relations among those who work together. For many Americans, there is almost as much friendship and mutuality with colleagues or buddies on the job as in the family. Indeed, for some, there may be a larger store of shared values with workmates than with the whole extended family at Thanksgiving dinner, at which they must sit down with persons whose politics they abhor, whose religious views they cannot abide, and whose occupational biases, ideas, values, and even social class may be far removed from their own. We may within limits choose our communities.[46]

The corporation—the workplace in general in a free, capitalist society—provides intervening socializing institutions that (to some extent) are taking the place of the splintering extended family. The shared experiences and beliefs that make for affectionate, natural attachments no longer reside solely or even principally in the family unit. But these natural relations may still be found, according to Novak, in the workplace—in the self-chosen community.

The workplace provides the sort of community necessary for a good life in Novak's view. It provides commonality and the motivation to act virtuously as well as affectionate attachments that transcend mere self-interest. It produces, in sum, "the communitarian individual." And for Novak, because it nurtures this individual, democratic capitalism is good.[47] In contemporary society the individual chooses his own communal relations, but chooses them nonetheless, and seeks to live up to the dictates of the community he has chosen. Even today man is a social being, and he must live up to the dictates of his occupational community if he is to live his proper, natural life. Thus Novak finds in contemporary society the life of conservative virtue—the life in which man serves the community to which he is attached out of habituated affection, in the capacities dictated by the position (or occupation) he occupies in that society. One's position may vary—in a capitalist society it is supposed to be the product of one's own choice, effort, and ability—but the sense of duty and the need for virtuous service remain.

Novak's reasons for deeming our society good certainly are not impervious to questioning. To call the welfare state virtuous, to say that paying the taxes that sustain welfare programs creates the habit of virtue (particularly in the absence of acts of real, or personal, charity) seems unconvincing on its face. And the community of the corporation, even if it does exist, may be viewed as an imposition upon the life of private and voluntary activity and community. Corporate community may be seen as dictatorial in nature since it is economic in its basis—as an imposition that has a questionable capacity for forming real affections. One need not disapprove of the corporation in order to wish one's personal life to be separate from it.

Yet Novak demonstrates the fundamental conservative impulse to find virtue in society as it exists, which lies at the heart of the conservative good life. To abandon the search for existing virtue is to abandon the conservative project itself—the defense of the good that is. According to Novak, "inattention to theory weakens the life of the spirit and in-

jures the capacity of the young to dream of noble purposes." This admonition seems to apply to conservatism in general. Inattention to the
nature of what is good in our society leads to an inability to set forth the
nobility of that which exists and renders all the more difficult the task
of fostering accepting virtue. "The first of all moral obligations is to think
clearly. Societies are not like the weather, merely given, since human
beings are responsible for their form. Social forms are constructs of the
human spirit."[48] Society may be torn asunder by imprudent theorizing,
whether or not theories actually are acted upon. But an imprudent hostility toward all theorizing weakens our ability to defend society against
those who would destroy its coherence.

Proper theorizing concerns, not how we might make society perfect,
but what it is about society as it exists that makes it worthwhile. To abandon the pursuit of virtue, on whatever grounds, seems then both imprudent
and self-defeating. If society loses its vision of the good life, it loses its
hold on its citizens—its ability to call forth unselfish service to that which
is loved because it is familiar.

KIRK AND THE CONSERVATIVE PATRIMONY

> When the old religious and literary culture trickles away, there is left a
> dreary vacuum, in little towns or in the biggest cities. In that vacuum, civic
> vigor expires. And presently some new system of compulsions is devised
> to substitute for the old voluntary commonwealth and the old loyalties
> of heart and mind.[49]

According to Kirk, the fundamental basis of the life of civic vigor, or
local virtue, lies in the religious and literary beliefs and practices of a
people. Unfortunately, we have ignored our traditions and allowed them
to be questioned and attacked for so long that we have all but lost sight
of them. We have cast ourselves adrift, with only orders from the state
to give us the illusion of proper direction.

While Americans' natural prudence remains, we must not only reclaim
but regain our patrimony, Kirk argues, if we are to make possible once
again any life of virtue. Skepticism and rationalism have deprived us of
the beliefs that make for a good life. Transcendent standards have fallen
victim to material desires and human pride. Kirk sees his task as that of
guiding us back to the traditional and thus natural path that follows the

dictates of natural law, a natural law embodied in the beliefs and practices, not of the moment, but of the consensus of the learned minds of our civilization.

Kirk spends precious little time discussing the particular habits and the particular ways in which affection and habit combine to make possible virtuous action. Kirk does not give any comprehensive picture of a conservative good life in contemporary America. What Kirk clearly is much more concerned to provide is a vision of what is necessary for the reinvigoration of the institutions and beliefs necessary for virtuous acceptance of and service to our given way of life.

Sacrifice and Virtuous Belief

Kirk tells us that our society has the skeptic, the rationalist, and the centralizer to blame for its current impoverishment. Those who question or dismiss traditional beliefs have succeeded in undermining them. Those who set up idealized notions of the perfectibility of man have paved the way for his envy, constant disappointment, and final degradation in merely material pursuits. Those who would solve all of our problems by founding an idealized utopia largely have achieved man's degradation by destroying the diverse, local training grounds of virtue.

Those who have sought to improve our nation through centralized planning have undermined its very legitimacy, for "who seeks guidance in time of crisis from the clerk of the federal district court . . . or the state administrator of the National Defense Education Act? A nation cannot be led by district agents of the Federal Bureau of Investigation, or even by generals operating upon contingent orders from Washington. Obedience and sacrifice, in such circumstances, may be obtained only by men generally recognized as the expression of state and local popular will: the responsible politician, if you will, not the civil servant or the commander of troops."[50]

If government is to promote rather than destroy virtue, it must find its basis in the locality, where loyalty and personal sacrifice themselves are based. The virtue of the citizenry is destroyed, not fostered, by centralized plans aimed at enforcing a uniform system of beliefs and practices on diverse communities. The beliefs and practices of local communities vary according to the dictates of local circumstances. Thus voluntary sacrifice—the only *virtuous* sacrifice—can be obtained from men only through natural, customary channels. One serves that which one loves because it is familiar.

Given Americans' natural independence and local attachments, Kirk argues, further centralization in America would have to rest on force and not on authority. In any "guided democracy," the "energies and loyalties of volition would have been supplanted by the compulsions of a latter-day Jacobinism, or of the Directory." As for Tocqueville, for Kirk tyranny and enervation would work together to degrade mankind.

In order to preserve the possibility of local, virtuous sacrifice, our traditional federal system must be preserved and reinvigorated. To bring this about, "the constitutional structure ought to be buttressed and helped to function." The only other alternative is an attempt to train new leaders for a new system and a new era of centralized coercion. Those who are unwilling to face this choice ("most of the Americans qualified to think about such matters") show themselves "willing to let the norms of politics shift for themselves—which is not in nature."[51]

For Kirk, our fundamental problem lies not so much with our habits or institutions as with our beliefs—or rather with our lack of genuine beliefs. His battle is one for our souls. "For the order of society is merely the order of souls writ large; there cannot be a good society without individual goodness of heart; and that goodness of heart is possible only when human beings perceive, with Socrates, that man is *not* the measure: God is the measure."[52] Our loss of trust in the goodness of God's will endangers our ability to live a good life in a good society. Only restoration of this trust (this "unsuspecting confidence") can restore to us our capacity for virtue.

Philosophy, Belief, and the Natural Order

> "Scientific" truth, or what is popularly taken to be scientific truth, alters from year to year—with accelerating speed, indeed, in our day. But poetic and moral truth changes little with the lapse of the centuries; and the norms of politics are fairly constant. Although virtue and wisdom are not identical, humane letters give to the imagination and the reason a moral bent.[53]

Scientific truth can provide no firm basis upon which to construct a true picture of the world or of our duty to our fellow man. Belief in the power of our independent reason is inherently delusive; it leads us to believe that the world, and not our perception, is inconstant. Only through reacquaintance with the permanent norms of natural law can we regain our ability to distinguish between truth and untruth, virtue and vice.

Our society retains its latent virtue, but our ability to act upon and within its horizons is inhibited by skepticism and by a childish belief in the powers of individual human reason. "We are dwarfs mounted upon the shoulders of giants," Kirk reminds us, quoting Bernard of Chartres. And our precarious position as such makes it foolish, to say the least, to cut the legs out from under our "giants" through dilettantish games of logic and skepticism. Philosophical games succeed only in lowering our own perspective and rendering us incapable of seeing as far as we once could. In such games "faith is destroyed by a Babel of opinions."[54]

Kirk's central concern is with books because it is through them that the norms necessary to any good society are transmitted. Our very natures are formed in large measure by what we read.

> Literature can corrupt; and it is possible, too, to be corrupted by an ignorance of humane letters, much of our normative knowledge necessarily being derived from our reading. The person who reads bad books instead of good may be subtly corrupted; the person who reads nothing at all may be forever adrift in life, unless he lives in a community still powerfully influenced by what Gustave Thibon calls "moral habits" and by oral tradition. And absolute abstinence from printed matter has become rare. If a small boy does not read *Treasure Island*, the odds are that he will read *Mad Ghoul Comics*.[55]

The moral habits that once might have maintained norms cannot serve this function in the era of *Mad Ghoul Comics*. Now more than ever we must rely on habits of good reading. If norms are not transmitted through the teachings of good books they will be corrupted through the teachings of bad books.

Our choice, for Kirk, is clear: normative education or corruption of the very souls of our youth. Thus Kirk thinks it "worthwhile to suggest the outlines of the literary discipline which induces some understanding of enduring standards. For centuries, such a program of reading—though never called a program—existed in Western nations. It strongly influenced the minds and actions of the leaders of the infant American Republic, for instance." The King James version of the Bible, Plutarch's

Lives, Shakespeare, something of Cicero, and something of Virgil played important, normative roles in the formation of the American Republic. These works tempered the actions of the framers (and could temper the character of ourselves and our children) by providing them with appropriate models of conduct and principles of government.

Unlike Burke and Tocqueville, Kirk emphasizes the role of books at the expense of any "moral habits." The normative understanding of the framers did not come solely from books, according to Kirk; "Their apprehension of norms was acquired in family, church and school, and in the business of life."[56] But the role of books was a large one.

> For we cannot attain very well to enduring standards if we rely simply on personal experience as a normative mentor. Personal experiment with first principles often is ruinous, and always is time-consuming; and as Newman wrote, "Life is for action." Therefore we turn to the bank and capital of the ages, the normative knowledge found in literature, if we seek guidance in morals, politics, and taste. Ever since the invention of printing, this normative understanding has been expressed increasingly in books, so that nowadays most people form their opinions, in considerable part, from the printed page.[57]

Kirk's almost exclusive emphasis on the printed page seems to deny him the fundamental basis on which both Burke and Tocqueville argued good character relies. The habits formed in daily interaction with circumstance and with neighbors are not necessarily "personal"; they need not exclude "the bank and capital of the ages." The habits formed in daily activity themselves transmit the knowledge of a people. Intervening institutions form human character, and quell the pride of supposedly self-made men, through the subtle rewards and punishments of manners, the intricate social interactions—with their elaborate rules of proper conduct—that prod members of a community to act properly so that they may gain the approval of their neighbors.[58] Such a view hardly seems a rejection of enduring standards in favor of individualism.

Kirk's failure to restate the traditional conservative emphasis on habit in the formation of proper character seems odd because it makes the institutions and practices he seeks to defend seem less important. If books are the primary transmitters of normative knowledge, then family, church, and locality are not so important a set of socializing institutions as Burke and Tocqueville argued. If books are sufficient to teach us how to act properly, it is unclear what role the habits of social interaction would play in the life of virtue.

Yet Kirk's preoccupation with books is itself a severe commentary on the corruption of our age. Burke and Tocqueville could assume in their audience a familiarity with the great books (and values) of the Western tradition. Today the very notion of a Western tradition is attacked by would-be founders ignorant of both the tradition and the dangers of their increasingly prevalent and intolerant "iconoclasm." The permanent things Kirk is so concerned to preserve—including natural law itself—are being lost beneath a sea of ideological charges of bias and demands for ever more, and ever more equally distributed, material goods. Egalitarian materialism has sapped the life from the very beliefs on which any good society must be based by delegitimizing the tradition of thought at their heart. Habits are essential, but if practice itself has been corrupted we require the aid of inherited knowledge and belief, in the written form, if we are to reconstruct the life of virtue.

Community and Freedom

> The American slum-dwellers may receive very good wages—when they work. Their trouble is that they are the uprooted, socially and morally. They have lost community, and many of them have lost any sort of moral coherence. Their failure, perhaps in the majority of cases, is a failure of will, complicated and in part produced by the destruction of family and the landmarks of community. Often they are the victims of certain public measures allegedly humanitarian in intent—"urban renewal," for instance, which destroys their neighborhoods without creating genuine new communities; and allowances for dependent children which, in application, make the rearing of bastards profitable and create a generation literally fatherless.[59]

According to Kirk, the poor suffer most from the centralizer's programs. Uprooted from their natural communities and given incentives to procreate and rear children outside the most natural of social institutions, the family (today it might be called the "male-headed household"), the poor live without standards. They are cast adrift, bereft of the means by which to judge their own conduct properly.

Kirk provides little in the way of discussion concerning the earthly impoverishment of the poor—the loss of the habits of local sociability. Although he refers to material causes of the poor's loss of will, Kirk leaves the nature of the relationship between circumstance and character largely unexamined. Instead he concentrates on the loss of spiritual community the poor experience in prefabricated buildings, dependent upon prefabricated programs for their sustenance, bereft of the will to forego both in the name of freedom and community.

The poor (not unlike the rest of us) are enslaved to normless centralizers and, more fundamentally for Kirk, to the materialistic rationalism promulgated by these centralizers. Freedom is the rendering of service to God. Thus our freedom and our virtue depend much more on ourselves and on our actions (and thoughts) than on the particular nature of the horizons within which we dwell.[60] Kirk's good life is very much a life of the mind, much closer to that of Aristotle on first glance than to that of Burke and Tocqueville. Yet Kirk does emphasize the natural order upon which any good life must be based. Indeed, "Evil, in essence, is the appetite to undo the natural order of things. It is the glorification of abnormity. And the price one pays for clutching at the unnatural is metamorphosis into a freak, or into a freak-master."[61]

Perhaps the greatest difference between Kirk and Aristotle lies in Kirk's emphasis upon the role, not of individual human reason, but of nonrational truth in transmitting normative knowledge. His educational program is based upon an opposition to both mere logicalism and the straightforward teaching of values. As Burke and Tocqueville emphasized the role of manners in painlessly but surely forming right character, Kirk emphasizes the role of stories (or "fantasies")in teaching truths deeper than those of would-be indoctrinators. "Now the modern masters of fantasy are not myth-makers, for that power expires with the childhood of the race. But fable, allegory, and parable are coming into their own once more; and as it was in the beginning, their purpose is ethical, rousing the moral imagination of a people long ensnared by idols." Analogies and stories that use material objects to convey spiritual meanings "show us the norms for man and society through conjuring up fanciful episodes in which our virtues and vices glimmer as in a looking glass. Were it not for the mirrored reflection, we should not take thought."[62]

Kirk's goal clearly is to make us take thought, to reexamine our beliefs in light of the understanding that individual reason is insufficient to the task of properly ordering our lives. And his project is obviously conservative. He seeks to reinvigorate existing institutions and practices (territorial democracy, traditional Western beliefs, virtuous voluntary service in the local community) by reestablishing our confidence in the God-given truth of natural law.

But, while Oakeshott and Kristol both seem to aim too low for the achievement of the life of accepting virtue, Kirk seems to aim, at least in part, too high. Oakeshott attempted to construct a life of virtue lacking transcendent justification. Apparently for him there is no natural law, there are only myths (seemingly, for Oakeshott, corollaries to Plato's noble lie) by which men should order their lives. The good life is achieved through the acceptance of what is clearly a myth (at least to the artist/philosopher) in the name of coherence, independent achievement, and proper pride.

Kristol seeks to maintain horizons he does not feel to be virtuous (although they seem justified in material terms). Our society's virtue lies in its material productivity, and we should acquiesce in it as a system that is not good but that lacks the squalor or hideousness of its alternatives. The hope is that some future philosopher or theologian will provide the necessary transcendent justifications for existing institutions and practices. It is this constructive task that Michael Novak undertakes, beginning within the horizons of democratic capitalism and within that most maligned of institutions, the corporation. He attempts to justify our existing intervening institutions on the ground that they foster virtue. The corporation has taken over, in part, the socializing role abandoned by the splintering extended family. Thus the corporation's character must be examined in light of its capacity to promote right action. Novak defends the corporation because he sees it as good and because it promotes a life of virtue within our existing set of institutions, beliefs, and practices.

Kirk is concerned most with the nature of our beliefs. Although intervening institutions are mentioned and defended as good, they are clearly subordinate to the transcendent beliefs that justify any given society. Perhaps Kirk's approach is a comment upon the existing state of our society; perhaps he feels that our institutions and practices are so corrupt that he must go beyond them to our very fundamental beliefs in order to reconstruct the bases of accepting virtue. Nonetheless he defends our fundamental institutions and practices; his goal is to reinvigorate, not to replace them.

The beliefs Kirk espouses are indeed fundamental to any conservative good life. But it would seem wise, given his desire to reinvigorate existing practices, for Kirk to place more emphasis on the interdependence of belief and practice, as explicated by both Burke and Tocqueville. In their view, man believes, in large measure, that which he does. Practice, habit—the factors forming our character—affect most men far more directly than does philosophy. And the tools of habit are necessary to combat the (rationalist) philosophy that undermines man's confidence in the good that is, by pointing out its logical fallacies.

Kirk clearly is concerned that we have the beliefs necessary to order our lives. But our lives themselves also must be ordered, according to Burke and Tocqueville (and Oakeshott and Kristol and Novak as well), if we are to be able to believe in what is right. The complex interaction between habit and reason must be mastered and fostered if the good life is to be possible. The all-too-common emphasis on man's material needs has sundered the fundamental link between normative belief and worldly action, a link that must be reforged in spiritual terms, taking into account the habitual nature of human character, if we are to reconstruct the life of accepting virtue.

The conservative good life remains elusive, but skepticism and materialism clearly do not provide the means with which to rebuild it. A fundamental truth is recognized by all the conservative thinkers whose work has been examined here: Man can conserve only what he can defend, and he can defend only what he believes, in his heart, to be good. What is needed in all political philosophy—today more than ever—is the humility to admit man's need for transcendent, objective moral truth. Courage is also needed if we are to submit to the rigors involved in reestablishing our recognition of the imperative truth of natural law, a law according to which justice is more than the equal distribution of sleeping pills.

Conclusion: The Material and the Eternal

Despair is an improper attitude, even in the face of the corruptions of our time. Man is not destined by God to pursue the "rewards" of envy and base appetite. The egalitarian materialism from which we suffer is the product of our own selfish choices—arrived at through our own free will. Providence may have dictated increasing equality, but man is no mere plaything of historical forces. We chose to undermine the standards of our civilization because they pronounced (and still pronounce) selfish materialism— and the self-idolatry at its root—to be bad. We chose to undermine our communities, our religious beliefs, our very families, in the name of an individual "growth" that is nothing more than a hypocritical mask for arrogant self-indulgence. We have, like good Babelians, redefined the institutions, practices, and beliefs of our society to make them serve our project of establishing a materialist paradise on earth.

Having chosen our own degradation, we may also choose our own salvation, but the second task will not be so easy as the first. Our degradation required only that we allow our base instincts to hold sway and to direct the rational intellect we mistook for the proper guiding force of life. To undo the damage done by our rationalistic hubris will require much more than the pragmatic tinkerings of would-be reformers. The corruption of our institutions is the product of a deeper corruption, that of our hearts. The change that is required today is one in the hearts (and *thence* the minds) of the people. Recognition that there are standards of conduct decreed by a higher power than the man in the street, the legislature, or the Supreme Court is the essential foundation of any proper reconstruction of virtue in our society.

To recognize the ordering power of religious belief is not enough. Oakeshott argued that religion plays an important role in human life, but his religion seems to be little more than another sleeping pill. "While religious faith may be recognized as a solace for misfortune and as a release from the fatality of wrongdoing, its central concern is with a less contingent dissonance in the human condition: namely, the hollowness, the futility of that condition, its character of being no more than 'un voyage au bout de la nuit.' What is sought in religious belief is not merely consolation for woe or deliverance from the burden of sin, but a reconciliation to nothingness."[1]

Religious truth, for Oakeshott, is little more than the truth of the existentialist's pit. The great truth, to which great men must be reconciled and from which most of us must be protected through myth, is that life ultimately has no higher meaning. Thus, bereft of faith in a transcendent, ordering God, the best even as brilliant a man as Oakeshott can offer us is the supposedly uncorrupted pursuit of earthly adventures—within the confines set by traditional belief. But conservatism is, and must be, more than the promotion of a peace enabling us to pursue our wants of the moment (which may include short-lived "encounters with eternity"). Conservatism is concerned intimately with the promotion, not of mere peace, and not of whatever institutions, practices, and beliefs happen to exist, but of the good life.

Societies are good and worthy of conservation if they allow for and promote a life of accepting virtue. If the people of a society are able to accept the existing institutions and serve them out of affection rather than out of mere self-interest or fear, on the basis of their own judgment and within the dictates of their given station in life, then this society is good. This vision of the good society must be maintained if conservatives are to reinvigorate the elements necessary for a good life.

The conservative good life requires a society that promotes recognizable stations and rules of conduct that may be fulfilled by men—of good will, to be sure—who are nonetheless neither angels nor saints. These stations and rules of conduct must also be authoritative. They must be such that men of good will, followers whenever possible of natural law, will recognize them as just, thus allowing men to fulfill their natures through affectionate attachments in family, church, and neighborhood.

The goal of a conservative good life and the very existence of a conservative political philosophy go unrecognized because they do not demand—indeed explicitly reject—detailed, rationalistic definition. The specifics of the conservative good life by nature are few in number. Conservatism requires respect for local prerogatives, concerning itself with promoting an atmosphere in which the duty to do unto others as you would have them do unto you will be recognized and acted upon. Local freedoms, well-ordered liberty, and means for advancement through the provision of public service (broadly defined) are essential practical elements to the conservative good life. But natural law provides standards of right conduct, not blueprints for utopian constructs. Above all what is needed is an attachment to virtue—to eternal standards of right conduct—in the face of material circumstances.

It is not the case that conservatism values all that exists, merely opposing all attempts at change. Skepticism alone provides neither the proper criteria by which to judge existing societies nor the appropriate basis on which to construct an adequate, accepting defense of any given way of life. Skepticism must be tempered and supplemented by considered thought and argument concerning the nature of man and the role of existing institutions, beliefs, and practices in fostering right action. Human reasoning must recognize and take place within the confines of transcendent, eternal standards as well as the exigencies of particular circumstances.

That conservatives find much of which they disapprove in contemporary society is not surprising, nor is this disapproval necessarily unconservative. Burke himself was considered a political reformer, seeking changes in the structure of parliamentary and royal offices in order to combat corruption, increase the legislature's independence, and bring rewards more in line with service to the community—to encourage virtuous public service.[2] Burke did not believe that English society was perfect. Some aspects of his society required reform so that impediments to virtue, that is, interferences with the good life, might be mitigated. Reform is not uniformly bad. Like statesmanship itself, reform is an art that must be practiced with care and with attention to the requirements of a coherent and stable life.

In speaking on behalf of his plan for economic reforms, Burke argued that

> whenever we improve, it is right to leave room for a further improvement. It is right to consider, to look about us, to examine the effect of what we have done. Then we can proceed with confidence, because we can proceed with intelligence. Whereas in hot reformations . . . the whole is gen-

erally so crude, so harsh, so indigested, mixed with so much imprudence and so much injustice, so contrary to the whole course of human nature and human institutions, that the very people who are most eager for it are among the first to grow disgusted at what they have done. Then some part of the abdicated grievance is recalled from its exile in order to become a corrective of the correction. Then the abuse assumes all the credit and popularity of a reform. The very idea of purity and disinterestedness in politics falls into disrepute, and is considered as a vision of hot and inexperienced men; and thus disorders become incurable, not by the virulence of their own quality, but by the unapt and violent nature of the remedies.[3]

Amid the clamor for "substantive justice," Burke's warning may show us the error of our ways. The attempt to cure the ills of the world—itself inherently prideful and dangerous—may lead to the destruction of our very society. Once the appetite for wholesale reform is stimulated, principles of civility and decency are cast aside as inconvenient; traditions of belief and practice are derided as reactionary and corrupt. The intemperate and foolish attempt to see to it that all men are treated in a perfectly just manner soon degenerates into a mocking parody of past injustice. The attempt to achieve equality of opportunity by judicial and bureaucratic fiat soon becomes the glorification of a "diversity" hostile to all standards save that of material equality. The cry for a mandated fair shake becomes the demand for an equal and unprincipled ("nonjudgmental") distribution of material goods. All men are degraded, not least because issues of justice and our duties to one another are lost in mutual resentment and conflict over the goods of material life.

"Society" cannot be just. "Society" is a descriptive abstraction used all too often to hide the replacement of material relations for the true basis of civilized life: friendship. Aristotle argued that friendship (*philia*) permeated the activities of any proper polis, from day-to-day commercial transactions to the most fundamental interactions of family life. Men *must* have a store of good will for their neighbors if they are to forgive inevitable human failings. Only acceptance and forgiveness make possible the daily sacrifice of narrow self-interest necessary for any civilized life.

Mutual affection, the heart of any good life, cannot exist if statistical distributions of racial, ethnic, or gender groups in given professions or economic classes (or any other redundantly statistical abstractions) are taken to be questions of justice. The desire to create a statistically defined materialist heaven on earth, by forcing all men to conform to a rigid and uniform conception of the good, poisons the heart as it deadens the mind to any realization of the true end of man. The desire to take the waiting out of wanting leaves life itself wanting. The destruction of traditional standards of conduct in the interest of material ("substantive") results corrupts the very idea of virtue and makes all but impossible the local diversity necessary for the good life.

The conservative is not faced with the choice of taking society exactly as it is or abandoning it. The conservative's duty is to find what is good in society and to protect and promote it. And prudent reforms that are in keeping with preexisting norms are an acceptable means of protecting and promoting the good. Kirk and Novak may argue conservatively for a rebirth of true philosophy, of investigation into the nature of the good and the right in (and of) our society. Indeed true philosophical thought is *required*, even in the view of a seemingly antiphilosophical conservative such as Kristol, if virtue is to be possible once again. Only the "philosophical" reconstruction of accepting virtue can provide the basis for the prudent reform needed in the face of our given circumstances. We require reform that does not call into question the unsuspecting confidence of the people in the goodness of their society. We require reform that maintains the essential link between the transcendent (the angelic realm mortals cannot achieve fully) and the merely material (the beastly realm to which those who aim too high and those who stoop too low in satisfying material desires necessarily must sink).

There are occasions when the conservative may despair of his ability to defend virtue in his society; he then must retire from the field of battle. Such was the case with Tocqueville after Louis Napoleon's coup d'etat. Tocqueville refused to associate himself in any way with Louis Napoleon after the latter dispensed with constitutional government and founded a personal, destructive, and ultimately short-lived dictatorship. Because Louis Napoleon had destroyed free and constitutional government, and as dictator controlled all of public life in France, Tocqueville felt constrained to retire to private life.[4]

When virtue is made impossible in public life, the conservative may abandon public life altogether, preserving his own honor even if he is incapable of preserving the honor and virtue of his society. But such abandonment is (and should be) the exception rather than the rule, even today. Our society is excessively dependent on the state and hostile toward the intermediate institutions necessary for virtue. Indeed our society, with its centralized administrative and welfare state, along with its blind adherence to idealized egalitarian notions, has come at least dangerously close to falling into the twin traps of soft despotism and tyranny of the majority about which Tocqueville warned. Yet the conservative still need not wholly abandon either virtue or our society. Rather than making materialist apologies for economic liberty, the conservative may seek to render coherent and fully active the virtues of liberty. Moderate reforms aimed at ameliorating improper impediments to local community—reforms aimed at strengthening the life of virtue—themselves are conservative in nature.

The proper aim of conservatism is to formulate a vision of the qualities in our society that make it worthy of conservation. The conservative must not merely defend society as it exists from reformist destruction. He must understand the conservative good life in order to promote it. We need, then, not so much a concrete set of policy proposals (many such are available) as a greater emphasis on coherent thought concerning the proper bases of the good life under current circumstances. We need thought that faces the circumstance of contemporary egalitarian materialism (and its institutional embodiment in a centralized administrative and welfare state) so as to defend intervening institutions and the accepting virtue they foster. Such an understanding accepts significant restraints on human thought and action, but it also recognizes the dignity of man and his need for a society that fosters—in some sense *requires*—virtuous action if his dignity is to be maintained.

THE CONSERVATIVE JOURNEY

The conservative is not an advocate of inaction and immobility, but he wishes the journey of life to traverse the immediate neighborhood, in mind as well as in body. He wants to find what is good in what is local, to find his enjoyments with those who are near and therefore dear to him. He seeks to take life's journey within a society that provides a familiar, affectionate community. Such a life is not without movement or activity. It most assuredly is not a life without virtue.

The particular structure of a particular society is not the central issue for the conservative. The good life, the life that allows us to live up to our potential, is his goal. Conservatives have defended caste-system India, traditionally Catholic Ireland, the mixed government of Great

Britain, revolutionary America, Jacksonian America, and even corporate America. There is a conservative vision, not of what the perfect government would be, but of what makes for a good life. What we must reconstruct, if this vision of the good life is to become in some sense a reality, is not a particular political system, but our understanding of and our desire to achieve virtue.

The conservative good life is not beyond criticism. Some may see the customs, attachments, and prejudices of its close-knit communities as intrusive or even servile. Caste systems may be social rather than political in nature, but they still infringe upon individual rights and distribute status and material rewards according to something other than that combination of talent and effort (and, of course, luck) that produces success in our own society. Caste systems prevent men from fulfilling their own potential in the name of preserving social stability.

Our own egalitarian circumstances present conservatives with a particularly difficult dilemma. Tocqueville saw equality as a mixed blessing. It is just because it does not award honor in as arbitrary a fashion as does aristocracy. It is dangerous because it may eliminate free thought and all forms of diversity through its promotion of materialism and the desire for conformity. To emphasize prejudice or unthinking belief as conservatism does, particularly in times of egalitarian materialism, may be to court the soft despotism Tocqueville so feared.

The conservative must treat with equality because it is an essential element of contemporary society. Basic egalitarian structures such as the welfare state and the almost infinitely malleable notion of equality of opportunity (which may be used to justify the affirmative-action programs conservatives oppose as well as the educational programs many of them support) have become integral, almost unquestioned parts of the administrative structure of our society. And egalitarian materialism and its concomitant social structures undermine the very bases of virtue. As Charles Murray points out, "Communities exist because they have a reason to exist, some core of functions around which the affiliations that constitute a vital community can form and grow. When the government takes away a core function, it depletes not only the source of vitality pertaining to that particular function, but also the vitality of a much larger family of responses."[5]

The centralized functioning—the abstract, impersonal, and mandatory charity—of the administrative and welfare state undermines the basic functions and so the very existence of local communities. The detailed regulations and dictates of such a state bind the individual to no one and replace personal attachments with impersonal (and amorphous) rules and duties. Since these rules and duties are aimed only at functional ends (efficiency and the redistribution of wealth), they render both community and individual "dysfunctional." It is the conservative's practical task to modify the contemporary state so that local community may be reconstructed. The particulars of policy positions are beyond the scope of this work, but it seems clear that any conservative acceptance of a welfare state must recognize its twin dangers: its emphasis on egalitarian materialism and its tendency to foster abstract notions that are opposed to local attachments. The welfare state itself is also a sign of lost virtue, for it reflects a desire on the part of recipients to redefine charity as a right (and thereby escape responsibility for their own actions) and a desire on the part of those who once tended the needs of the poor to dispense with the inconveniences of charity—the time, effort, and affectionate service true charity entails.

Tocqueville praised Americans for tempering the egalitarianism of their society with local participation and particularly with an accepted natural aristocracy. So long as public assistance is considered a matter of abstract right rather than of local duty, no natural aristocracy can function. Without some form of Great Chain there can be no eternal links between men. Mandatory charity must at least be local and meaningfully personal if habit is to breed affection and affection virtue.[6]

THE CONSERVATIVE CHOICE

The conflict between visions of right action—of what makes for a good life—lies at the heart of differences in political philosophy. One's choice of political philosophies—of views of the nature and meaning of life—necessarily is based on the belief that the vision one chooses provides the means for a good life. To choose on any other basis simply does not make sense. Such a choice denies the validity of choice itself because it denies the value of the search for what is good.

There are indeed choices in this life, and these choices are philosophical as well as practical. The conservative choice properly involves consideration of the elements in our society that constitute a virtuous journey through this life. Such thoughts may make certain reforms in existing structures appear useful, but the more important task is to encourage a particular kind of thought, a certain (accepting) attitude toward that which exists. Only on the basis of such an attitude may conservative reform and virtue itself exist.

It is understandable that some should despair of America. Virtue is not easy to find in a culture of selfishness, a culture in which personal responsibility and the proper demands of the community are subjugated to convenience, self-indulgence, and envy. But man's selfish nature is not the product of modernity; it is an integral aspect of his nature. If we are to fulfill our own duties to our community we must seek, in whatever ways we can, to reawaken the nobler side of man's nature to the pressing needs of the community and of the individual spirit.

This is not a hopeless task. Americans, more perhaps than any other people, have a vast store of decency that has seen them through times of trouble and times of temptation. We are a confused people. Having been told that it is our duty to guarantee, through centralized state programs, a "minimum" standard of living to everyone, we have come to confuse regulatory schemes for "systems" of caring and justice. Yet the impulse to do right, to love our neighbors as ourselves, remains alive within our people. It must be encouraged and fostered.

The solution to our dilemma lies not in new legislative schemes but in a call to service. After decades of mass murder, impoverishment, and degradation, the fallacies of Marxism—the reductio ad absurdum of egalitarian materialism—have become apparent to all but the most myopic and self-involved intellectuals. Despite mass rejection of its methods, the *goals* of Marxism—after all merely the most virulent form of the prevalent sickness of our age—continue to enthrall. Even with the hopeful signs coming from the fall of despotism in the East and the resurgence of long-suffering communities there, it would be foolish to suppose that changes in political systems will solve the problems of mankind. Today man requires, more than at perhaps any other time, not a change of system but a change of heart.

Tocqueville, whose life and times gave him more right than most to despair, warned the pre-1848 governors of France of impending disaster. But, while he endorsed prudent reforms, Tocqueville pointed out that "I am not, gentlemen, so mad as not to know that no laws can affect the destinies of nations. No, it is not the mechanism of laws that produces great events, gentlemen, but the inner spirit of the government. Keep the laws as they are, if you wish. I think you would be very wrong to do so; but keep them. Keep the men, too, if it gives you any pleasure. I raise no objection so far as I am concerned. But, in God's name, change the spirit of the government; for, I repeat, that spirit will lead you to the abyss."[7]

Both man and society are held together by the spirit. If the spirit of our society is changed, the laws will follow, for we then will have the ability to change laws as we ought. Ours is a corrupt society, one mired in materialist thought and practice. To change the hearts of men, to persuade them that they have lost and must regain a precious heritage of belief and practice, would be no easy task. But to fail even to make the attempt, to despair and resign from society altogether, unless one resigns from temporal life itself in pursuit of God, is to fail to do God's will. It is to deny that man was made to be perfected by society, and by his attachment to his society.

To promote affirmation in a time of cynicism, in a time during which iconoclasm has formed a new and intolerant intellectual orthodoxy, is to be truly "revolutionary." But such promotion is the essence of conservatism. We must understand *and cherish* whence we come so that we may determine in which direction we should travel in the journey of life, and in our attempt to extract ourselves from our current predicament.

There remains virtue in our society. There remain men willing and able to promote virtue. There remains even a reservoir of good will and civility ready to come to the fore—if called upon. Thus the good life remains possible even in the seeming twilight of Western Civilization.[8] The oncoming night of envy and selfishness, of egalitarian materialism, will fall only if it is allowed to fall. The fault for our current dilemma, and for the oncoming night if we fail to change heart, lies and will lie nowhere else but in our selves. The price man has always paid for his free will is that of suffering from his mistakes; it was perhaps to escape this truth that man cast himself under the spell of egalitarian materialism in the first place. But man remains free to reshoulder his responsibility for himself, and for his neighbor, and so make possible his own salvation.

Notes

INTRODUCTION

1. Certainly there are partial exceptions. Natural law thinkers such as Russell Kirk and Peter Stanlis occasionally comment on the contemporary conservative movement; see, for example, Kirk, "Enlivening the Conservative Mind," *Intercollegiate Review* 21 (1986): 25–28. But, overall, studies purporting to give a comprehensive view of all or part of contemporary conservatism concern themselves primarily with policy positions and conservative opposition to reform; see, for example, Charles R. Kesler's introduction to *Keeping the Tablets: Modern American Conservative Thought*, ed. William F. Buckley, Jr., and Charles R. Kesler (New York: Harper & Row, 1980); George H. Nash, *The Conservative Intellectual Movement in America since 1945* (New York: Basic Books, 1976); Clinton Rossiter, *Conservatism in America: The Thankless Persuasion* (New York: Vintage Books, 1962); Peter Steinfels, *The Neoconservatives: The Men Who Are Changing America's Politics* (New York: Simon & Schuster, 1979); and Noel O'Sullivan, *Conservatism* (New York: St. Martin's Press, 1976).

2. Ralph Waldo Emerson, *Essays & Lectures* (New York: Library of America, 1983), 189.

3. Eric Voegelin, *The New Science of Politics* (Chicago: University of Chicago Press, 1952), 110.

4. Ibid., 129.

5. Ibid., 120.

6. Ibid., 178.

7. Ibid., 179.

8. Ibid., 132.

9. Leo Strauss, *Natural Right and History* (Chicago: University of Chicago Press, 1953), especially 176–77.

10. Ibid., 186.

11. Ibid., 188; fittingly enough, Strauss quoted Burke in making his point.

12. Ibid., 184.

13. Ibid., 189.

14. Strauss, *Natural Right*, 36–44; Voegelin, *New Science*, 13–26. It is interesting to note that Voegelin saw opportunity in the unquestioned status of Weberian "demonic" standards. Appeal to hitherto neglected standards—no less logically compelling than those of the social sciences—might, for Voegelin, be used as the logical basis for a reversal of scientific nihilism.

15. See Voegelin, *New Science*, 124.

16. Ibid., 122.

17. Strauss, *Natural Right*, 171–73.

18. Leo Strauss, *Liberalism Ancient and Modern* (New York: Basic Books, 1968), viii; see also chapter 1 of this book.

19. Voegelin, *New Science*, 188.

20. Any full study of Voegelin's and Strauss's views of the proper response to the contemporary conservative dilemma would require not only an extensive discussion of their historical arguments but also a piecing together of scattered and at times intentionally obscure references and unfinished writings in an attempt to reconstruct a prescriptive argument for change. I am not saying that such a project is not worthwhile—I do, in fact, discuss Strauss's view of the proper role and importance of philosophy in chapter 1—but a full discussion of these works constitutes a separate project from this one.

21. On Burke see, for example, C. B. MacPherson, *Burke* (New York: Hill & Wang, 1980), and J. G. A. Pocock, *Politics, Language and Time: Essays on Political Thought and History* (New York: Atheneum, 1971). Frederick A. Dreyer even claims that Burke is a disciple of John Locke; see *Burke's Politics: A Study in Whig Orthodoxy* (Waterloo, Ontario: Wilfrid Laurier, 1979). On Tocqueville see, for example, E. J. Hobsbawm, *The Age of Revolution: 1789–1848* (New York: New American Library, 1962). L. L. Wade, in "Tocqueville and Public Choice," *Public Choice* 47 (1985): 491–508, argues that Tocqueville's reliance on self-interest essentially defines his thought and project.

22. On Burke see, for example, Frank O'Gorman, *Edmund Burke: His Political Philosophy* (Bloomington: Indiana University Press, 1973). Antecedents of this view are many. Historian Lewis Namier pictures Burke as an out-of-power politician whose sole concern, like all such politicians, is to acquire political position; see especially *The Structure of Politics at the Accession of George III*, 2 vols. (London: Macmillan, 1929). John MacCunn, in *The Political Philosophy of Burke* (London: Edward Arnold, 1913), argues that Burke was a forerunner of Bentham. The view of Burke as a utilitarian has its origins in Henry Buckle, *The History of Civilization in England*, 2 vols. (New York: D. Appleton, 1875). On Tocqueville see, for example, Marvin Zetterbaum, *Tocqueville and the Problem of Democracy* (Stanford, Calif.: Stanford University Press, 1967), in which Tocqueville's views of natural law and of justice itself are interpreted in terms of material interest. See also Max Lerner, "Tocqueville's *Democracy in America*: Politics, Law and the Elite," *Antioch Review* 25 (Winter 1965–66): 543–63. Jean-Claude Lamberti, in *Tocqueville and the Two Democracies*, trans. Arthur Goldhammer (Cambridge: Harvard University Press, 1989), argues that Tocqueville's central concern was to oppose the "revolutionary spirit" in France while

reconciling increasing governmental activity with the structures and mores of (for Lamberti) a pluralist, egalitarian, and largely interest-based liberty. See also Raymond Aron, *Main Currents in Sociological Thought*, vol. 1, trans. Richard Howard and Helen Weaver (Garden City, N.Y.: Doubleday, 1968), and Jack Lively, *The Social and Political Thought of Alexis de Tocqueville* (Oxford: Oxford University Press, 1962), for the view that Tocqueville was an early theorist of the (sociological) workings of pluralism.

23. See, for example, Russell Kirk, *The Conservative Mind from Burke to Eliot*, 7th ed. (Chicago: Regnery, 1986); Peter Stanlis, *Edmund Burke and the Natural Law* (Ann Arbor: University of Michigan Press, 1958); Gerald W. Chapman, *Edmund Burke: The Practical Imagination* (Cambridge: Harvard University Press, 1967); and Harvey C. Mansfield, Jr., *Statesmanship and Party Government: A Study of Burke and Bolingbroke* (Chicago: University of Chicago Press, 1965). Burleigh Taylor Wilkins, in *The Problem of Burke's Political Philosophy* (Oxford: Clarendon Press, 1967), argues that Burke was a natural law thinker, but Wilkins further argues that Burke recognized the legitimacy of Lockean natural rights. The result, ultimately, is a collapsing of conservatism into a rather hesitant liberalism.

24. See, for example, Russell Kirk, *Conservative Mind*, and J. P. Mayer, *Alexis de Tocqueville: A Biographical Essay in Political Science*, trans. M. M. Bozman and C. Hahn (New York: Viking Press, 1940).

25. See, for example, Bruce James Smith, *Politics and Remembrance: Republican Themes in Machiavelli, Burke and Tocqueville* (Princeton, N.J.: Princeton University Press, 1985). See also John P. Diggins, *The Lost Soul of American Politics: Virtue, Self-Interest and the Foundations of Liberalism* (Chicago: University of Chicago Press, 1984), and Roger Boesche, *The Strange Liberalism of Alexis de Tocqueville* (Ithaca, N.Y.: Cornell University Press, 1987), for treatments of Tocqueville that present him as a liberal with certain republican proclivities.

26. Chapman, *Edmund Burke*, provides an excellent discussion of these major issues of Burke's career.

27. For a comprehensive treatment of Tocqueville's career, see Andre Jardin, *Tocqueville: A Biography*, trans. Lydia Davis with Robert Hemenway (New York: Farrar Straus Giroux, 1988).

28. George F. Will, *Statecraft as Soulcraft: What Government Does* (New York: Simon & Schuster, 1983), 154–55. This is not to say that Will is, in any coherent sense, a conservative. See the notes in chapters 6 and 7 in this book.

29. Irving Kristol, *Two Cheers for Capitalism* (New York: Basic Books, 1978).

30. One rather telling example of current attitudes toward friendship is Isaac F. Kramnick's *The Rage of Edmund Burke: Portrait of an Ambivalent Conservative* (New York: Basic Books, 1971). Based on the assumption that intimate relations between men must be homosexual in nature, Kramnick's work subjects Burke's lifelong friendship with Will Burke to page after page of vulgarized Freudian innuendo. His intent is to prove that Burke must have had a deep ambivalence toward heterosexuality that translated somehow into an equally deep ambivalence toward the upper classes, with which Kramnick identifies conservatism.

CHAPTER ONE: NATURAL LAW AND VIRTUE

1. Thomas Aquinas, *Treatise on Law: (Summa Theologica Questions 90–97)* (Washington, D.C.: Regnery, 1987), 97; emphasis in original.
2. Leo Strauss, *Liberalism Ancient and Modern* (New York: Basic Books, 1968), vii.
3. Ibid., viii.
4. Ibid.
5. A clarification seems in order at this point. It is not my goal to read out of the conservative movement anyone who happens to disagree with any of the tenets that I argue constitute the fundamental bases of conservative political philosophy. But if one is to achieve any kind of coherence in dealing with the debates and problems of today, it is necessary to be clear on the distinction between political allies and adherents to the same political philosophy. Libertarians, neoconservatives, and traditionalists belong to the conservative movement as it is defined today. This does not mean that they share the same political philosophy (although many of them in fact may); neither does it mean that there is no basis for cooperation and genuine friendship among men of good will who happen to disagree on certain important moral and philosophical matters.
6. The best discussion of Aquinas's rationalism and indeed of his philosophy in general is provided in Etienne Gilson, *The Christian Philosophy of Saint Thomas Aquinas* (London: Victor Gollancz, 1957); see especially 59. For a discussion of the history of natural law doctrine—and its roots in Roman Stoic and Thomistic thought—see especially Peter Stanlis, *Edmund Burke and the Natural Law* (Ann Arbor: University of Michigan Press, 1958), chap. 1.
7. Aquinas, *Treatise*, 18. Strauss was certainly correct in pointing out that natural law is necessarily theological—based on the reasonable recognition of the primacy of divine law. Yet this does not mean that human reason is powerless in those areas in which divine law has not spoken, or even in those areas where it has, since man must always seek to interpret correctly what God demands. See Leo Strauss, *Natural Right and History* (Chicago: University of Chicago Press, 1953), 163–64.
8. Aquinas, *Treatise*, 3–4. See also Gilson, *Christian Philosophy*, pt. 2, chap. 7.
9. For a rather hostile discussion of Aquinas's view of the limits and uses of reason, see D. J. O'Connor, *Aquinas and Natural Law* (London: Macmillan, 1967), especially around 35.
10. The *New Catholic Encyclopedia* (New York: McGraw-Hill, 1967), 882, notes Aquinas's separation of *synderesis* from the concept of the will. Aquinas "regarded [*synderesis*] as an innate habit of practical reason (not a faculty itself), by which man comes to know immediately the first principles of the moral order." Neither inborn nor merely willed, conscience is learned through education, that is, by living a proper life.
11. Aquinas, *Treatise*, 60.
12. Ibid., 82.
13. Ibid., 78.

14. Ibid., 98. Revolution is, of course, a far different matter than mere disobedience, for it necessarily involves grievous hurt and so for Aquinas cannot be justified, save in the most extreme circumstances.

15. Aquinas, *Treatise*, 74–75.

16. See O'Connor, *Aquinas*, 36.

17. See ibid., 5.

18. Stanlis, *Burke*, 9–10.

19. None of this is to question whether Aquinas was a devout and holy man, but Thomistic philosophy perhaps owes more to Aristotle's philosophy—a philosophy that did not recognize the existence, let alone the authority, of revelation—than the conservative might wish.

20. Stanlis, *Burke*, app. 1.

21. Ibid., 17.

22. Ibid., 10–11. In *The Problem of Burke's Political Philosophy* (Oxford: Clarendon Press, 1967), Burleigh Taylor Wilkins makes the important point that Strauss's bifurcation of classical natural law from modern natural-rights theory is an oversimplification. And Wilkins is correct to point out that the transition from classical to modern thought was much more one of emphasis than of category—of degree rather than kind (24). But Wilkins, who seeks to place Burke within the Lockean tradition, overlooks important aspects of this difference of degree, for Wilkins reads natural law in a modern, rationalistic manner. He questions the ability of any thinker to approve of both prejudice and natural law—and "saves" Burke's natural law credentials by downplaying his emphasis on habit and by exaggerating his rather limited commitment to notions of natural rights. The emphasis that differentiates classical from modern thinkers—or, more properly, natural law from non-natural law thinkers—concerns human reason and will. Natural law thinkers emphasize the natural limits of the former and the proper limits of the latter; truly modern thinkers place sufficient faith in reason to justify, in their minds, the assertion of human over divine will. The replacement of what is given (our circumstances and natures) by what is asserted ("rationally," to be sure) to be correct—and thence willed—sets modern thought apart from its natural law moorings. The propriety of Locke's status as a natural law thinker need not concern us here, but to argue that Burke fits within a tradition of thought emphasizing natural (rational as opposed to historical) rights is to ignore or to misread fundamentally the clear emphases in Burke's own work.

23. This is not an intellectual biography of either Burke or Tocqueville. But it is not unimportant that Burke's education as a youth and his (short-lived) study of law left him with an abiding love of classical writers (especially Cicero, from whom Burke quoted extensively and whose style pervades his work) and in particular with a firm respect for the wisdom embodied in the English common law; see Stanlis, *Burke*, chap. 3. Neither is it unimportant that Tocqueville's upbringing was aristocratic—punctuated by reminders and examples of the obligations of high station—and Catholic (in some ways Jansenist); that his childhood friend, tutor, and confidant was a Jesuit steeped in the "old" moral wisdom; and that his legal training was, for him, as much a preparation in moral

history as in the practice of law. See Andre Jardin, *Tocqueville: A Biography*, trans. Lydia Davis with Robert Hemenway (New York: Farrar Straus Giroux, 1988), around 43, and especially 62, for Tocqueville's own statement of his moral confusion on witnessing the chasm between the lessons of his youth and the corruptions and teachings of his university days.

24. Isaac F. Kramnick, "Skepticism in English Political Thought from Temple to Burke," *Studies in Burke and his Time* 12 (Fall 1970): 1656.

25. For a full discussion of this concept, see Arthur O. Lovejoy, *The Great Chain of Being* (Cambridge: Harvard University Press, 1936).

26. Alexis de Tocqueville, *Democracy in America*, ed. J. P. Mayer, trans. George Lawrence (Garden City, N.Y.: Doubleday, 1969), 433–34.

27. Stanlis, *Burke*, 77.

28. Tocqueville, *Democracy*, 62.

29. See also the discussion in chapter 4 of this book concerning Tocqueville's criticism of the French Old Regime for usurping the role of the upper classes and so destroying the proper bases for hierarchical distinctions.

30. Quoted, from Edmund Burke, *Reflections on the Revolution in France* (New York: Macmillan, 1955), 98–99, in Kramnick, "Skepticism," 1657.

31. Isaac F. Kramnick, *The Rage of Edmund Burke: Portrait of an Ambivalent Conservative* (New York: Basic Books, 1971), 25.

32. Ibid., 77.

33. I am not attempting here to recreate the venerable medieval or early modern conceptions of virtue—knowledge of which was once well-nigh universal. Neither space nor the scope of this work allows for such a (much needed) historical discussion. Instead I aim to reconstruct the conservative vision of virtue, looking to its (often less than overt) formulations, which are made as much in response to existing circumstances as to historical precept. None of this is intended to imply, however, that earlier formulations of the virtues, any more than earlier formulations of natural law, were in any way "less true" than those presented here. For an introduction to Aquinas's conception of virtue, see Gilson, *Christian Philosophy*, pt. 3.

34. Ibid., 27–29.

35. Aristotle, *Nicomachean Ethics*, trans. H. Rackham (Cambridge: Harvard University Press, 1933), bk. 5, 33.

36. Ibid., bk. 2, 111.

37. Ibid., bk. 6, 339.

38. Ibid., 345–46.

39. Ibid., 367.

40. Ibid., bk. 5, 257–61.

41. Ibid., 293–95.

42. Clearly the notion that slavery makes justice irrelevant is no longer accepted, but the relationship between one's station in life—one's profession as well as social status—and the proper treatment to be accorded one, remains important to this day.

43. Aristotle, *Nicomachean Ethics*, bk. 2, 71.

44. Ibid., 85.

45. Ibid., 89.
46. Ibid., bk. 3, 147.
47. Ibid., bk. 1, 47.
48. Ibid., bk. 10, 631.
49. Ibid., 631–33.
50. Ibid., bk. 5, 319.
51. Ibid., bk. 10, 365–69.
52. Ibid., bk. 6, 347.
53. Ibid., bk. 10, 613.
54. Ibid.
55. Ibid., 617.
56. Ibid.
57. Ibid.
58. See especially Aristotle, *Politics*, trans. Ernest Barker (London: Oxford University Press, 1958), bk. 7, chaps. 4–17, for his discussion of the physical, structural, and educational requirements for the ideal state—the one in which the citizens (though not, of course, all residents) enjoy a life of leisure, furnished with those things that are necessary for it—to be achieved and maintained.
59. J. G. A. Pocock, *The Machiavellian Moment: Florentine Political Thought and the Atlantic Republican Tradition* (Princeton, N.J.: Princeton University Press, 1975), 66–67. The use of Pocock as the primary interpreter of republican theory is intended to divorce the argument made here from any republican reading of modern thinkers, be they Machiavelli, Montesquieu, or certain of the American Founders. For a cogent critique of republican theory and scholarship, see Thomas L. Pangle, *The Spirit of Modern Republicanism: The Moral Vision of the American Founders and the Philosophy of Locke* (Chicago: University of Chicago Press, 1988).
60. Pocock, *Machiavellian Moment*, 67.
61. Ibid., 68.
62. Ibid., 69–70.
63. Ibid., 71.
64. Ibid., 73.
65. Ibid., 74.
66. Ibid., 316.
67. Forrest McDonald, *Novus Ordo Seclorum: The Intellectual Origins of the Constitution* (Lawrence: University Press of Kansas, 1985), 70–71. McDonald refers to Pocock, noting particularly his emphasis upon the republican concern with corruption.
68. Pocock, *Machiavellian Moment*, 249.
69. Ibid., 184.
70. Ibid., 184–85.
71. Harvey C. Mansfield, Jr., *Statesmanship and Party Government: A Study of Burke and Bolingbroke* (Chicago: University of Chicago Press, 1965), 214.
72. Tocqueville, *Democracy*, 618.
73. Edmund Burke, *Reflections on the Revolution in France*, in vol. 3 of *Works* (London: John C. Nimmo, 1899), 477.

74. Ibid., 478–79.
75. Ibid., 476–77.
76. Ibid., 361.
77. Aristotle, *Politics*, bk. 1.

CHAPTER TWO: PHILOSOPHY, MAN, AND SOCIETY

1. Plato, *The Republic*, trans. Allan Bloom (New York: Basic Books, 1968), 290, 607b.
2. Edmund Burke, *Appeal from the New to the Old Whigs*, in vol. 4 of *Works* (London: John C. Nimmo, 1899), 176.
3. Edmund Burke, *Reflections on the Revolution in France*, in vol. 3 of *Works*, 338.
4. Burke, *Appeal*, *Works*, 4: 192.
5. Edmund Burke, *Letters on a Regicide Peace*, *Letter 1*, in vol. 5 of *Works*, 341.
6. Ibid.
7. Burke, *Reflections*, 3: 240.
8. Ibid., 241.
9. Ibid., 242; emphasis in original.
10. Ibid., 313.
11. Ibid., 4–5.
12. Onora O'Neill, "Ethical Reasoning and Ideological Pluralism," *Ethics* 99 (July 1988): 9.
13. Ibid., 10; emphasis in original.
14. Edmund Burke, "Letter to a Member of the French National Assembly," *Works*, 4: 51–52.
15. Edmund Burke, "Speech on American Taxation," *Works*, 2: 72–73.
16. Burke, *Reflections*, 3: 307–8.
17. Burke, *Regicide Peace*, *Letter 4*, in vol. 6 of *Works*, 28.
18. Burke, *Regicide Peace*, *Letter 2*, in vol. 5 of *Works*, 362.
19. Ibid., 106; emphasis added.
20. Burke, *Reflections*, 3: 350.
21. Ibid., 311.
22. Ibid., 309.
23. Ibid., 477.
24. Burke, *Appeal*, 4: 176.
25. Ibid., 175; emphasis in original.
26. Ibid., 176.
27. Burke, *Reflections*, 3: 274; emphasis in original.
28. Ibid., 450.
29. Burke, "Letter to a Member of the French National Assembly," 4: 51.
30. Burke, *Reflections*, 3: 271–72; emphasis in original.
31. Ibid., 272–73; emphasis in original.
32. J. G. A. Pocock, "Burke and the Ancient Constitution," in *Politics, Lan-*

guage and Time: Essays on Political Thought and History (New York: Atheneum, 1971), 208.

33. Burke, *Reflections*, 3: 259–60.

34. Ibid., 361.

35. Ibid., 346–47.

36. Ibid., 347.

37. Burke, *Appeal*, 4: 205.

38. Burke, *Reflections*, 3: 527.

39. Ibid., 559.

40. See especially *Regicide Peace, Letter 1*, 5: 320, for a discussion of Jacobinism's inherent hostility to the "community of Europe."

41. Ibid., 314.

42. See Harvey C. Mansfield, Jr., *Statesmanship and Party Government: A Study of Burke and Bolingbroke* (Chicago: University of Chicago Press, 1965), 204–7, for a discussion of Burke's comments, particularly in his "Letter to a Noble Lord," concerning his own (unfulfilled) desire to found a family and his views on the necessary role of such families in providing "presumptive" virtue.

43. Burke, *Reflections*, 3: 317–18.

44. Edmund Burke, *Fragments of a Tract Relative to the Laws against Popery In Ireland*, in vol. 6 of *Works*, 330.

45. Burke, *Regicide Peace, Letter 3*, in vol. 5 of *Works*, 466.

46. Burke, *Appeal*, 4: 115.

47. Burke, *Fragments of a Tract*, 6: 340.

48. Ibid., 323.

49. Burke, *Regicide Peace, Letter 1*, 5: 302.

50. Burke, *Fragments of a Tract*, 6: 339–40.

51. Edmund Burke, "Letter to Sir Hercules Langrishe," *Works*, 4: 257–58; emphasis in original.

52. Burke, *Regicide Peace, Letter 1*, 5: 310; emphasis in original.

53. Burke, "Letter to a Member of the French National Assembly," 4: 30.

CHAPTER THREE: ACCEPTING VIRTUE IN BURKE

1. Edmund Burke, "Letter to the Sheriffs of Bristol," *Works* (London: John C. Nimmo, 1899), 2: 234; emphasis in original.

2. Edmund Burke, *Reflections on the Revolution in France*, in vol. 3 of *Works*, 260.

3. Edmund Burke, "Letter to a Member of the French National Assembly," in vol. 4 of *Works*, 26.

4. Burke, *Reflections*, 3: 294–95; emphasis in original.

5. See Burke's "Letter to a Member of the French National Assembly," 4: 13.

6. Ibid., 335.

7. See, for example, C. B. MacPherson, *Burke* (New York: Hill & Wang, 1980), and J. G. A. Pocock, *Politics, Language and Time: Essays on Political Thought and History* (New York: Atheneum, 1971).

8. Burke, *Reflections*, 3: 336.

9. Ibid., 332.

10. Ibid., 331.

11. Ibid., 426.

12. Ibid., quoted in Isaac F. Kramnick, *The Rage of Edmund Burke* (New York: Basic Books, 1971), 64.

13. Edmund Burke, "Speech on a Motion Made in the House of Commons, the 7th of May 1782, for a committee to inquire into the state of representation of the Commons in Parliament," quoted in Kramnick, *Rage*, 64. It is also interesting to note Burke's repeated use of familial imagery in arguing that England had not lived up to its paternal responsibilities in dealing with its American colonies (see p. 121).

14. Edmund Burke, "Letter to a Noble Lord," *Works*, 5: 124–25.

15. Edmund Burke, *The Correspondence*, in vol. 3 of *Works*, 192–93 (22–23), Burke to Marquess of Rockingham. The reference here is to Rockingham's repeal of the Stamp Act in 1766. Quoted in Kramnick, *Rage*, 118.

16. Edmund Burke, *Observations on a Late Publication on the Present State of the Nation*, in vol. 1 of *Works*, 271–72; emphasis added.

17. Edmund Burke, *Appeal from the New to the Old Whigs*, in vol. 4 of *Works*, 174.

18. Ibid., 175.

19. Edmund Burke, *Regicide Peace, Letter 3*, in vol. 5 of *Works*, 457–58.

20. Ibid., 455.

21. Burke, *Reflections*, 3: 296.

22. Ibid., 284.

23. Ibid., 285.

24. Quoted in Harvey C. Mansfield, Jr., *Statesmanship and Party Government: A Study of Burke and Bolingbroke* (Chicago: University of Chicago Press, 1965), 209.

25. Quoted in ibid., 201.

26. Edmund Burke, *Speech on Conciliation with America*, in vol. 2 of *Works*, 127.

27. Burke, "Letter to Sheriffs of Bristol," 2: 225.

28. Burke, *Observations*, 1: 271–72.

29. Burke, *Regicide Peace, Letter 4*, in vol. 6 of *Works*, 43.

30. Ibid.

31. Burke, *Appeal*, 4: 206–7.

32. Ibid., 207.

33. Ibid.

34. Burke, *Observations*, 1: 417.

35. Edmund Burke, *Thoughts on the Cause of the Present Discontents*, in vol. 1 of *Works*, 517.

36. Ibid., 518.

37. See Edmund Burke, "Speech on the Plan for Economical Reform," *Works*, vol. 2, especially p. 287.

38. See Edmund Burke, "Motion Relative to the Speech from the Throne," *Works*, 2: 539–76.

39. See Edmund Burke, "Speech on Mr. Fox's East India Bill," *Works*, 2: 525.

40. Burke, *Reflections*, 3: 313.

41. Quoted in Mansfield, *Statesmanship*, 181.

42. Burke, "Speech on Mr. Fox's East India Bill," 2: 531.

43. Quoted in Mansfield, *Statesmanship*, 181.

44. Burke, *Observations*, 1: 417.

45. Ibid., 418; emphasis in original.

46. See Edmund Burke, "Speech at the Conclusion of the Poll," *Works*, 2: 96–97, for Burke's classic defense of the parliamentary representative's prerogative and responsibility for independent judgment.

47. Burke, *Reflections*, 3: 559–60.

48. Ibid., 292.

49. Burke, "Letter to a Member of the French National Assembly," 4: 29.

50. Ibid., 27.

51. Ibid., 27–28.

52. Burke, *Reflections*, 3: 292.

CHAPTER FOUR: TOCQUEVILLE AND THE CONSERVATION OF LIBERTY IN AMERICA

1. Edmund Burke, *Reflections on the Revolution in France*, in vol. 3 of *Works* (London: John C. Nimmo, 1899), 296.

2. It is interesting to observe in this regard that Tocqueville, in one of his rare references to Burke, noted that his "clear-sighted" conservative predecessor failed to grasp the true nature and intent of the French Revolution. Burke sought to convince the French that proper reforms could be made based on French tradition and on "the ancient common law of Europe." But it was precisely this ancient common law, and indeed all remnants of Europe's aristocratic and feudal institutions, that the Revolution sought to destroy. In this task the Revolution's success was inevitable, according to Tocqueville, for the age of equality had dawned. The question now was how man might retain his virtue in the face of radically changed circumstances—Alexis de Tocqueville, *The Old Regime and the French Revolution*, trans. Stuart Gilbert (Garden City, N.Y.: Doubleday, 1955), 20–21.

3. Alexis de Tocqueville, *Democracy in America*, ed. J. P. Mayer, trans. George Lawrence (Garden City, N.Y.: Doubleday, 1969), xiv.

4. Ibid.

5. Ibid., 315.

6. Ibid., 12; note also Tocqueville's letter to his English translator, Henry Reeve, xi. "I am writing in a country and for a country where the cause for equality is from now on won—without the possibility of a return toward aristocracy." Tocqueville also declared himself a friend toward democracy in this letter. The

friendship, no doubt real, was nonetheless partly of necessity. And friendships of necessity, though they often blossom, begin and often end with less trust than do those of choice. Note as well George Armstrong Kelly's insightful observation: "Tocqueville's speculative religious *telos* was equality, not progress and prosperity—and he advances this proposition with delicate irony: 'We may naturally believe that it is not the singular prosperity of the few, but the greater well-being of all that is most pleasing in the sight of the Creator and Preserver of men. What appears to me to be man's decline is, to His eye, advancement; what afflicts me is acceptable to Him.' It is by this subtle and wistful turn of phrase that this giant among nineteenth-century prophets parts company with the rising messianic discourse of his time" (*Politics and Religious Consciousness in America* [New Brunswick, N.J.: Transaction Books, 1984], 124). One need not approve of the spread of equality in all its aspects, let alone unequivocally, in order to recognize its status as the will of God and also to recognize one's duty to promote virtue in its face.

7. Edmund Burke, "Speech on Mr. Fox's East India Bill," *Works*, 2: 509.

8. See especially Tocqueville, *Democracy*, chapters 4–6 of volume 2 (2 vols. in 1).

9. Ibid., 315; emphasis in original.

10. John P. Diggins, *The Lost Soul of American Politics* (Chicago: University of Chicago Press, 1986), 239.

11. Tocqueville, *Democracy*, 517.

12. Ibid., 506.

13. Diggins, *Lost Soul*, 231. See also Robert P. Kraynak, "Tocqueville's Constitutionalism," *American Political Science Review* 81 (Dec. 1987), for a discussion of Tocqueville's attempt to adapt the American Constitution so that it would be possible to inculcate a kind of moral virtue in the citizens by teaching them to act freely but with moral responsibility. Although Kraynak sees Tocqueville's achievement as being unique, the argument here is that attempts to promote this kind of virtue in the face of changing circumstances are quintessentially conservative.

14. Tocqueville, *Democracy*, 237–38.

15. Ibid., see especially 507–8.

16. Tocqueville, *Old Regime and the French Revolution*, xiv.

17. See especially Bruce James Smith, *Politics and Remembrance* (Princeton, N.J.: Princeton University Press, 1985), and Roger Boesche, *The Strange Liberalism of Alexis de Tocqueville* (Ithaca, N.Y.: Cornell University Press, 1987). It should be noted that Smith writes of "republican themes" in Tocqueville, and Boesche describes Tocqueville as a liberal (if a "strange" one with republican leanings). Particularly in the case of Boesche, however, there is a curious emphasis on Tocqueville's desire for public spirit and his use of the words "virtue," "glory," and "turmoil" that fails to take into account the meaning that *Tocqueville*—as opposed to the other republican authors on whom Boesche relies so heavily—attaches to these words. Tocqueville's use of these terms must be viewed in the context of his passionate desire for order and for the com-

munity of a largely *social* rather than an explicitly political life. On Boesche, see especially *Strange Liberalism*, chap. 11.

18. Andre Jardin, *Tocqueville: A Biography*, trans. Lydia Davis with Robert Hemenway (New York: Farrar Straus Giroux, 1988), 416. See also Alexis de Tocqueville's *Recollections on the French Revolution of 1848*, ed. J. P. Mayer, trans. Alexander Teixeira de Mattos (Cleveland, Ohio: World Publishing, 1959), for his pointed attacks against both the greedy and indolent middle classes who allowed the revolution to occur and the envious and hubristic intellectuals who brought it about.

19. Quoted in Jardin, *Tocqueville*, 193.

20. Tocqueville, *Recollections*, 223–24.

21. Ibid., 68. Although commentators such as John Koritansky fault Tocqueville for his "modernist," supposedly egalitarian beliefs, his insistence that liberty must be "held in check" by religion, custom, and law places Tocqueville at odds with radical democratic theorists such as Rousseau. Indeed, of the three thinkers whom Tocqueville referred to as his "constant companions," his debt to Rousseau seems least systematic and concrete. Tocqueville's thought shows a deep affinity for the skepticism and religious spirit of Pascal; it also shares Montesquieu's concern that political regimes reflect the circumstances of their people and check themselves through a balancing of powers. Tocqueville's sharing of Rousseau's yearning for community, if balanced against other aspects of his thought, seems to indicate as much of an analytic concern with the problems of democracy as a desire to foster the life of the spirit in democratic times. There is no general will in Tocqueville's thought—save perhaps that degradingly perpetrated by the tyranny of the majority; Tocqueville's conservative life of the spirit is neither merely a matter of the general will's demanding the suppression of individuality nor of aristocratic class particularism but of a concern that the general and the specific be integrated as much as possible within human society through recognition of man's universal sociability and the role of habit in the formation of character. See John Koritansky, *Alexis de Tocqueville and the New Science of Politics* (Durham: Carolina Academic Press, 1986).

22. Tocqueville, *Old Regime*, x–xi.

23. Ibid., x.

24. Ibid., 157.

25. Ibid., 167.

26. Tocqueville, *Recollections*, 214; emphasis added. The remainder of the passage is also enlightening: "And this [way of governing] could not allow us to remain popular for long, since everybody wanted to evade the Constitution. The [socialist Montagnard] Mountain wanted more, the Monarchists much less."

27. Jardin, *Tocqueville*, 305. For an extensive discussion of Tocqueville's opposition to revolutionary politics and ideas, see Jean-Claude Lamberti, *Tocqueville and the Two Democracies*, trans. Arthur Goldhammer (Cambridge: Harvard University Press, 1989), especially pt. 3.

28. Tocqueville, *Democracy*, 252.

29. Ibid., 254.

30. Ibid., 256–57.

31. Quoted in Seymour Drescher, *Tocqueville and England* (Cambridge: Harvard University Press, 1964), 15.

32. Tocqueville, *Democracy,* 284.

33. Ibid., 433–34.

34. Ibid., 437.

35. Ibid., 441.

36. Ibid., 304.

37. Ibid., 438.

38. Tocqueville, *Old Regime,* 167.

39. Ibid., pt. 2, chap. 3, especially 157–59.

40. Ibid., 162.

41. Peter Augustine Lawler, "Was Tocqueville a Philosopher?" *Interpretation* 17 (1990): 405–6; see also 401–3, for a discussion of Tocqueville's view of Platonism. For Tocqueville, Platonic philosophy spoke to man's permanent need and desire for truth and thereby enriched his soul but was fundamentally misguided in its view of the natural limitations of human reason. Lawler notes Tocqueville's debt to the antirationalist thinker Blaise Pascal, who observed that "we desire truth and find in ourselves nothing but uncertainty. . . . We are incapable of not desiring truth and happiness, and incapable of either certainty or happiness." Platonism is at heart a (beautiful) illusion.

42. Ibid., 404.

43. Tocqueville, *Democracy,* 239.

44. Ibid., 210.

45. Ibid.

46. Ibid., 169.

47. Ibid., 305.

48. Ibid., xiv.

49. See, for example, Doris Goldstein's discussion of Tocqueville's correspondence with Gobineau in *Trial of Faith* (New York: Elsevier, 1975), chap. 2. Tocqueville chastised Gobineau for his excessively biological arguments concerning national characters, stating that such theories ignore and interfere with necessary notions of free will and with Christian belief itself.

50. Tocqueville, *Democracy,* 32.

51. Ibid., 36.

52. Ibid., 47; emphasis in original.

53. Ibid., 35.

54. Ibid., 50.

55 Ibid., 79.

56. Ibid., 62.

57. Ibid., 167.

58. Ibid., 307.

59. Drescher, *Tocqueville and England,* 92. Tocqueville's concern with locality may also be seen in his discussions of class. Whether in America, Britain, or France, Tocqueville examined the shared circumstances, motivations, and

mores of particular, often conflicting, social classes. Indeed, *The Old Regime and the French Revolution* is at heart a discussion of how administrative centralization under the Old Regime destroyed local freedoms dating from the Middle Ages, set up barriers to class and thence to national solidarity, and thus paved the way for the French Revolution by creating a nation of uniform, petty individualists.

60. Tocqueville, *Democracy*, 285.

61. Ibid., 318.

62. Ibid., 318–19.

63. Ibid., 375.

64. Ibid.

65. Ibid., 308.

66. Ibid., 318.

67. Ibid., 318–19.

68. Ibid., 319–20.

69. Ibid., 360.

70. Ibid., 363.

71. Edmund Burke, "Letter to the Right Honorable Henry Dundas, with the Sketch of a Negro Code," *Works*, 6: 259.

72. Tocqueville, *Democracy*, 268–69.

73. Ibid., 268.

74. Ibid., 102–3.

75. Ibid., 103.

76. Ibid., 243.

77. Ibid., 75.

78. This is in sharp contrast to the practice of the Old Regime—a practice carried over to revolutionary France—of establishing tyrannical laws and administrative practices to which frequent exceptions were made. In this way law itself became contemptible to Frenchmen and freedom seemed an unnatural alternative to the established despotisms. See Tocqueville, *Old Regime*, pt. 2, especially chaps. 3 and 4.

79. Tocqueville, *Democracy*, 139.

80. Ibid., 96.

81. Ibid., 698.

82. Ibid., 442–43.

83. Ibid., 444.

84. Ibid., 17.

85. Ibid., 298.

86. See, for example, ibid., 446, where Tocqueville presents the spread of Christianity as one with historical and therefore divine sanction. Goldstein also discusses Tocqueville's attachment to Christianity and Catholicism and his support of attempts to convert the Hindus; see *Trial of Faith*, 114.

87. Tocqueville, *Democracy*, 189.

88. Ibid., 62–63.

89. Once again, Tocqueville's argument in *The Old Regime* is cogent: The ancient, free, and participatory communities of the Middle Ages were destroyed

by the centralizing grip of the Old Regime. By the time of the revolution, Frenchmen had utterly forgotten what freedom was and were capable of pursuing it for only a brief, shining moment in the midst of tyranny, hubris, and bloodshed.

90. Tocqueville, *Democracy*, 308.
91. Ibid., 274.
92. Ibid., 543.
93. Ibid., 457.
94. Ibid.
95. Ibid., 457–58.
96. Ibid., 555–58.
97. Tocqueville, *Recollections*, 69.
98. Ibid., 79.

CHAPTER FIVE: VIRTUE PROPERLY UNDERSTOOD

1. See, for example, Melvin Richter, "Tocqueville on Algeria," *Review of Politics* 25 (July 1963): 396–98.
2. Alexis de Tocqueville, letter to J. S. Mill, March 18, 1841, quoted in ibid., 383–84.
3. See especially ibid., 391.
4. Alexis de Tocqueville, letter to Henry Reeve, April 12, 1840, quoted in ibid., 385.
5. See ibid., 393–94.
6. Alexis de Tocqueville, ed. Beaumont, 9, 448, quoted in ibid., 394.
7. Alexis de Tocqueville, *Selected Letters on Politics and Society*, trans. James Toupin and Roger Boesche (Berkeley: University of California Press, 1985), 101–2.
8. Ibid., 150–51.
9. Alexis de Tocqueville, *Democracy in America*, ed. J. P. Mayer, trans. George Lawrence (Garden City, N.Y.: Doubleday, 1969), 616–17.
10. Alexis de Tocqueville, *The Old Regime and the French Revolution*, trans. Stuart Gilbert (Garden City, N.Y.: Doubleday, 1955), 119; emphasis added.
11. Ibid., 14.
12. Tocqueville, *Democracy*, 642–43.
13. "The passions that stir the Americans most deeply are commercial and not political ones, or rather they carry a trader's habits over into the business of politics. They like order, without which affairs do not prosper, and they set an especial value on regularity of mores, which are the foundation of a sound business; they prefer the good sense which creates fortunes to the genius which often dissipates them; their minds, accustomed to definite calculations, are frightened by general ideas; and they hold practice in greater honor than theory" (ibid., 285).
14. Tocqueville, *Old Regime*, 118.
15. See, for example, Tocqueville, *Democracy*, 457.

16. Ibid., 626.

17. Ibid., 526.

18. Alexis de Tocqueville, *Recollections on the French Revolution of 1848*, ed. J. P. Mayer, trans. Alexander Teixeira de Mattos (Cleveland, Ohio: World Publishing, 1959), 12–13.

19. Ibid., 79–80.

20. Ibid., 11.

21. Tocqueville, *Democracy*, 95.

22. Ibid., 511.

23. Ibid., 512–13.

24. Ibid., 515.

25. It is also likely to be shoddy and funded inequitably. Tocqueville discussed the deleterious effects of governmental intervention in local affairs of improvement and charity throughout *The Old Regime*; see especially 40–41.

26. Tocqueville, *Democracy*, 522.

27. Ibid.

28. Tocqueville, *Old Regime*, 40.

29. Ibid., 124.

30. Tocqueville, *Democracy*, 239.

31. Note also Tocqueville's own attempts to found conservatively (and to form a constitution of limited, balanced powers) in the aftermath of the Revolution of 1848; see *Recollections*, 214.

32. Tocqueville, *Democracy*, 395.

33. Ibid.

34. See, for example, ibid., 196.

35. Ibid., 250–51.

36. Ibid., 201.

37. Ibid., 202.

38. Ibid., 692.

39. Ibid., 224.

40. Ibid., 258.

41. Ibid., 633.

42. Tocqueville discussed aristocratic and monarchical as well as democratic peoples in this context. Place hunting, the harmful use of self-interest, is particularly dangerous in a democracy because there will be far more place seekers than governmental positions. Thus a perpetual class of disgruntled men will be opposed to the government because it has failed to give them what they want and feel they deserve (see ibid., 633–34).

43. Ibid., 262–63.

44. Tocqueville, *Old Regime*, 41.

45. See especially ibid., pt. 2, chap. 9.

46. Ibid., 111.

47. Tocqueville, *Democracy*, 95.

48. Ibid., 44.

49. Ibid., 511.

50. Ibid.

51. Ibid.

52. Tocqueville, *Old Regime*, 121–22.

53. Ibid., 122–23.

54. Alexis de Tocqueville, *The European Revolution and Correspondence with Gobineau*, ed. and trans. John Lukacs (Garden City, N.Y.: Anchor, 1959), 169–70; quoted, with amendments, in Marvin Zetterbaum, *Tocqueville and the Problem of Democracy* (Stanford, Calif.: Stanford University Press, 1967), 150.

55. Tocqueville, *Old Regime*, 47.

56. Ibid., 48; see also the preceding pages of pt. 1, chap. 3, for further discussion of the democratic nature of the local community in feudal France.

57. Ibid., 44–45.

58. To be sure, Aristotle characterized man as a *political* animal. But it is significant that Aristotle's notion of *philia* or friendship was both central to his analysis of man's social and political life and, one might say, extrapolitical in nature. Indeed, *philia* both transcends and makes possible more strictly political activity, for it is the basis of all human associations—from the political community to economic relations to the very foundation of civilization—affection. All communities and all human interaction depend upon a basic friendship or good will. See *Nicomachean Ethics*, trans. Martin Ostwald (New York: Macmillan, 1962), bk. 8.

CHAPTER SIX: THE DILEMMA OF CONTEMPORARY CONSERVATIVE HORIZONS

1. Leo Strauss, *Natural Right and History* (Chicago: University of Chicago Press, 1953), 300.

2. Ibid., 317.

3. Ibid., 319.

4. Marvin Zetterbaum, *Tocqueville and the Problem of Democracy* (Stanford, Calif.: Stanford University Press, 1967), 147.

5. Ibid., 153–55.

6. Ibid., 112. Clearly, this critique has much in common with that of Marxists such as MacPherson who claim that conservatives such as Burke sought to protect propertied interests by convincing those who sought change that reform could bring only disaster. See C. B. MacPherson, *Burke* (New York: Hill & Wang, 1980), 35.

7. As will become clear, the connection between libertarianism and conservatism is much more tenuous than many would like to believe. The libertarian values individual choice and action above all else—including custom, tradition, and any life of accepting virtue. Free market conservatism is not, however, an oxymoron. Economic liberty has a long tradition and enjoys strong acceptance in many (particularly Western) societies and so may be defended quite consistently on both conservative and libertarian grounds.

8. One obvious objection to this choice of method is that it fails to examine the thought of many prominent conservatives—including some thinkers who

may be seen as more important than one or more of those men chosen. One significant case in point is that of William F. Buckley, Jr. But Buckley himself prefers, in dealing with fundamental philosophical issues, to defer to other thinkers—significantly to Russell Kirk and particularly to Michael Oakeshott. See, for example, the preface to the reissue of *Up from Liberalism* (New York: McDowell, Obolensky, 1959), in which Buckley eloquently restates the antiphilosophical conservative argument—"To indict the law-breaker shouldn't require that the prosecutor define the good life"—and then cites Oakeshott's argument that the purpose of govenment is to damp down rather than to stoke the fires of desire. Although Kristol also is no philosopher, his is a studied rejection of abstract argument fundamental to neoconservative thought, quite different from Buckley's deference to the philosophical arguments of others. As a more general point, it would be impossible to treat seriously the thought of significant numbers of contemporary conservatives in the space allowed here. Indeed, no single volume has done so. Instead, such volumes (George H. Nash's *The Conservative Intellectual Movement in America since 1945* [New York: Basic Books, 1976]) is a particularly competent example) treat contemporary conservatism as an ideological movement best dealt with through an examination of historically held policy positions and a general opposition to change. It necessarily is up to the reader to determine if the "paradigm" set up in the following pages "fits" his view of the thought of particular contemporary conservatives not covered here. In fact, I will refer to some other contemporary conservatives in this and the following chapter in an attempt to show the validity of my argument. My central defense here is that it is at least highly significant that three prominent thinkers from diverse groups within the conservative movement share fundamental assumptions and goals partaking of and potentially fulfilled by the life of accepting virtue.

9. In addition to Buckley, *Up from Liberalism*, see, for example, Irving Kristol, "Rationalism in Economics," in *Reflections of a Neoconservative: Looking Back, Looking Ahead* (New York: Basic Books, 1983).

10. Paul Franco, "Michael Oakeshott as Liberal Theorist," *Political Theory* 19 (Aug. 1990): 411.

11. David R. Mapel, "Civil Association and the Idea of Contingency," *Political Theory* 19 (Aug. 1990): 405.

12. Michael Oakeshott, *The Voice of Liberal Learning: Michael Oakeshott on Education*, ed. Timothy Fuller (New Haven, Conn.: Yale University Press, 1989), 64.

13. Mapel's essay makes much of the notion, which he ascribes to Oakeshott, that "law and morality are human inventions whose authority is ultimately grounded only in the continuing acknowledgment of those who participate in them" (Mapel, "Civil Association," 393). According to Mapel, this lack of "any necessary foundations for human practices" allows each individual to question and criticize whatever rules and practices happen to exist. In essence, Mapel ascribes to Oakeshott the notion that each man has the ability to step back from his social context and judge it rationally. Of all notions, this is the one for which Oakeshott held the greatest disdain. Precisely because authority depends upon

consensus, for Oakeshott, the individual, if he is to act properly rather than commit moral enormities, must see his task in life as that of learning how best to maintain the coherence of the existing order. Mapel's essay purports to be a critical reading of Oakeshott's *On Human Conduct* (Oxford: Clarendon Press, 1975). This is convenient because it allows him to ignore the bulk of Oakeshott's criticism of Rationalism. But, even in *On Human Conduct*, Oakeshott explicitly rejects the notion that society should be treated as the malleable (one might say disposable) construct Mapel wishes it to be. The clearest expression of this is Oakeshott's portrait of the theoretician who, mistaking his proper, limited investigatory role for that of an arbiter of society's proper character, attempts to direct those engaged in the practices of daily life through the use of blustering lies. See Oakeshott, *On Human Conduct*, 26, and also the discussion of Oakeshott's vision of right conduct and his *substantive* conception of virtue in the next chapter of this book.

14. Franco's claim that Oakeshott is some (perhaps "strange") sort of liberal rests on his assertion that Oakeshott's "theory of civil association, in its concern with liberty, its appreciation for individuality, and its defense of the rule of law cannot but be characterized as liberal" ("Michael Oakeshott as Liberal Theorist," 411). That a conservative may, indeed must, value well-ordered liberty, individuality, and the rule of law should by now be clear. Furthermore, Oakeshott's treatment of these terms is far afield from that of any coherent conception of liberalism (he does not even use the term liberal in other than a pejorative sense outside the realm of education). Acknowledging that Oakeshott rejects "the more questionable metaphysical and ethical assumptions" of liberalism (411), including the fundamental liberal constructs of "atomism and negative individualism" (430), Franco ends up resting his liberal interpretation on Oakeshott's favorable view of Hobbes (though not of Locke, who apparently is a "bad" liberal [415]). But Oakeshott's Hobbes is no liberal. Indeed, in making his argument Franco winds his way through a number of assertions of questionable validity or relevance to liberalism. According to Franco, Oakeshott's liberal Hobbes "put will, the individual will, as the basis of the state" (414). Oakeshott's Hobbes "put" nothing anywhere; rather, he *recognized* the dependence of the state (and of human conduct) on self-willed action—*including the action of acquiescence*. More problematical, Franco ascribes to some form of idealist philosophical liberalism, and even to Oakeshott, the notion that men consent to government through a general or rational will completely divorced from contractarian theory. To assert that liberalism may include that cover for totalitarian control known as the general will is to stretch its meaning beyond the bounds of coherence. Further, Oakeshott recognized the distinction between consent and moral rectitude (or rational will) only in the sense that he argued that civil association rests on the consent of its members to the existing rules—whatever they might think of the morality of those rules. Most important, Franco provides a stunning misreading of Oakeshottean tradition (or "living tradition") completely divorced from Oakeshott's emphasis on the role of habit and convention. It might also be noted that Oakeshott is openly hostile to the

very notion of natural rights (see Michael Oakeshott, *Rationalism in Politics and Other Essays* [London: Methuen, 1967], 120 and 135).

15. Oakeshott, *On Human Conduct*, 41. Quoted in Robert Grant, *Oakeshott* (London: Claridge Press, 1990), 75. Grant's book provides the best introduction to Oakeshott's work and in particular to the idealist roots of his philosophy.

16. See, for example, *The Voice of Liberal Learning*, 47–48; Oakeshott argues that "'self-realization' for human beings is not, of course, the realization of an exactly pre-determined end which requires only circumstances favourable to this end in order that it should be achieved; but nor is this self an infinite, unknown potentiality which an inheritance of human achievement is as likely to thwart as to promote. Selves are not rational abstractions, they are historic personalities, they are among the components of this world of human achievements; and there is no other way for a human being to make the most of himself than by learning to recognize himself in the mirror of this inheritance."

17. Oakeshott, *Rationalism*, 184.

18. Oakeshott, "On Misunderstanding Human Conduct: A Reply to My Critics," *Political Theory* 4 (Aug. 1976): 361.

19. Oakeshott, *On History and Other Essays* (Totowa, N.J.: Barnes & Noble, 1983), 129. It is true, as Grant argues, that the necessary "indifference" of Oakeshott's *lex* (or law, properly so-called) "to its subjects' moral beliefs signifies only a reluctance to defy or to interfere with them. If so, Oakeshott's position turns out after all to be genuinely conservative. The difficult distinction between 'private' and 'public' morals . . . is ultimately decided not by governments or political thinkers but by subjects. If the latter expect morals to be enforced, then a government which disregards their wishes, or attempts to impose some other morality upon them ([*Rationalism*] 186–87), puts itself, and *respublica*, in jeopardy. On the other hand, it will also be an 'uncivil', and above all an unwise, society which calls for a degree, or kind, of conformity to which any sizeable minorities in its midst may be expected to take serious (and not merely selfish) exception. To make it impossible for citizens who would otherwise do so to identify themselves with *lex* is to free them, in their own eyes, from any obligation save that which they feel to their own 'community', and to store up obvious trouble for the future" (Grant, *Oakeshott*, 86). Yet missing from this characterization is any notion of proper limits to the sensibilities of the subjects. That natural law posits such limits is clear; that Oakeshott also seeks to limit the scope of such sensibilities will be argued in chapter 7.

20. Oakeshott, "On Misunderstanding Human Conduct," 366–67.

21. Oakeshott, *Rationalism*, 40.

22. Josiah Lee Auspitz, "Individuality, Civility, and Theory: The Philosophical Imagination of Michael Oakeshott," *Political Theory* 38 (Aug. 1976): 262–64; Oakeshott, *Experience and Its Modes* (Cambridge: Cambridge University Press, 1933), 347.

23. Oakeshott, *On History*, 11.

24. Oakeshott, *Rationalism*, 101.

25. Grant argues that Oakeshott "is resolutely opposed to transcendental explanations, because the transcendental is not the premise or 'cause' of experience, but rather something to which, under certain conditions, experience seems inconclusively to point" (*Oakeshott*, 35). It is difficult to take issue with this point given Oakeshott's reticence to give even religious experience any transcendent cast. See *Oakeshott*, 38, for Grant's restatement of Oakeshott's characterization of religion as merely one part of the mode of practice in his early work. Yet Grant's near dismissal of religion's role in Oakeshott's thought also seems inappropriate. Grant recognizes that Oakeshott did come to value religion as "aesthetic" rather than as merely practical (106), but that the role of religious experience in this life reflects a theological reality beyond human experience is at the least more of an open question than Grant allows.

26. Oakeshott, *Rationalism*, 103.

27. Ibid., 100.

28. Ibid., 98.

29. Ibid., 97.

30. Ibid., 48.

31. Ibid., 89.

32. Ibid., 102.

33. Oakeshott, *On History*, 14–15.

34. Oakeshott, *Rationalism*, 99.

35. Oakeshott, *Hobbes on Civil Association* (Oxford: Basil Blackwell, 1975), 30–31.

36. Kristol, *Reflections*, 90.

37. Ibid., 179.

38. See, for example, ibid., 199.

39. Ibid.

40. Ibid., 29.

41. Ibid., 76.

42. See, for example, Michael Novak's argument in *The Spirit of Democratic Capitalism* (New York: Simon & Schuster, 1982), 218–20, that a minimal amount of compulsory charity might be justified in order to see to it that the deserving poor may be assured sustenance.

43. Kristol, *Reflections*, 30.

44. Ibid., 37.

45. This argument, following Weber of course, is made most fully by Daniel Bell. For Bell, capitalism is faced with a dire prospect: The moral basis on which it was built, that of short-term self-denial and Protestant morality, has died out because of the temptations of consumerist capitalism. "The Protestant ethic had served to limit sumptuary (though not capital) accumulation. When the Protestant ethic was sundered from bourgeois society, only the hedonism remained, and the capitalist system lost its transcendental ethic" (Daniel Bell, *The Cultural Contradictions of Capitalism* [New York: Basic Books, 1976], 21). Perhaps not insignificantly, Bell has cut his ties with neoconservatism in favor of overtly social democratic allies and positions.

46. Kristol, *Reflections*, 27.

47. Irving Kristol, *Two Cheers for Capitalism* (New York: Basic Books, 1978), 257.

48. Bell's solution to the loss of the transcendental ethic of capitalism—the basis, for him, of modern Western society—is not the replacement of this ethic with another ethic or set of mores fitting the new circumstances. Unlike Tocqueville's attempt to maintain virtue in the face of changed conditions, Bell's prescription is the acceptance of a life of extremely limited virtue: "In trial and defeat—and there has been defeat—a virtue emerges: the possibility of a self-conscious maturity (which the stoics called the tragic sense of life) that dispenses with charismatic leaders, ideological doctrines, and manifest destinies, and which seeks to redefine one's self and one's liberal society on the only basis on which it can survive. This basis must be created by conjoining three actions: the reaffirmation of our past, for only if we know the inheritance from the past can we become aware of the obligation to our posterity; recognition of the limits of resources and the priority of *needs*, individual and social, over unlimited appetite and wants; and agreement upon a conception of equity which gives all persons a sense of fairness and inclusion in the society and which promotes a situation where, within the relevant spheres, people *become* more equal so that they can be *treated* equally" (Bell, *Cultural Contradictions*, 281–82; emphasis in original). Egalitarianism and the pursuit of material goods (on an equal basis) are to replace the pursuit of virtue.

49. Kristol, *Two Cheers*, xiii.

50. The Marxist past of Kristol (as well as of many of his fellow neoconservatives) clearly has much to do with his choice of vocabulary. But the concern here is with the present form of Kristol's thought rather than with its genesis; Kristol himself has written on this latter topic. See especially the opening chapters of *Reflections*.

51. Russell Kirk, *Enemies of the Permanent Things: Observations of Abnormity in Literature and Politics* (Peru, Ill.: Sugden, 1984), 255.

52. Ibid., 17.

53. Ibid.

54. Russell Kirk, *The Conservative Mind from Burke to Eliot*, 7th ed. (Chicago: Regnery, 1986), 7–8.

55. Ibid., 8.

56. Ibid., 8–9.

57. Kirk, *Enemies*, 288–89.

58. Ibid., 168.

59. Ibid., 177–78. In several places Kirk modifies his emphasis on the Christian faith by including its "Judaic roots"; see especially 30.

60. Ibid., 235.

61. Ibid., 249.

62. Ibid., 252.

63. Ibid., 290.

64. Ibid., 226.

65. Ibid., 285–86.

66. See, for example, ibid., 189.

67. Ibid., 145.
68. Ibid., 36.
69. Ibid., 34.
70. Ibid., 37–38.
71. Ibid., 68.
72. Ibid., 41.

CHAPTER SEVEN: THE QUEST FOR VIRTUE

1. Russell Kirk, *Enemies of the Permanent Things* (Peru, Ill.: Sugden, 1984), 167.
2. Michael Oakeshott, *On Human Conduct* (Oxford: Clarendon Press, 1975), 26.
3. Michael Oakeshott, *Hobbes on Civil Association* (Oxford: Basil Blackwell, 1975), 150.
4. Michael Oakeshott, *Rationalism in Politics and Other Essays* (London: Methuen, 1967), 197.
5. Ibid., 198.
6. Hannah Pitkin, "Inhuman Conduct and Unpolitical Theory: Michael Oakeshott's *On Human Conduct*," *Political Theory* 8 (Aug. 1976): 301.
7. Oakeshott, *Rationalism*, 199.
8. Ibid., 198.
9. Oakeshott, *Hobbes*, 289–90.
10. See Robert Grant, *Oakeshott* (London: Claridge Press, 1990), especially 65–70 and 84–86, for an introduction to Oakeshott's conception of civility. Oakeshott's *On Human Conduct* is principally concerned with civility, a conception of extreme importance to conservatism in general as well as to Oakeshott in particular because it embodies the customs that allow for friendly interaction and the formation of the attachments that hold society together. Unfortunately, as with much else of importance in Oakeshott's work (in particular the influence of his early attachment to idealist philosophy on his later work), a full discussion of civility is beyond the scope of this book and so must await another opportunity. As to the role of idealism in Oakeshott's thought, Paul Franco, in *The Political Philosophy of Michael Oakeshott* (New Haven, Conn.: Yale University Press, 1990), shows how difficult the subject can be.
11. Oakeshott, *Hobbes*, 150–51.
12. Friedrich Nietzsche, *The Use and Abuse of History*, trans. Adrian Collins (Indianapolis: Bobbs Merrill, 1957).
13. Michael Oakeshott, *On History and Other Essays* (Totowa, N.J.: Barnes & Noble, 1983), 165.
14. Oakeshott, *Hobbes*, 151.
15. Ibid., 151–52.
16. Ibid., 153.
17. Ibid., 153–54.
18. Oakeshott, *Rationalism*, 59.

19. Ibid., 72.

20. Ibid., 76–77.

21. Ibid., 79.

22. Oakeshott, *On History*, 176.

23. Ibid., 179–80.

24. Ibid., 181–87.

25. Ibid., 191.

26. Ibid., 193.

27. Ibid., 193–94.

28. This moral view makes Oakeshott's choice of Hobbes as the exemplary artist/philosopher seem odd. Generally recognized as the theorist of selfish, calculating fear, Hobbes would seem a much more likely candidate as an exemplar of the problem of modern rationalism than of its solution.

29. Oakeshott's emphasis on the independent pursuit of individual wants may be seen as contributing to the picture of him as a rather unconservative libertarian, emphasizing individual will over community service. But again Oakeshott's emphasis is on the necessary acceptance by men of the structures and practices of their society, an acceptance that clearly takes precedence over individual initiative as it makes it possible.

30. Timothy Fuller, "The Work of Michael Oakeshott," *Political Theory* 19, (Aug. 1991): 330.

31. For a more complete explication of this character, see Bruce Frohnen, "Oakeshott's Hobbesian Myth: Pride, Character and the Limits of Reason," *Western Political Quarterly* 27 (Dec. 1991).

32. Fuller, "Work of Michael Oakeshott," 330.

33. Oakeshott, *On Human Conduct*, quoted in ibid.

34. Quoted in Patrick Riley, "The Voice of Michael Oakeshott in the Conversation of Mankind," *Political Theory* 18 (Aug. 1991): 335.

35. Fuller, "Work of Michael Oakeshott," 331.

36. Irving Kristol, *Reflections of a Neoconservative* (New York: Basic Books, 1983), 40–41.

37. George Will, often referred to as a conservative in the neoconservative mold, also accepts the Weberian view of the cultural and intellectual weakness of contemporary society. Much like Kristol and Bell, Will argues that "the dynamics of capitalist society undermine the sense of a permanent order in the world, a sense that is highly useful to the transmission of settled beliefs." Will, however, sees himself as being personally engaged in the rebuilding of the bases for a conservative good life, one transcending mere economic liberty. "Reflection about how the individual should live is inseparable from reflection about the nature of the good society. Today we need an argument about the connection between the society we have and the kind of individuals we want American life to nurture. . . . All economic arrangements, whatever the mixture of free trade and protection and subsidies and entitlements, should be discussed as expedients. They should be evaluated in terms of the contributions they make to the things we value fundamentally, the things involving important political principles: equality of opportunity, neighborliness, equitable material allocation, hap-

piness, social cohesion, justice" (George F. Will, *Statecraft as Soulcraft: What Government Does* [New York: Simon & Schuster, 1983], 150–51 and 135–36). These principles do not seem to have their basis in the natural operations of American society; they are indeed abstract and even mutually contradictory principles predicated upon the notion that the government has a central role in determining the institutions and practices (and character) that are proper to a given society. Such assumptions contradict the fundamental conservative reliance on natural socializing institutions and the preexisting practices and prejudices of a people for the formation of proper character.

38. Kristol, *Reflections,* 41.

39. Irving Kristol, *Two Cheers for Capitalism* (New York: Basic Books, 1978), 262.

40. Kristol, *Reflections,* 41–42.

41. Will seems in agreement with Kristol in this area. For Will, "statecraft *is* soulcraft. . . . Statecraft . . . need not affect the citizens' inner lives skillfully, or creatively, or decently. But the one thing it cannot be, over time, is irrelevant to those inner lives." The emphasis once again is on the role of the state as the primary guardian of the soul. Will argues that an "aim of prudent statecraft is to limit the state by delegating many of its chores to intermediary institutions. . . . Conservative soulcraft has as its aim the perpetuation of free government by nurturing people so they can be comfortable and competent in society." That is, government should delegate some of the duties Will clearly sees as naturally belonging to it. Intermediary institutions are to be given particular, subsidiary roles in the formation of character, as dictated by the (assumedly prudent) statesman entrusted with the health of the body politic and the souls of its members (*Statecraft,* 144 [emphasis in original], 145).

42. Michael Novak, *The Spirit of Democratic Capitalism* (New York: Simon & Schuster, 1982), 18.

43. Ibid., 133.

44. Ibid., 132.

45. Ibid., 131–32.

46. Ibid., 142.

47. Ibid., 143.

48. Ibid., 20.

49. Kirk, *Enemies,* 66.

50. Ibid., 243.

51. Ibid., 252.

52. Ibid., 259.

53. Ibid., 51.

54. Ibid., 107.

55. Ibid., 44–45.

56. Ibid., 45.

57. Ibid., 45–46.

58. For a concise and useful discussion of Kirk's view of the role of pride in the progressive decadence of contemporary society, see John P. East, *The Amer-*

ican Conservative Movement: The Philosophical Founders (Chicago: Regnery, 1986), especially 23–25.

59. Kirk, *Enemies*, 128–29.

60. Ibid., 97. This is particularly true, according to Kirk, for the philosopher and the writer.

61. Ibid., 123.

62. Ibid., 112.

CONCLUSION: THE MATERIAL AND THE ETERNAL

1. Michael Oakeshott, *On Human Conduct* (Oxford: Clarendon Press, 1975), 83.

2. See Edmund Burke, "Speech on Economical Reform," *Works* (London: John C. Nimmo, 1899), 2: especially 286–87.

3. Ibid., 243.

4. Doris Goldstein, *Trial of Faith* (New York: Elsevier, 1975), 82. But see Andre Jardin, *Tocqueville: A Biography,* trans. Lydia Davis with Robert Hemenway (New York: Farrar Straus Giroux, 1988), chaps. 24–25, for an account of Tocqueville's courageous actions in person and in print during Louis Napoleon's coup that contradicts the official version.

5. Charles Murray, *In Pursuit of Happiness and Good Government* (New York: Simon & Schuster, 1988), 274.

6. Those readers who might see in this statement an acceptance of any notion of the inherent worth of those people who happen to possess large sums of money are referred to the beginning of chapter 5, where the necessary link between the ability to make (or inherit) wealth and virtue (or even common decency) is questioned. A natural aristocrat, like a hereditary one, fulfills his duties largely because they are generally recognized to be just that—duties naturally belonging to his particular station. The issue is not whether the concept of noblesse oblige accords those in positions of prominence unearned prestige; the question is how we could possibly compel those in prominent positions to care for the less fortunate through any means other than habitual duty and attachment—unless, of course, one desires to resort to (necessarily repeated and institutionalized) threats and brute force.

7. Alexis de Tocqueville, *Recollections on the French Revolution of 1848*, ed. J. P. Mayer, trans. Alexander Teixeira de Mattos (Cleveland, Ohio: World Publishing, 1959), 14.

8. The rise of which, *contra* Voegelin, I do not regret.

Selected Bibliography

Aquinas, Thomas. *Treatise on Law: (Summa Theologica Questions 90–97)*. Washington, D.C.: Regnery, 1987.

Aristophanes. *The Clouds*. In *Four Texts on Socrates*. Trans. Thomas G. West and Grace Starry West. Ithaca, N.Y.: Cornell University Press, 1984.

Aristotle, *Nicomachean Ethics*. Trans. H. Rackham. Cambridge: Harvard University Press, 1933.

———. *Nicomachean Ethics*. Trans. Martin Ostwald. New York: Macmillan, 1962.

———. *Politics*. Trans. Ernest Barker. London: Oxford University Press, 1958.

Aron, Raymond. *Main Currents in Sociological Thought*. Trans. Richard Howard and Helen Weaver. 2 vols. Garden City, N.Y.: Doubleday, 1968.

Auspitz, Josiah Lee. "Individuality, Civility, and Theory: The Philosophical Imagination of Michael Oakeshott." *Political Theory* 38 (Aug. 1976): 261–94.

Bell, Daniel. *The Cultural Contradictions of Capitalism*. New York: Basic Books, 1976.

Boesche, Roger. *The Strange Liberalism of Alexis de Tocqueville*. Ithaca, N.Y.: Cornell University Press, 1987.

Buckle, Henry. *The History of Civilization in England*. 2 vols. New York: D. Appleton, 1875.

Buckley, William F., Jr. *Up from Liberalism*. New York: McDowell, Obolensky, 1959.

Burke, Edmund. *Works*. 12 vols. London: John C. Nimmo, 1899.

Chapman, Gerald W. *Edmund Burke: The Practical Imagination*. Cambridge: Harvard University Press, 1967.

Diggins, John P. *The Lost Soul of American Politics: Virtue, Self-Interest and the Foundations of Liberalism*. Chicago: University of Chicago Press, 1986.

Drescher, Seymour. *Tocqueville and England*. Cambridge: Harvard University Press, 1964.

Dreyer, Frederick A. *Burke's Politics: A Study in Whig Orthodoxy*. Waterloo, Ontario: Wilfrid Laurier, 1979.

East, John P. *The American Conservative Movement: The Philosophical Founders*. Chicago: Regnery, 1986.

Emerson, Ralph Waldo. *Essays and Lectures*. New York: Library of America, 1983.

Franco, Paul. "Michael Oakeshott as Liberal Theorist." *Political Theory* 19 (Aug. 1990): 411–36.

————. *The Political Philosophy of Michael Oakeshott*. New Haven, Conn.: Yale University Press, 1990.

Frohnen, Bruce. "Oakeshott's Hobbesian Myth: Pride, Character and the Limits of Reason." *Western Political Quarterly* 27 (Dec. 1991): 789–809.

Fuller, Timothy. "The Work of Michael Oakeshott." *Political Theory* 19 (Aug. 1991): 326–33.

Gilson, Etienne. *The Christian Philosophy of Saint Thomas Aquinas*. London: Victor Gollancz, 1957.

Goldstein, Doris. *Trial of Faith*. New York: Elsevier, 1975.

Grant, Robert. *Oakeshott*. London: Claridge Press, 1990.

Hobsbawm, E. J. *The Age of Revolution: 1789–1848*. New York: New American Library, 1962.

Jardin, Andre. *Tocqueville: A Biography*. Trans. Lydia Davis with Robert Hemenway. New York: Farrar Straus Giroux, 1988.

Kelly, George Armstrong. *Politics and Religious Consciousness in America*. New Brunswick, N.J.: Transaction Books, 1984.

Kesler, Charles R., and William F. Buckley, Jr., eds. *Keeping the Tablets: Modern American Conservative Thought*. New York: Harper & Row, 1980.

Kirk, Russell. *The Conservative Mind from Burke to Eliot*. 7th ed. Chicago: Regnery, 1986.

————. *Enemies of the Permanent Things: Observations of Abnormity in Literature and Politics*. Peru, Ill.: Sugden, 1984.

————. "Enlivening the Conservative Mind." *Intercollegiate Review* 21 (Spring 1986): 25–28.

Koritansky, John. *Alexis de Tocqueville and the New Science of Politics*. Durham: Carolina Academic Press, 1986.

Kramnick, Isaac F. *The Rage of Edmund Burke: Portrait of an Ambivalent Conservative*. New York: Basic Books, 1971.

————. "Skepticism in English Political Thought from Temple to Burke." *Studies in Burke and his Time* 12 (Fall 1970): 1627–60.

Kraynak, Robert P. "Tocqueville's Constitutionalism." *American Political Science Review* 81 (Dec. 1987): 1175–96.

Kristol, Irving. *Reflections of a Neoconservative: Looking Back, Looking Ahead*. New York: Basic Books, 1983.

————. *Two Cheers for Capitalism*. New York: Basic Books, 1978.

Lamberti, Jean-Claude. *Tocqueville and the Two Democracies*. Trans. Arthur Goldhammer. Cambridge: Harvard University Press, 1989.

Lawler, Peter Augustine. "Was Tocqueville a Philosopher?" *Interpretation* 17 (1990): 401–14.

Lerner, Max. "Tocqueville's *Democracy in America*: Politics, Law and the Elite." *Antioch Review* 25 (Winter 1965–66): 543–63.

Lively, Jack. *The Social and Political Thought of Alexis de Tocqueville*. Oxford: Oxford University Press, 1962.

Lovejoy, Arthur O. *The Great Chain of Being*. Cambridge: Harvard University Press, 1936.

MacCunn, John. *The Political Philosophy of Burke*. London: Edward Arnold, 1913.

McDonald, Forrest. *Novus Ordo Seclorum: The Intellectual Origins of the Constitution*. Lawrence: University Press of Kansas, 1985.

MacPherson, C. B. *Burke*. New York: Hill & Wang, 1980.

Mansfield, Harvey C., Jr. *Statesmanship and Party Government: A Study of Burke and Bolingbroke*. Chicago: University of Chicago Press, 1965.

Mapel, David R. "Civil Association and the Idea of Contingency." *Political Theory* 19 (Aug. 1990): 392–410.

Mayer, J. P. *Alexis de Tocqueville: A Biographical Essay in Political Science*. Trans. M. M. Bozman and C. Hahn. New York: Viking Press, 1940.

Murray, Charles. *In Pursuit of Happiness and Good Government*. New York: Simon & Schuster, 1988.

Namier, Lewis. *The Structure of Politics at the Accession of George III*. 2 vols. London: Macmillan, 1929.

Nash, George H. *The Conservative Intellectual Movement in America since 1945*. New York: Basic Books, 1976.

Nietzsche, Friedrich. *The Use and Abuse of History*. Trans. Adrian Collins. Indianapolis: Bobbs Merrill, 1957.

Novak, Michael. *The Spirit of Democratic Capitalism*. New York: Simon & Schuster, 1982.

Oakeshott, Michael. *Experience and Its Modes*. Cambridge: Cambridge University Press, 1933.

———. *Hobbes on Civil Association*. Oxford: Basil Blackwell, 1975.

———. *On History and Other Essays*. Totowa, N.J.: Barnes & Noble, 1983.

———. *On Human Conduct*. Oxford: Clarendon Press, 1975.

———. "On Misunderstanding Human Conduct: A Reply to My Critics." *Political Theory* 4 (Aug. 1976): 353–68.

———. *Rationalism in Politics and Other Essays*. London: Methuen, 1967.

———. *The Voice of Liberal Learning: Michael Oakeshott on Education*. Ed. Timothy Fuller. New Haven, Conn.: Yale University Press, 1989.

O'Connor, D. J., *Aquinas and Natural Law*. London: Macmillan, 1967.

O'Gorman, Frank. *Edmund Burke: His Political Philosophy*. Bloomington: Indiana University Press, 1973.

O'Neill, Onora. "Ethical Reasoning and Ideological Pluralism." *Ethics* 99 (July 1988): 705–22.

O'Sullivan, Noel. *Conservatism*. New York: St. Martin's Press, 1976.

Pangle, Thomas L. *The Spirit of Modern Republicanism: The Moral Vision of the American Founders and the Philosophy of Locke*. Chicago: University of Chicago Press, 1988.

Pitkin, Hannah. "Inhuman Conduct and Unpolitical Theory: Michael Oakeshott's *On Human Conduct*." *Political Theory* 8 (Aug. 1976): 301–20.

Plato. *The Republic*. Trans. Allan Bloom. New York: Basic Books, 1968.

Pocock, J. G. A. *The Machiavellian Moment: Florentine Political Thought and the Atlantic Republican Tradition*. Princeton, N.J.: Princeton University Press, 1975.
———. *Politics, Language and Time: Essays on Political Thought and History*. New York: Atheneum, 1971.
Richter, Melvin. "Tocqueville on Algeria." *Review of Politics* 25 (July 1963): 369–98.
Riley, Patrick. "The Voice of Michael Oakeshott in the Conversation of Mankind." *Political Theory* 18 (Aug. 1991): 334–35.
Rossiter, Clinton. *Conservatism in America: The Thankless Persuasion*. New York: Vintage Books, 1962.
Smith, Bruce James. *Politics and Remembrance: Republican Themes in Machiavelli, Burke and Tocqueville*. Princeton, N.J.: Princeton University Press, 1985.
Stanlis, Peter. *Edmund Burke and the Natural Law*. Ann Arbor: University of Michigan Press, 1958.
Steinfels, Peter. *The Neoconservatives: The Men Who Are Changing America's Politics*. New York: Simon & Schuster, 1979.
Strauss, Leo. *Liberalism Ancient and Modern*. New York: Basic Books, 1968.
———. *Natural Right and History*. Chicago: University of Chicago Press, 1953.
Tocqueville, Alexis de. *Democracy in America*. Ed. J. P. Mayer, trans. George Lawrence. 2 vols. in 1. Garden City, N.Y.: Doubleday, 1969.
———. *The European Revolution and Correspondence with Gobineau*. Ed. and trans. John Lukacs. Garden City, N.Y.: Anchor, 1959.
———. *The Old Regime and the French Revolution*. Trans. Stuart Gilbert. Garden City, N.Y.: Doubleday, 1955.
———. *Recollections on the French Revolution of 1848*. Ed. J. P. Mayer. Trans. Alexander Teixeira de Mattos. Cleveland, Ohio: World Publishing, 1959.
———. *Selected Letters on Politics and Society*. Trans. James Toupin and Roger Boesche. Berkeley: University of California Press, 1985.
Voegelin, Eric. *The New Science of Politics*. Chicago: University of Chicago Press, 1952.
Wade, L. L. "Tocqueville and Public Choice." *Public Choice* 47 (1985): 491–508.
Wilkins, Burleigh Taylor. *The Problem of Burke's Political Philosophy*. Oxford: Clarendon Press, 1967.
Will, George F. *Statecraft as Soulcraft: What Government Does*. New York: Simon & Schuster, 1983.
Zetterbaum, Marvin. *Tocqueville and the Problem of Democracy*. Stanford, Calif.: Stanford University Press, 1967.

Index